Safeguarding Critical E-Documents

Safeguarding Critical E-Documents

Implementing a Program for Securing Confidential Information Assets

ROBERT F. SMALLWOOD

WILEY

John Wiley & Sons, Inc.

Library of Congress Cataloging-in-Publication Data:
Smallwood, Robert F., 1959–
    Safeguarding critical e-documents : implementing a program for securing confidential
information assets / Robert F. Smallwood.
        pages   cm
    Includes index.
    ISBN 978-1-118-15908-8 (hardback); ISBN 978-1-118-28227-4 (ebk);
ISBN 978-1-118-28281-6 (ebk); ISBN 978-1-118-28687-6 (ebk)
    1. Computer security.   2. Document Management.   3. Electronic records.
4. Cyberspace–Security measures.   I. Title.
    QA76.9.A25S627 2012
    005.8–dc23   2011048567

Printed in the United States of America

10   9   8   7   6   5   4   3   2   1

For Araceli

Contents

Foreword

Today, yet another organization will be forced to admit that it has lost control of its information. The admission will be elicited by a court, a regulator, a reporter, or even a hacker. The company will admit that it has no clear understanding of what information it owns, where that information resides, or what value it has. Finally, it will admit that a fundamental lack of information oversight has put the company and its shareholders, customers, and partners at risk.

Worldwide, businesses and their clients are plagued by the effects of information mismanagement. Each year, they spend more on hardware and software to protect their data, but information security continues to be compromised. What's broken?

Let's start here.

Imagine a world where your chief privacy officer doesn't care about privacy. Where your chief operations officer thinks operations are someone else's problem. Or where your chief financial officer thinks that her job is managing spreadsheets, not money.

Welcome to the world of information management: a world where C-level executives—chief information officers (CIOs)—who, despite having the word *information* in their title, are not actually responsible for information. Most organizations have had chief information officers for at least two decades, and yet, most still cannot answer this question: "Who owns databases—those who maintain them or those who produce them?"

A question, which by the way, was raised in 1984 by *Modern Office Technology Magazine*.

The failure of institutions worldwide to clearly answer this question is at the root of the problems Robert Smallwood addresses here. It's not the CIO's fault; in fact, most CIOs are very clear about their role. Most view themselves more as chief *infrastructure* officers, stewards of the information *systems*; the people who keep the lights on but who do not generate the electricity; the owners of the storage tanks, pipes, and faucets, but not of the water itself. Pick your analogy.

Rather, fault lies with chief executive officers (CEOs) and boards, who have failed to understand that *information* governance (IG) lies at the heart of *corporate* governance; who fail to listen to the CIO when he talks about the real scope of his job; who are stuck in a different decade (even century) because they think the problem is about moving boxes of paper from facility to facility; and who, finally, have failed to adapt the CIO role, delegate the problem to another C-level executive, or create a new assignment.

This is the world that this book seeks to illuminate. And it couldn't be more timely.

In the book, Robert lays out a framework for understanding this problem, and a plan for dealing with the details—from strategy to software. Both elements are essential. We need to redefine the way we look at the information problem, which Robert helps us to do. But we also need a practical manual for active information governance, which he also provides in the form of authoritative and seasoned guidance.

The path to successful information governance is long. This book should help make your journey shorter and less painful. Safe travels!

Barclay T. Blair
Founder and President, ViaLumina Ltd.
www.vialumina.com

Preface

If you reveal your secrets to the wind, you should not blame the wind for revealing them to the trees.

—Khalil Gibran, writer and artist (1883–1931)

E lectronic document security has come to the forefront of the business and political world with the 2010 exposure of classified U.S. military documents by the website WikiLeaks and its founder Julian Assange. With the threat of more disclosures, and plenty of examples of leaked information in the corporate realm, organizations are scrambling to plug gaps in electronic document security to protect critical information assets.

Protecting confidential electronic documents (e-documents) goes far beyond protecting military secrets. In the private sector it means safeguarding blueprints, software, price lists, financial data, strategic plans, legal documents, personnel files, and other private corporate data, which have real economic implications. According to the U.S. Commerce Department, intellectual property (IP) theft has been estimated at more than $250 billion and costs over 750,000 jobs annually. The International Chamber of Commerce has estimated the global fiscal loss to intellectual property theft is more than $600 billion per year—and rising.

After reading this book you will know why any breach of internal information—even one like the WikiLeaks scandal—can be prevented by leveraging *information governance (IG)* policies and processes. Some IG technologies have been in existence for almost a decade, and implementing them can ensure that e-document and communications security measures are followed and enforced. These technologies are maturing and some are sophisticated enough to remotely control and monitor access to confidential documents, even after such documents leave the organization or an employee in possession of them is terminated. The following chapters provide key steps and insights for protecting critical e-documents and securing confidential information assets.

This book lays out the threats that may compromise the critical electronic documents of an enterprise across various types of computing applications, from e-mail and instant messaging (IM) to mobile and cloud computing to social networking; then it offers advice and solutions for countering these threats.

This book will assist CEOs, senior managers, CIOs, records managers, information technology (IT) managers, compliance and risk managers, and others involved in information governance, e-document security, records management, and e-records implementations to make intelligent, informed decisions. For those seeking to implement a program for securing confidential information assets, bulk pricing for the book and e-book are available. Contact: safeguard@electronic-records-management.com.

Acknowledgments

I would like to thank Andy Han, Bud Porter-Roth, Barclay Blair, Bill Broddy, Charmaine Brooks, and Paula Lederman for their contributions to this book. Special thanks to Adi Ruppin for his time and unique insights.

Safeguarding Critical
E-Documents

PART I

The Problem and Basic Tools

CHAPTER 1

The Problem: Securing Confidential Electronic Documents

The element of surprise has accounted for more victories throughout history than any other tactic, according to Sun Tzu in *The Art of War*. In 1941, the United States military was surprised by the attack on Pearl Harbor and, as a result, would learn a valuable lesson about preparedness and vulnerability.[1]

WikiLeaks: A Wake-Up Call

Today, attacks on organizations' information infrastructure occur daily, siphoning off confidential information. The most well-known cybersecurity breach is that associated with the WikiLeaks incident, in which confidential military, diplomatic, and corporate information was accessed and exposed online. This is perhaps the most visible example of an information security failure, but all types of organizations—not just the government and military—are at risk. And such breaches can be difficult to discover. Many times these types of incursions take place undetected for months, or even years, compromising the position of the victim organization and eroding the value of its information and stakeholder equity.

Since it is now widely known and accepted that the impact of leaked confidential information is real and the consequences are serious, organizations must constantly be on guard to protect confidential documents. There are specific steps that can be taken to counter the ongoing threat.

A number of countermeasure steps and processes that support information governance (IG) are available. These must be implemented alongside new technologies to enforce electronic document security (EDS). IG deals with the policies that control access to and use of information. They are a critical first step. For instance, in the case of WikiLeaks, a U.S. Army private allegedly provided classified military information to Julian Assange. A policy should have been in place to disallow low-level personnel from accessing the Secret Internet Protocol Router Network (SIPRNet), which is used to transmit classified information. Protecting confidential e-documents begins with robust and thorough policy analysis, starting with the questions "How are we going to govern the use of our confidential information? Who gets access to which information? Where? And when?"

> Ironically, the technology that could have secured documents and prevented them from leaking is used by WikiLeaks itself to control access.

Once these key questions are answered, newer EDS technologies can be applied to enforce the policies and control the access and use of information. Commercial and defense software providers have created systems that can safeguard electronic documents and records, wherever they may reside or be transported. The latest generation of this technology has advanced so that policy management is more streamlined and control over e-documents can occur remotely, anytime or anyplace, whether on a hard drive, thumb drive, mobile device, website, or in transit.

The goal of a program to secure confidential information assets is to provide complete document lifecycle security (DLS) for critical electronic documents and records, from their creation and use to their final archiving or destruction.

In 2010, the federal government took steps to better protect its information infrastructure by launching United States Cyber Command (CYBERCOM). The mission of the project is to "synchronize the Defense Department's various networks and cyberspace operations to better defend them against the onslaught of cyber attacks."[2] Unfortunately, it does little to address the issue of misuse of authorized data retrievals by insiders with security clearance. That is where clear and enforced IG, and technology tools, are critical to securing internal information assets.

> The goal of a program to secure confidential information assets is to provide complete document lifecycle security (DLS) for critical electronic documents and records, from their creation and use to their final archiving or destruction.

This book details the specific policies that need to be created for various information delivery platforms as well as the specific technologies that are needed to control, manage, and audit the use of electronic documents. These solutions are available; they simply take time, a focused effort, an adequate budget, and strong management resources to accomplish. And IG is not a one-off, one-time effort; once the program is in place, it must be consistently monitored, audited, and reviewed. *Leaving an organization vulnerable to data spills and breaches is due to poor management, and presents an avoidable business risk.* This risk can be avoided with proper policy analysis, planning, communication, and auditing as part of an overall IG program, and by leveraging security technologies.

U.S. Government Attempts to Protect Intellectual Property

The theft of intellectual property (IP), which includes software source code, patented designs and blueprints, research, customer lists, and business methods, is a growing problem, and the U.S. government stepped in to combat it. In early 2010, the Department of Justice (DoJ) formed an IP task force to focus law enforcement efforts on the nettlesome and increasing problem of IP theft.[3]

The DoJ is trying to coordinate at multiple levels to streamline efforts between state, federal, and international law enforcement agencies to address IP theft, which has real economic consequences, especially for providers of software which is commonly illegally copied. Access to proprietary software source code must be securely monitored as it is a critical information asset for software development companies. The same is true of other providers of IP, such as law firms, consulting firms, advertising agencies, research companies, and the like.

Threats Persist across the Pond: U.K. Companies on Guard

The problem of inappropriate or criminal access of confidential information assets spans the globe. In the United Kingdom, it was reported that cases involving employees taking confidential data from the workplace tripled from 2008 to 2009, and they have continued to increase today.[4]

Hard economic times may have contributed to the rise, as employees moved to new jobs or started new businesses using confidential information (e.g., client contact information) stolen from their previous employer. But many of these cases could have been prevented with proper IG polices and enforcement using EDS technologies.

Increase in Corporate and Industrial Espionage

Corporate espionage is not new, and it has tangible costs. Ford is reported to have suffered a loss estimated at $50–$100 million as a result of the theft of confidential documents by one of its own employees. A former product engineer who had access to thousands of trade secret documents and designs sold them to a competing Chinese car manufacturer.

In another case of industrial espionage, the car manufacturer Renault filed a criminal complaint, asserting that another company tried to buy secrets related to its electric car program.[5] Several executives were ultimately suspended, showing that in our highly competitive business environment, ethics may be cast to the wayside if it means gaining an advantage—or, in the case of the complicit executives, financial gain. This can occur at the highest levels of enterprises, not just in the trenches.

Some schemes can be quite deceptive and devious, masked by standard operating procedures. Granting remote access to confidential information assets for key personnel is common. Granting medical leave is also common. But a deceptive and dishonest employee could feign a medical leave while downloading volumes of confidential information assets for a competitor—and that is exactly what happened at Accenture, a global consulting firm. During a fraudulent medical leave, an employee was allowed access to Accenture's Knowledge Exchange (KX), a detailed knowledge base containing previous proposals, expert reports, cost-estimating guidelines, and case studies. The employee went to work for a direct competitor and continued to download the confidential information from Accenture, estimated to be as many as 1,000 critical documents. While the online access to KX was secure, the use of the electronic documents could have been restricted even *after* the documents were downloaded, if newer technologies were deployed to secure them. Software security protections can be employed to seal the documents and control their use—even after they leave the organization.

> Ford's loss from stolen documents in a single case of IP theft was estimated at $50–$100 million.

Other recent high-profile industrial espionage and document leakage cases include:

- Hybrid car trade secrets were stolen from General Motors by an engineering employee in a scheme to sell them to rival Chinese car manufacturers.

- Huawei Technologies, the largest networking and mobile communications company in China, was sued by U.S.-based Motorola for allegedly conspiring to steal trade secrets through former Motorola employees.
- Health information of 1,600 cardiology patients at Texas Children's Hospital was compromised when a doctor's laptop was stolen. The information included personal and demographic information about the patients, including their names, dates of birth, diagnoses, and treatment histories.[6]
- Car burglars made off with personal records of 4,000 patients of a Portland, Oregon, psychologist and the names and Social Security numbers of 2,900 jobless residents in the county.
- MI6, the U.K. equivalent of the U.S. Central Intelligence Agency (CIA), learned that one of its agents in military intelligence attempted to sell confidential documents to the intelligence services of The Netherlands for £2 million GBP ($3 million USD).
- U.K. medics lost the personal records of nearly 12,000 National Health Service (NHS) patients in just eight months. Also, a hospital worker was suspended after it was discovered he had sent a file containing pay-slip details for *every* member of staff to his home e-mail account.[7]
- Personal information about more than 600 patients of the Fraser Health Authority in British Columbia, Canada, was stored on a laptop stolen from Burnaby General Hospital.

The list of breaches and espionage could go on and on, more than filling the pages of this book. It is clear that it is occurring and that it will continue. Safeguarding confidential information assets cannot rely solely on the trustworthiness of employees and basic security measures. It takes up-to-date information governance efforts and newer technology sets. Executives and senior managers can no longer avoid the issue, as it is abundantly clear that the threat is real and the costs of taking such avoidable risks can be high. A single security breach can cost the entire business.

Risks of Medical Identity Theft

Rising medical identity theft is alarming and damaging to consumers and represents a liability for health care organizations. The U.S. government has become more involved, establishing the President's Task Force on Identity Theft and a medical-specific program in conjunction with the Office of the National Coordinator for Health Information Technology (ONC).[8] There are new initiatives and incentives for health care providers and institutions to automate health records. However, this move toward electronic patient records carries new medical identity theft risks. ONC commissioned technology consulting firm Booz Allen Hamilton to conduct a study of the extent and impact of medical identity theft, the results of which were published in a January 2009 report. It stated, in part:

> *The consumer has the greatest potential for loss as well as key roles in prevention, detection, and remediation. Of course, many other parties may be involved or affected by medical identity theft. An individual may inappropriately access health data when it is held by many participants in the health care delivery chain, including the insurer, health care provider, a third party (e.g., lab, pharmacy), or the consumer. When these misappropriations result in medical identity theft, however, the impact on the consumer has the possibility of being the most severe.*

> Some potential effects on the consumer include compromise of patient care as a result of inaccurate health information entering his or her health record; inability to receive health insurance or other benefits; or financial obligations for services that were never received. *In turn, the consumer is most knowledgeable about his or her own health record and, therefore, is the first line of defense for protecting against medical identity theft and identifying a potential issue early, which may help to reduce the damage.* [emphasis added] [9]

> The consumer has the most to lose from medical identity theft.

Why Don't Organizations Safeguard Their Information Assets?

A leading document security software provider has issued this statement, which sums up the problematic irony in most organizations, regarding their internal documents:

> *Despite repeated examples of data loss the industry has witnessed over the past few years, and despite their disastrous consequences, many organizations still lack clear data security policies and fail to deploy the right security arsenal to prevent them. While they take all the necessary measures to protect their physical infrastructure and facilities—controlling and restricting access to their physical sites—they fail to protect their informational and digital assets. Yet, this is where a company's innermost secrets, intellectual property and value resides—confidential files, financial documentation, acquisition plans, customer information, sensitive e-mails, exclusive product releases and other corporate records. All are ultra-capital assets that need to be shielded from the outside world.* [10]

Organizations lacking in the policies and technologies necessary to protect their internal confidential documents and communications should begin an IG initiative and investigate technologies that can assist in enforcing policies, such as endpoint security tools like information rights management (IRM) that can secure electronic documents from their creation through their entire lifecycle.[11]

But it's not all about technology. It is also about leadership, communications, and corporate culture. Leveraging and enforcing IG policies to create a culture of security and compliance may be the best weapon senior management has to combat internal theft and industrial espionage. Communications and training must be planned, methodical, and regular. Safeguarding information assets is not a project—it is a constant process.

One thing is painfully true: Corporate espionage will continue to increase. Most of it will go undetected, quietly eroding information assets over time. The biggest question is whether or not your organization has put in place the necessary steps to counter it and mitigate its risk, or whether it will suffer steep losses like so many others.[12]

> The most effective way to prevent industrial espionage is by embedding data and document security into an organization's culture.

The Blame Game: Where Does Fault Lie When Information Is Leaked?

When information is spilled through an unintentional disclosure or data breach the most frequent scapegoat is the employee who was closest to it. He or she could be the person who lost a thumb drive or laptop, or the one responsible for securing a particular document type in their functional area. The higher-ups zero in on this person and place the blame squarely on them, but what level of responsibility does the employer share? Are they not responsible for corporate governance, and therefore IG? Are they not responsible for providing the technology and tools to help secure confidential information assets?

There are policies that must be formed and technologies that must be deployed, and these are the responsibility of the employer and senior management. In the event of a data breach, they need to *first* look at their IG policies and business processes. Were the procedures (and enabling technologies)—the tools employees need—in place to protect critical documents and data? Are lines of responsibility clear? Is there auditability and accountability?

Accidental or unintentional data breaches can be as damaging as malicious or intentional ones. So IG policies must be set and tested and audited regularly to ensure compliance and effectiveness. Only certain employees should have access to confidential information assets, and always at the proper time. Also, employees must be made aware of possible ways to lose or compromise data. Training should be ongoing. Communication should consistently enforce the message over a variety of media, week after week, month after month. As Peter Abatan states in his blog, "It is only after an organisation has employed the right tools that it can begin to hold its employees responsible for a security breach."[13]

Consequences of Not Employing E-Document Security

A senior executive pondered what could happen if his organization did not use EDS software for safeguarding critical documents. What are the potential consequences? The following are six ways an organization can be negatively impacted, according to Abatan:

1. *The perceived value of your business is eroded slowly through the loss of your intellectual property to competitors that former employees join or new startups by former employees.*
2. *Investor confidence in your business' ability to safeguard trade secrets begins to wane.*
3. *You really don't have full control of where your information assets are located and as such you cannot know when your confidential information gets into the wrong hands.*
4. *You cannot control how your confidential information or sensitive data is used once you send it to a third party.*
5. *Staff could mail confidential documents or sensitive data to the wrong recipient after which you have no control.*
6. *You might never know when your intellectual property is taken without permission and used in a way that is counter-intuitive to your business.*[14]

In addition, there is the potential direct cost of fines and legal fees for compliance failures.[15] To mitigate this risk, managers need to find out how technologies, such as IRM and data loss prevention (DLP)—which are discussed in detail later in this book—can prevent the flow of confidential information and intellectual property to competitors, and also develop and enforce IG to implement the policies needed to protect confidential e-documents.

Chapter Summary: Key Points

- Electronic document security (EDS) came to the forefront with the revelation of leaked documents openly published by WikiLeaks. This should be a wake-up call to all organizations.
- The goal of a program to secure confidential information assets is to provide complete document lifecycle security (DLS) for critical electronic documents.
- Industrial espionage and loss of confidential documents is rising, and will continue to increase.
- Loss of confidential documents and intellectual property causes real economic damage to organizations, and erodes information asset value.
- Organizations should first take a serious look at the business processes that support information governance when there is a data breach or loss/misuse of confidential information assets.
- Leakage and misuse of internal e-documents can be avoided by developing information governance strategies to create and enforce policies for EDS, and by deploying specific technologies to monitor compliance.

Notes

1. Bill Blake, "WikiLeaks, the Pearl Harbor of the 21st Century," *edocument Sciences, LLC*, posted December 6, 2010, http://edocumentsciences .com/wikileaks-the-pearl-harbor-of-the-21st-century, retrieved July 10, 2011.
2. Ibid.
3. Antone Gonsalves, "Justice Department Launches IP Task Force," *InformationWeek Government*, posted February 15, 2010, www.infor mationweek.com/news/government/policy/showArticle.jhtml?articleID =222900277, retrieved March 9, 2012.
4. James Hurley, "Companies Warned as Data Theft Disputes Surge," *The Telegraph*, posted November 24, 2010, www.telegraph.co.uk/finance /businessclub/8157244/Companies-warned-as-data-theft-disputes-surge .html, retrieved March 9, 2012.
5. Peter Abatan, "Corporate and Industrial Espionage to Rise in 2011," Enterprise Digital Rights Management, www.enterprisedrm.info/post/ 2742811887/corporate-espionage-to-rise-in-2011, retrieved March 9, 2012.

6. Todd Ackerman, "Laptop Theft Puts Texas Children's Patient Info at Risk," *Houston Chronicle*, July 30, 2009, http://www.chron.com/news/houston-texas/article/Laptop-theft-puts-Texas-Children-s-patient-info-1589473.php, retrieved March 2, 2012.

7. Jonny Greatrex, "Bungling West Midlands Medics Lose 12,000 Private Patient Records," *Sunday Mercury,* September 5, 2010, http://www.sundaymercury.net/news/sundaymercuryexclusives/2010/09/05/bungling-west-midlands-medics-lose-12-000-private-patient-records-66331-27203177, retrieved March 2, 2012.

8. U.S. Department of Health & Human Services, "ONC Commissioned Medical Identity Theft Assessment" http://healthit.hhs.gov/portal/server.pt?open=512&objID=1177&parentname=CommunityPage&parentid=12&mode=2&in_hi_userid=10732&cached=true, retrieved August 1, 2011.

9. Booz Allen Hamilton, "Medical Identity Theft Final Report," January 15, 2009, www.nachc.com/client/Medical%20Identity%20Theft%20Final%20Report-ONC.pdf.

10. Quoted in Robert Smallwood, "Securing Documents in the Wiki-Leaks Era," *KM World*, posted May 28, 2011, www.kmworld.com/Articles/Editorial/Feature/Securing-documents-in-the-WikiLeaks-era-75642.aspx, retrieved August 1, 2011.

11. Peter Abatan, "Corporate and Industrial Espionage to Rise in 2011," Enterprise Digital Rights Management, www.enterprisedrm.info/post/2742811887/corporate-espionage-to-rise-in-2011, retrieved March 9, 2012.

12. Ibid.

13. Peter Abatan, "Who Should Be Blamed for a Data Breach?" Enterprise Digital Rights Management, retrieved February 2, 2012.

14. Peter Abatan, "What Could Happen If You Don't Employ Enterprise Rights Management," Enterprise Digital Rights Management, www.enterprisedrm.info/, retrieved March 9, 2011.

15. Adi Ruppin, e-mail to the author on August 30, 2011.

CHAPTER 2

Information Governance: The Crucial First Step

G ood information management is critical to succeed in today's fast-paced, competitive global business environment. Having trusted and reliable data in reports and databases allows managers to make key decisions with confidence.[1] And accessing that information and business intelligence in a timely fashion can yield a long-term sustainable competitive advantage, creating more agile enterprises.

To do this, enterprises must standardize and systematize their handling of information; that is, how it is accessed, controlled, managed, shared, stored, and audited. This is *information governance (IG)*.

First, Better Policies; Then, Better Technology for Better Enforcement

Typically, some policies governing the use and control of information may have been established for financial and compliance reports, and perhaps e-mail, but they are often incomplete and out-of-date, and have not been adjusted for changes in the business environment, such as new technology platforms (e.g., Web 2.0, social media), changing laws (e.g., U.S. FRCP 2006 changes), and additional regulations.

Further adding to the challenge is the rapid proliferation of mobile devices like tablets and smartphones used in business—information can be more easily lost or stolen—so IG efforts must be made to preserve and protect the enterprise's information assets.

Proper IG requires that policies are flexible enough not to hinder the proper flow of information in the heat of the business battle yet strict enough to control and audit for misuse, policy violations, or security breaches. This is a continuous iterative policy-making process, which must be monitored and fine-tuned. Even with the absolute best efforts, some policies will miss the mark and need to be reviewed and adjusted.

Getting started with IG awareness is the first step. It may have popped up on an executive's radar at one point or another and an effort might have been made, but many organizations leave these policies on the shelf and do not revise them regularly, so, when new platforms like social media arrive, they may find themselves on their heels and in the throes of new policy-making and enforcement efforts.

This reactive, tactical *project* approach is not the way to go about it—haphazardly swatting at technological, legal, and regulatory flies. A proactive, strategic *program,* with a clear, accountable sponsor, an ongoing plan, and regular review process is the only way to continuously adjust IG policies to keep them current so that they best serve the organization's needs.

> Information governance is a subset of corporate governance.

The information that companies are busy generating, collecting, and mining offers a wealth of potential benefits; however, its use also carries substantial risks. As a result, some organizations have created formal governance bodies to establish strategies, policies, and procedures surrounding the distribution of information inside and outside the enterprise. These governance bodies may include members from many different functional areas, since proper IG necessitates input from a variety of stakeholders. Representatives from information technology (IT), records management, risk management, compliance, operations, security, legal, finance, and perhaps knowledge management are frequently a part of IG teams. Often these efforts are jump-started and organized with third-party consulting resources that specialize in IG efforts.

Defining Information Governance

What is information governance? According to "The Rise of Information Governance" by The 451 Group:

> *There's no single answer to that question. At a high level, information governance encompasses the policies and leveraged technologies meant to dictate and manage what corporate information is retained, where and for how long, and also* how *it is retained (e.g., protected, replicated and secured). Information governance spans retention, security and lifecycle management issues.*[2]

Information governance is a subset of corporate governance, which has been around as long as corporations have existed. IG is a rather new multidisciplinary field which is still being defined, but has gained traction in the last several years. The focus on IG comes not only from compliance, legal, and records management functionaries but also from executives who understand they are accountable for the governance of information and that theft or erosion of information assets has real costs and consequences.

IG is an all-encompassing term for *how an organization manages the totality of its information.*

IG is more than simply the governance of information technology. It goes much further than controlling and managing IT and its development; IG focuses on the output, the *result* of applying IT. That means it focuses on the actual documents, reports, and records (created from raw data and applications), and controlling their use and security.

IG is a hybrid field, using a set of multidisciplinary methods and technologies to support an organization's operational and compliance requirements.

> Information governance is more than governing IT—rather it focuses more on managing and controlling the output of IT.

IG includes elements of records management, information security and privacy, IT governance, corporate governance, enterprise content management (ECM), e-discovery, and e-mail archiving. This also means that it includes technology subcategories such as document management, enterprise search, knowledge management, business continuity, and disaster recovery.

IG is the set of policies, processes, and controls to manage information in compliance with external regulatory requirements and internal governance frameworks. Specific policies apply to specific document types, records, and other business information such as e-mail and reports. Simply put, information governance is "the way in which an organisation handles, uses and manages its information in an efficient, effective and secure manner to all the appropriate ethical, legal and quality standards."[3]

> Information governance is how an organization maintains security, complies with regulations, and meets ethical standards when managing information, data, and documents.

Industry thought leader Barclay T. Blair explains that IG is a "relatively new term for which the precise meaning is still being shaped by the market and those that promote its use. However, it is clear that the term incorporates (in whole or in part) concepts from disciplines such as:

- Records Management
- Compliance
- Information Management
- IT Governance (such as COBIT and ITIL)
- Corporate Governance (such as COSO, SOX, PCAOB Standards)
- Information Security/Information Protection
- Privacy
- Enterprise search, portals, and knowledge management
- Enterprise content management
- Document management
- Archiving
- Business continuity, backup and disaster recovery
- E-Discovery

This is why IG is a multidisciplinary pursuit."[4]

Essentially, information governance is "a quality-control discipline for managing, using, improving and protecting information."[5]

IG requires inclusion and consultation with stakeholders and a holistic thought process to improve the quality and security of information throughout its lifecycle. The result is not only more secure information, but also better information to base decisions on, and closer adherence to regulatory and legal demands.[6]

As previously stated, IG is a part of corporate governance and it draws on IT governance, but it goes much further. IG is expansive and amorphous and difficult to get one's arms around to understand but the key is that *IG involves creating, maintaining, monitoring, and enforcing policies for the use of information*—including unstructured information such as electronic documents—*to meet external compliance demands and internal governance controls.*

The scope of this book is in developing and leveraging IG in the narrower context of managing electronic documents, records, and communications in a secure fashion.

Accountability Is Key

According to Debra Logan at Gartner Group, *none of the proffered definitions of IG include "any notion of coercion, but rather ties governance to accountability* [italics added] that is designed to encourage the right behavior. . . . The word that matters most is *accountability* [italics in the original]." The root of many problems with managing information is the "fact that there is no accountability for information as such."[7]

Establishing policies, procedures, processes, and controls to ensure the quality, integrity, and security of confidential documents are the fundamental steps needed to protect critical documents in this age of überhackers and WikiLeaks. Then, the auditing, testing, maintenance, and improvement of IG and e-document security software installation become essential.

Why IG Is Good Business

IG is a tough sell. It can be difficult to make the business case for it, unless there has been some colossal data breach or loss of documents. In fact, *the largest impediment to IG adoption is simply identifying its benefits and costs,* according to The Economist Intelligence Unit. Sure, the enterprise needs better control over its information, but how much better? At what cost? What is the payback period and the return on investment (ROI)?[8]

It is challenging to make the business case for IG, yet making that case is fundamental to getting IG efforts off the ground.

Here are eight reasons why IG makes good business sense, from Barclay Blair:

1. **We can't keep everything forever.** *IG makes sense because it enables organizations to get rid of unnecessary information in a defensible manner. Organizations need a sensible way to dispose of information in order to reduce the cost and complexity of IT environment. Having unnecessary information around only makes it more difficult and expensive to harness information that has value.*
2. **We can't throw everything away.** *IG makes sense because organizations can't keep everything forever, nor can they throw everything away. We need information—the right information, in the right place, at the right time. Only IG provides the framework to make good decisions about what information to keep.*
3. **E-discovery.** *IG makes sense because it reduces the cost and pain of discovery. Proactively managing information reduces the volume of information exposed to e-discovery and simplifies the task of finding and producing responsive information.*
4. **Your employees are screaming for it—just listen.** *IG makes sense because it helps knowledge workers separate "signal" from "noise" in their information flows. By helping organizations focus on the most valuable information, IG improves information delivery and improves productivity.*
5. **It ain't gonna get any easier.** *IG makes sense because it is a proven way for organizations to respond to new laws and technologies that create new requirements and challenges. The problem of IG will not get easier over time, so organizations should get started now.*

6. ***The courts will come looking for IG.*** *IG makes sense because courts and regulators will closely examine your IG program. Falling short can lead to fines, sanctions, loss of cases, and other outcomes that have negative business and financial consequences.*

7. ***Manage risk: IG is a big one.*** *Organizations need to do a better job of identifying and managing risk. The risk of information management failures is a critical risk that IG helps to mitigate.*

8. ***Email: reason enough.*** *IG makes sense because it helps organizations take control of email. Solving email should be a top priority for every organization.*[9]

Impact of a Successful IG Program

When making the business case for IG, and articulating its benefits, it is useful to focus on its central impact. *Putting cost-benefit numbers to this may be difficult, unless you also consider the worst-case scenario of loss or misuse of confidential information assets.* How much is a new patented design worth? How much are confidential merger and acquisition (M&A) documents worth? How much are customer lists worth? Internal price lists? Frequently, organizations do not understand the value of IG until trade secrets are stolen, an expensive legal battle is lost, heavy fines are imposed for non-compliance, or executives go to jail.

A successful IG program should enable organizations to:

- **Use common terms across the enterprise.** This means that departments must agree on how they are going to classify document types, which relies on a cross-functional effort. With common enterprise terms, searches for information are more productive and complete. This begins with developing a standardized corporate taxonomy, which defines the terms (and substitute terms in a custom corporate thesaurus), document types, and their relationships in a hierarchy.

- **Map information creation and usage.** This effort can be buttressed with the use of technology tools such as data loss prevention (DLP), which can be used to discover the flow of information within and out of the enterprise. You must first determine *who* is accessing *which* information *when,* and *where* it is going. Then these information flows can be monitored and analyzed. The goal is to stop the erosion or misuse of information assets and to stem data breaches with monitoring and security technology.

- **Obtain "information confidence."** That is, the assurance that information has integrity, validity, accuracy, and quality; this means being able to *prove* that the information is reliable, and its access, use, and storage meets compliance and legal demands.

- **Harvest and leverage information.** Using techniques and tools like data mining and business intelligence, new insights may be gained that provide an enterprise with a sustainable competitive advantage over the long term, since managers will have more and better information as a basis for business decisions.[10]

Critical Factors in an IG Program

When presenting a proposed IG program, it is helpful to clarify the keys to making it successful. Listed below are the most important factors to a successful IG program, adapted from the MIKE2.0 open framework for information management, created by the consulting firm BearingPoint. This definition provides the "target scope" for an IG solution offering:

- **Accountability.** Because of the ways in which information is captured—and how it flows across the enterprise, *everyone* has a role to play in how it is governed. Many of the most important roles are played by individuals fairly junior in the organization. They typically play a key role in the data capture stage and often cause—or see—errors on a first-hand basis. Certain key individuals need to be dedicated to IG. These roles are filled by senior executives such as the CIO, Information Architects, and Data and Content Stewards.
- **Efficient operating models.** The IG approach should define an organizational structure that most effectively handles the complexities of both integration *and* information management (IM) across the whole of the organization. Of course, there will typically be some degree of centralization as information flows across the business. However, this organizational model need not be a single, hierarchical team. The common standards, methods, architecture, and collaborative techniques so central to IG allow this model to be implemented in a wide variety of models: physically central, cloud or virtual, or offshore. *Organizations should provide assessment tools and techniques to progressively refine these new models over time*.
- **A common methodology.** An IG program should include a common set of activities, tasks, and deliverables. Doing so builds specific IM [information management]-based competencies. This enables greater reuse of artifacts and resources, not to mention higher productivity out of individuals. It also manifests the commonalities of different IM initiatives across the organization.

- **Standard models.** A common definition of terms, domain values, and their relationships is one of the fundamental building blocks of IG. This should go beyond a traditional data dictionary. It should include a lexicon of unstructured content. Defining common messaging interfaces allows for easy inclusion of "data in motion." Business and technical definitions should be represented and, just as important, the lineage between them easy to navigate.
- **Architecture.** An IM architecture should be defined for the current-state, transition points, and target vision. The inherent complexity of this initiative will require the representation of this architecture through multiple views. This is done in Krutchen's Model. Use of architectural design patterns and common component models are key aspects of good governance. This architecture must accommodate dynamic and heterogeneous technology environments that, invariably, will quickly adapt to new requirements.
- **Comprehensive scope.** An IG approach should be comprehensive in its scope, covering structured data *and* unstructured content. It should also include the entire lifecycle of information. This begins with its initial creation, including integration across systems, archiving, and eventual destruction. This comprehensive scope can only [be] achieved with an architecture-driven approach and well-defined roles and responsibilities.
- **Information value assessment (IVA).** Organizations (should) place a very high value on their *information assets*. As such, they will view their organization as significantly de-valued when these assets are unknown—or poorly defined. An IVA assigns an economic value to the information assets held by an organization. The IVA also [shows] how IG influences this value. It must also measure whether the return outweighs the cost, as well as the time required to attain this return. In this vein, current methods are particularly immature, although some rudimentary models do exist. In this case, industry models must greatly improve, much like what has occurred in the past ten years in the infrastructure space.
- **Senior leadership.** *Senior leaders need to manage their information*, and deal with related issues. CIOs, for example, must face a host of business users who increasingly demand relevant, contextual information. At this same time, leadership teams often blame failures on "bad data." In the post Sarbanes-Oxley environment, CFOs are asked to sign off on financial statements. To this end, *the quality of data and the systems that produce that data are being scrutinized now more than ever before*. CMOs are being asked to grow revenues with less human resources. New regulations around the management of information have prevented many organizations from being effective. Senior leaders must

work towards a common goal of improving information while concurrently appreciating that IM is still immature as a discipline. The bottom line is that there will be some major challenges ahead.

- **Historical quantification.** In the majority of cases, the most difficult aspect of IM [and information governance] can be stated very simply: most organizations are trying to fix decades of "bad behavior." The current-state is often unknown, even at an architectural or model level. The larger the organization, the more complex this problem typically becomes. Historical quantification through common architectural models and quantitative assessments of data and content are key aspects of establishing a known baseline. Only then can organizations move forward. For such a significant task, this assessment must be conducted progressively—not all at once.
- **Strategic approach.** An IG program will need to address complex issues across the organization. Improvements will typically be measured over months and years, not days. As a result, a strategic approach is required. A comprehensive program can be implemented over long periods of time through multiple release cycles. The strategic approach will allow for flexibility to change. However, the level of detail will still be meaningful enough to effectively deal with complex issues.
- **Continuous improvement.** It is not always cost-effective to fix all issues in a certain area. Sometimes, it is best instead follow the 80/20 rule. An IG program should explicitly plan to revisit past activities. It should build on a working baseline through audits, monitoring, technology re-factoring, and personnel training. Organizations should look for opportunities to "release early, release often." At the same time, though, they should remember what this means from planning and budgeting perspectives.
- **Flexibility for change.** While an IG program involves putting standards in place, it must utilize its inherent pragmatism and flexibility for change. A strong governance process does *not* mean that exceptions can't be granted. Rather, key individuals and groups need to know exceptions are occurring—and why. The Continuous Improvement approach grants initial workarounds. These then have to be re-factored at a later point in order to balance short-term business priorities.
- **Governance tools.** Measuring the effectiveness of an IG program requires tools to capture assets and performance. Just as application development and service delivery tools exist, organizations need a way to measure information assets, actions, and their behaviors.[11]

By focusing an IG program proposal on its resultant impact, senior managers can more readily understand the business case to implement and its crucial benefits.

Who Should Determine IG Policies?

When forming an information governance steering committee or board, it is essential to include representatives from cross-functional groups and at differing levels of the organization. It must be driven by an executive sponsor (see Chapter 14 on securing and managing executive sponsorship) and include active members from key business units, as well as other departments including IT, finance, risk, compliance, records management, and legal. Then, corporate training/education and communications must be involved to keep employees trained and current on IG policies. This function may be performed by an outside consulting firm if there is no corporate education staff. Knowledge workers, those who work with sensitive information in any capacity, must understand the risks of document leakage and data loss, and must be cognizant of these risks as they perform their day-to-day functions. *Policies are worthless if people do not know or understand them, or how to comply.* And training is a crucial element that will be examined in any compliance hearing or litigation that may arise. "Did senior management not only create the policies, but provide adequate training on them, on a consistent basis?" This will be a key question raised. So a training plan is a necessary piece of IG and education should be heavily emphasized.[13]

The need for IG is increasing due to the increased incidence of theft and misuse of internal documents and communications. But also the need for IG is increasing because of more rigorous legal and regulatory requirements. *Organizations that do not have active IG programs should reevaluate IG policies and their internal processes following any security breach or theft.* If review boards include a broad section of critical players on the IG committee and leverage executive sponsorship, they *may* be able to fend off any future attacks on their confidential information assets.

Chapter Summary: Key Points

- Although organizations vigilantly protect their physical assets, most do *not* properly secure and govern their information assets.
- Information governance (IG) is how an organization maintains security, complies with regulations, and meets ethical standards when managing information, data, and documents.
- IG is a subset of corporate governance and encompasses the policies and leveraged technologies meant to manage *what* corporate information is retained, *where*, and *for how long*, and also *how* it is retained.

- Implementing an IG program requires a multidisciplinary approach with representatives from a broad cross section of the organization.
- Training and communications are key components of an IG program to secure confidential information assets. Knowledge workers must be apprised of the risks of document and data loss so they can actively counter them daily.

Notes

1. The Economist Intelligence Unit, "The Future of Information Governance," www.emc.com/leadership/business-view/future-information-governance.htm, retrieved March 10, 2012.
2. Kathleen Reidy, "The Rise of Information Governance," *Too Much Information: The 451 Take on Information Management* (blog), August 5, 2009, http://blogs.the451group.com/information_management /2009/08/05/the-rise-of-information-governance/, retrieved March 28, 2012.
3. "Information Governance Framework," *Adventures in Records Management,* posted November 12, 2007, http://adventuresinrecordsm anagement.blogspot.com/2007/11/information-governance-framework .html, retrieved December 14, 2011.
4. "What is Information Governance?" Via Lumina, http://vialumina .com/our-services/what-is-information-governance/, retrieved July 15, 2011.
5. Arvind Krishna, "Three Steps to Trusting Your Data in 2011," CTO Edge, posted March 9, 2011, www.ctoedge.com/content/three-steps-trusting-your-data-2011, retrieved July 12, 2011.
6. Ibid.
7. Debra Logan, "What Is Information Governance? And Why Is It So Hard?" posted January 11, 2010, http://blogs.gartner.com/debra_logan/ 2010/01/11/what-is-information-governance-and-why-is-it-so-hard/, retrieved July 12, 2011.
8. Barclay T. Blair, "Making the Case for Information Governance: Ten Reasons IG Makes Sense," ViaLumina Ltd, 2010, http:// barclaytblair.com/making-the-case-for-ig-ebook/, retrieved September 7, 2011.
9. Barclay T. Blair, "8 Reasons Why Information Governance (IG) Makes Sense," posted June 29, 2009, http://aiim.typepad.com/aiim_blog /2009/06/8-reasons-why-information-governance-ig-makes-sense.html, retrieved July 12, 2011.

10. Arvind Krishna, "Three Steps to Trusting Your Data in 2011," CTO Edge, posted March 9, 2011, www.ctoedge.com/content/three-steps-trusting-your-data-2011, retrieved July 12, 2011.
11. MIKE2.0, "Information Governance Solution Offering," http://mike2.op enmethodology.org/wiki/Information_Governance_Solution_Offering, retrieved July 20, 2011.
12. Ibid.
13. "Governance Overview (SharePoint Server 2010)," http://technet .microsoft.com/en-us/library/cc263356.aspx, retrieved April 19, 2011.

PART II

Information Platform Risks and Countermeasures

CHAPTER 3

Managing E-Documents
and Records

This chapter provides an overview of the types of software applications that manage electronic documents—and their security vulnerabilities—to afford a basic understanding of the fundamental challenges enterprises face in securing their confidential information assets.

Electronic documents and records can be managed by a few different types of software, which overlap in functionality and are often implemented in more than one instance in an organization.

Enterprise Content Management

Enterprise content management (ECM) software (sometimes referred to as content management systems, or CMS) manages the totality of an organization's content, from web content to internal e-documents, reports, and business records. So, when a document is rendered in various forms (e.g., web, electronic, print), only one file of the content is needed. This one file is kept up-to-date for access across departments or the entire enterprise.

ECM can manage all types of content in the enterprise, although in practice its focus is on managing unstructured content, while databases usually manage structured content. Structured content consists of numbers in rows and columns that can be manipulated arithmetically in calculations. This data is primarily financial and is often used in financial reports and business intelligence (BI) applications. Unstructured content is everything else—*and accounts for roughly 90 percent of an organization's total information*—including those e-documents, e-records, e-mail, and other content that is not expressed in numbers but exists as digital files. This may include scanned copies of documents like contracts or customer letters, loan or insurance applications, bills of lading, and land deeds, or internally created documents, like letters and memos, spreadsheets, audio-visual presentations, and other common business outputs.

ECM systems provide powerful document management support for managing versioned e-documents and ensure that users can easily retrieve the latest versions, while tracking revisions. *But many users will still use out-of-date versions they have stored locally, outside the repository* (e.g., from their desktop PC, tablet, smartphone, or in their e-mail inbox). This can result in costly errors, wasted work, and, most important, failure to comply with current regulations and operating procedures.

Information governance (IG) measures and additional technology are needed to find those errant e-documents that are scattered about the enterprise. In addition, e-documents and other content are no longer secure once they are accessed by authorized users, so protections must be added to the e-documents directly, to maintain persistent security wherever they are routed.

The glaring weakness of ECM systems is that, by and large, once a document is accessed by an authorized user it has no protections at all outside the repository to track and secure it. Another layer of information technology is necessary.

Document Management Principles

Document management is a subset and component of the broader discipline of ECM and is related to document imaging (scanning paper to digital), workflow, records management (RM), and digital asset management (DAM).

To safeguard critical e-documents that comprise key information assets, it is essential to have an understanding of the *document lifecycle*, the entire span of use of e-documents, from creation to final disposition (i.e., archiving or storage) and how they are controlled through those processes.

Document lifecycle management (DLM), a subset of information lifecycle management (ILM), *is the concept that a document must be managed through its entire cycle of use, from its original creation (or delivery to the enterprise) to final disposition.*

This seems obvious. Of course documents must be managed as they are used throughout the organization. But the *management* part of DLM includes specific actions or processes that are invoked automatically as the document works its way through its lifecycle.

For instance, when a document's *draft* state is complete, it may be automatically routed for approval to the next-level employee responsible. Once it is approved, it becomes a *final* document, and that may invoke an automatic routing of a copy to the document management repository. If it is an actual business record (as defined by the organization itself), it may be routed to the electronic records management (ERM) system.[1]

Once a document is in the ERM system, a record retention schedule will be applied, based on its document type and all business, legal, and regulatory requirements. As the document reaches the end of its required retention period, a decision must be made as to whether to archive it permanently or to destroy it. This routing and these decisions can be completely automated or can allow for human review between steps. In any case, it is best if this document routing and processing is performed transparently, so the knowledge worker who created it may work unimpeded.

But the policies on how the document is routed, handled, stored, and ultimately archived or destroyed must first be developed, and they must be kept up to date. This is the hard part of DLM.

The Goal: Document Lifecycle Security

The goal of efforts to secure critical e-documents is complete *document lifecycle security (DLS)*, a term that is coined in this book.

DLS ensures that documents are protected and secured from creation, through their entire lifecycle of use to final disposition. During that time, the ability to edit, forward, copy, print, or otherwise manipulate a document can be restricted and completely secured, with new technologies available today, like information rights management (IRM). Many technologies can secure perimeters, and some can secure documents in transit, but to secure them during editing and use—even if the documents are copied and moved to mobile media or other desktops outside the organization and then routed back—that is the challenge and goal.

Electronic Document Management Systems

An *electronic document management system* (*EDMS* or *DMS*) is software designed to store and track electronic documents. It manages electronic documents such as word processing and spreadsheet files, digital report files, and scanned images of paper documents.

> Document management software is used to track and store electronic documents throughout their lifecycle.

Document management [software] controls the lifecycle of documents in your organization—how they are created, reviewed, and published, and how they are ultimately disposed of or retained.[2]

A well-designed DMS allows knowledge workers to more easily find and share documents. First, it organizes documents in a logical way, by using standardized terms in a corporate taxonomy, making them easy to search for; standardized metadata fields describe the document's characteristics. Second, a DMS standardizes content creation and its presentation across an enterprise. Such standardization components must be worked out ahead of time in an initial document governance plan. This plan should lay out which types of documents will be managed, which file types will be accepted, what restrictions will be placed on file size, and other parameters of the DMS's operation.

This standardization and organization makes it easier to meet required legal and compliance obligations, while reducing the cost of doing so. Documents requested by legal counsel or regulators can be searched for and found faster, and at a lower cost. Knowledge workers can be confident that the documents they are working on are the most current, and their searches for documents are complete and thorough. And having an efficient document management system in place can be strategic in that it helps feed other high-level business activities that can give an organization a competitive edge.[3]

According to TechNet:

[A]n effective document management solution controls, manages and tracks:

- *What types of [electronic] documents and other content can be created.*
- *What templates to use for each type of document.*
- *What metadata (descriptive information) to provide for each type of document.*
- *Where to store documents at each stage of a document's life cycle.*
- *How to control access to a document at each stage of its life cycle.*
- *How to move documents within the organization as team members contribute to document creation, review, approval, publication, and disposition.*
- *What policies to apply to documents so that document-related actions are audited, documents are retained or disposed of properly, and content important to the organization is protected.*
- *How documents are converted as they transition from one stage to another during their life cycles.*
- *How [electronic] documents are treated as corporate records, which must be retained according to legal requirements and corporate guidelines.[4]*

As with ECM systems, the vulnerability that document management systems have is that once a document is legitimately accessed by an authorized user, it has few if any protections to track and secure it. So, if a document is checked out from the corporate document library, and is outside the confines of the document management system, it is exposed to not only malicious threats but also accidental or unintentional loss or misuse. Additional IG policies and another layer of technology are needed in order that the documents may be secured, wherever they may be.

Records Management Principles

Not all documents are records. In business, a *record* is a document or other physical or electronic item that serves as evidence of a transaction or business activity performed by the organization. Records management is the process by which an organization determines what types of information are records, how to manage them through their retention periods, and how to ultimately destroy or archive them. The same principles that apply in records management apply in the management of electronic records.

Electronic Records Management

Electronic records management (ERM) software—often referred to by the newer, expanded moniker, electronic document and records management system (EDRMS)—manages all business records and documents regardless of their physical form. This means that both paper and electronic records are tracked in an ERM/EDRMS. Electronic forms of records can be e-documents, e-forms, video files, voice files, CD, DVD, audio tape, or any other type of electronic record.

ERM systems enforce record retention and disposition policies according to established retention schedules (e.g., ensuring that critical business records are retained for seven years), during which time they cannot be modified, and after which they are deleted so that they are no longer subject to the risk of legal discovery during a potential litigation. *But deleting records from a records management repository will often still leave dozens of copies scattered around internal and external servers and desktops.* This creates a liability for the organization and exposes it to potential misuse of confidential information assets.

So again, further IG measures and additional technology are necessary to ensure full compliance when destruction of a record is called for at the end of its lifecycle. Those errant, unfiled, or misfiled records can be easily found using modern enterprise search and data-mapping tools.

ERM systems are particularly vulnerable, since protections like document encryption may be considered an alteration of the record, and protections like IRM would not allow access to the needed metadata, indexing, and file records, as this information is typically encrypted. So securing the records would mean that some ERM functionality, such as full-text search of the records, would be disabled.

Chapter Summary: Key Points

- Electronic documents and records can be managed by a few different types of software applications that overlap in functionality and often are implemented in more than one instance in an organization. These include enterprise content management (ECM) systems, document management systems (DMS), electronic document and records management systems (EDRMS), and electronic records management (ERM) systems.
- Enterprise content management (ECM) systems manage unstructured content, from web content to internal documents, reports, and business records. Databases manage structured content that is expressed numerically in rows and columns.
- ECM systems typically manage repositories of e-documents and lack security once content has been legitimately accessed, so additional information governance (IG) measures and layers of technology are needed.
- A critical problem is that in the normal course of business, many copies of these documents are stored and used on laptops, tablets, and other devices outside the repository, where they are no longer managed and controlled.
- Document lifecycle security (DLS) means protecting a document from its creation through its editing, routing, and final disposition. DLS is the goal of a program to secure confidential information assets.
- A document management system (DMS) is software designed to store and track electronic documents. A DMS is used to track and store electronic documents such as word processing and spreadsheet files, digital report files, and scanned images of paper documents. Documents are vulnerable once outside the repository.
- ERM systems manage all business records and documents, regardless of their physical form. This means that both paper and electronic records are tracked in an ERM (or EDRMS). ERM systems present new challenges for records security since most approaches would encrypt needed data and not allow for indexing and full-text searching.

Notes

1. Don Lueders, "The Information Lifecycle Model," October 21, 2009, http://sharepointrecordsmanagement.com/2009/10/21/the-information -lifecycle-model/, retrieved August 5, 2011. Used with permission from Microsoft.
2. "Document Management Overview (SharePoint Server 2010)," May 12, 2010, http://technet.microsoft.com/en-us/library/cc261933.aspx, retrieved October 6, 2011. Used with permission from Microsoft.
3. "Document Management," Kofax, www.kofax.com/glossary/Document-Management/, retrieved October 6, 2011. Used with permission from Microsoft.
4. "Document Management Overview (SharePoint Server 2010)," May 12, 2010, http://technet.microsoft.com/en-us/library/cc261933.aspx, retrieved October 6, 2011. Used with permission from Microsoft.

CHAPTER 4

Information Governance and Security for E-mail Messages

E-mail is the most common business software application and the backbone of business communication today. Employees utilize it all day, including during their personal time. Social media use has skyrocketed in recent years and has actually surpassed e-mail for personal use, but the fact remains that in business, knowledge workers rely on e-mail for almost all communications, *including those of a sensitive nature*.

A 2011 survey of 2,400 corporate e-mail users worldwide found that nearly two-thirds preferred e-mail as their favorite form of business communication, surpassing not only social media but also telephone and in-person contact.[1]

These e-mail communications may contain confidential information assets such as strategic plans, financial spreadsheets and reports, product price lists, marketing plans, competitive analyses, safety data, recruitment and salary details, progressing contract negotiations, and other sensitive information.

E-mail systems can be hacked, monitored, and compromised and cause far-reaching damage to a victimized organization. The damage may occur slowly, and go undetected, while information assets—and business value—are eroded.

In mid-2011, it was reported that the "hacktivist" group AntiSec claimed responsibility for hacking a U.S. government contractor, Booz Allen Hamilton, and publically exposing 90,000 military e-mail addresses and passwords from the contractor by posting them online. It was the second attack on a government defense contractor in a single week.[2]

Booz Allen employees "maintain high government security clearances" working with the defense sector, yet AntiSec penetrated the communications systems with relative ease and noted it "basically had no security measures in place."[3]

AntiSec was able to go even further by running its own rogue application to steal software source code and to search and find access credentials to steal data from other servers, which the group said would help it to infiltrate other federal contractors and agencies. It even stated it might pass the security information on to other hackers.

The attack didn't stop there. Later that week, another federal defense and FBI contractor, IRC Federal, was hacked, databases were invaded, the website was modified, and information from internal e-mail messages was posted online.[4]

Employees Regularly Expose Organizations to E-mail Risk

A 2011 global e-mail survey, commissioned by a leading hosted e-mail services provider, found that nearly 80 percent of all employees send work e-mail to and from their personal accounts, and 20 percent do so regularly, which means that critical information assets are exposed to uncontrolled security risks.[5]

"Awareness of the security risks this behavior poses does not act as a deterrent" (italics added). Over 70 percent of people questioned recognize that there is an additional risk in sending work documents outside the corporate e-mail environment, but almost half of "these same respondents feel it is acceptable to send work emails and documents to personal email accounts anyway." According to the survey, the reasons for using personal e-mail accounts for work purposes range from working on documents remotely (71 percent), to sending files that are too big for the company mailbox (21 percent), taking documents with them when they leave a company (18 percent), and those who simply don't want to carry a laptop home (9 percent).[6] The top two frustrations users had with work e-mail were restrictions on mailbox size, which has a negative impact on e-mail management, and the inability to send large attachments. This second issue often forces workers to use a personal account to send and receive necessary files. If size limits are imposed on mailboxes and attachments, companies must provide a secure alternative to file storage and transfer. Otherwise, employees are pushed into risking corporate information assets via personal e-mail. This scenario not only complicates things for e-mail administrators but it also has serious legal and regulatory implications. Clearly, as stated by Paul Mah, "email retention and archival becomes an impossible task when emails are routed in a haphazard manner via personal accounts."[7]

This means that security, privacy, and records management issues must be addressed by first creating information governance (IG) policies to control and manage the use of e-mail. These policies can utilize the e-mail system's included security features and also employ additional monitoring and security technologies where needed.

The e-mail survey also found an overall lack of clear e-mail policies and weak communication of existing guidelines. Nearly half of the respondents stated that either their company had no e-mail policy or that they were unaware of one. Among those aware of a corporate e-mail policy, four in ten think it could be communicated better. Among companies that have a policy, most (88 percent) deal with the appropriate use of e-mail as a business tool, but less than one-third (30 percent) address e-mail retention from a security standpoint.

Generally, employees are aware that sending work documents outside of their corporate network is unsafe, and yet they continue to do so. It is abundantly clear that *e-mail policies have to be updated and upgraded to accommodate and manage the increasingly sophisticated and computer-savvy generation* of users who are able to find ways to work around corporate e-mail restrictions. (These users have been dubbed *Generation Gmail*.) In addition, new e-mail monitoring and security technologies need to be deployed to counter this risky practice, which exposes information assets to prying eyes or malicious attacks.

E-mail Policies Should Be Realistic and Technology Agnostic

E-mail policies must not be too restrictive. It may be tempting to include catch-all policies that attempt to tamp down user behavior, but such efforts cannot succeed.[8] An important step is consulting with stakeholders to understand their usage patterns and needs and then going through a series of drafts of the policy, allowing for input. It may be determined that some exceptions and changes in technologies need to be factored in, and that some additional technology is needed to accommodate users while keeping information assets safer and meeting compliance and legal demands. Specifics of these policies and tools should be progressively tightened down on a regular basis as the process moves forward.

These new IG guidelines and policies need to refer to technology in a generic sense—a "technology-neutral" sense—rather than specifying proprietary software programs or features.[9] That is to say, they should be written so that they are *not* in need of revision as soon as new technologies are deployed.

Developing organization-wide IG policies is time-consuming and expensive; they are a defensive measure that does not produce revenue, so managers, pressed for performance, often relegate policy-making to the low-priority list. Certainly, it is a tedious, difficult task, so organizations should aim to develop policies that are flexible enough to stand the test of time. But it is also necessary to establish a review process to periodically revise policies to accommodate changes in the business environment, the law, and technology.

Here is an example of a technology-agnostic policy directive:

All confidential information must be encrypted before being transmitted over the Internet.

This statement does not specify the technology to be used or the mode of transmission. The policy is neutral enough to cover not only e-mail and instant messaging (IM) but also social media, cloud computing, mobile computing, and other means of communication. The policy also does not specify the method or brand of the encryption technology, so the organization can select the best method and technology available in the future without adapting the policy.[10]

Is E-mail Encryption the Answer?

Not all corporate e-mail contains trade secrets, and much of it is innocuous. The most security-conscious organizations utilize e-mail encryption (scrambling the contents using advanced algorithms) to protect sensitive and confidential e-mail. But it isn't a simple matter of selecting the technology and implementing it. Users have to buy in, and they must understand why the policy is necessary since it will affect their day-to-day jobs. This is especially true if the technology that supports a policy is difficult to use or requires extra steps; otherwise employees will resist using it.

A study conducted by Princeton University entitled "Secrecy, Flagging, and Paranoia: Adoption Criteria in Encrypted E-Mail" found that "users saw universal, routine use of encryption as paranoid." Encryption flagged a message not only as confidential but also as urgent, so users found the encryption of mundane messages annoying.[11]

Interestingly, *the Princeton team also found that social factors influenced encryption decisions along with technical factors such as usability.* The findings suggest that understanding these social factors is necessary so that encryption technologies can be more widely accepted and adopted. In other words, these social factors should be considered when developing e-mail policies, conducting IG training, and following up regularly with positive reinforcement messages. On the flip side, any IG program must also include monitoring, audits, negative sanctions, and, ultimately, termination of employees who continue to expose the organization to unnecessary risk by not following established IG guidelines.

In summary, the Princeton study found:

- *The belief that encryption is not needed because a company is too small*
- *Encryption flags a message as being important or secret*

- *Encryption solutions are too complicated for users*
- *Email encryption solutions are too hard to implement and set up*
- *Using encryption makes the company look paranoid*
- *Receiving encrypted messages can be annoying*

To quote one respondent of the study, "normal people don't encrypt normal email messages." [12]

The average knowledge worker may not understand or appreciate the need for encrypting e-mail, but 99 percent of the time, e-mail travels around unsecured over the Internet. Surely information assets are being exposed, and an organization must zero in on those messages that are most at risk and contain the most sensitive information and consider updating IG policies and implementing e-mail encryption for them.

Critical to this effort will be clear communication of the secured e-mail policy on a consistent basis and training support for end users.

Common E-mail Security Mistakes

In just one week in 2011,

> *Google, the International Monetary Fund (IMF) and Citigroup all made headlines as a result of email associated with them being under attack. The reason we continue to see companies make the news as a result of email attacks is that email security is sometimes ignored when it comes to training users properly and making good decisions. In some cases, having the latest and greatest when it comes to security tools even creates a false sense of security that causes IT [information technology] staff and users, to overlook the little things.* A multi-layered defense that has been properly configured with all the best technology can be rendered useless if the little things are forgotten [emphasis added].[13]

For e-mail security governance, start with the basics, that is, communicating the importance of complex passwords and changing them frequently, instead of using ones that are static and easy to guess. This should not only be a part of an e-mail policy directive, but it can be encouraged by regularly sending reminders. A vigilant, security-conscious organization may even spot check by randomly sifting through e-mail passwords.

More training is needed to keep users aware that one simple error, such as hitting Reply All can mistakenly pass on sensitive information. Employees also need to understand that executable files in attachments (those with a .exe or .msi extension) can spread viruses, and that no one should blindly open attachments, even if they are from a known business contact, friend, or family member. This also applies to compressed zip files, which can release viruses when they are unzipped. Malware is often spread unknowingly by people who are in constant contact with each other. If attachments (or zip files) become a critical concern, the ability to open attachments with executable files can be turned off. In fact, some hidden malicious files can automatically execute when a simple e-mail message is opened, and this automatic execution must be disallowed by the e-mail system administrator.

Enterprises with sophisticated network security and firewalls can easily forget that desktop security is a necessity, too. Scanning a desktop, laptop, or tablet computer for viruses can prevent malware from becoming embedded. Once a malicious program is installed, it can use a simple keystroke logger to capture even the most complex of passwords, and it can be extremely difficult to detect that a computer has been compromised.

Prevention is the best medicine, and being proactive with users means having a detailed and up-to-date e-mail policy that weighs the enterprise's risks. And remember, "It is safer to disallow certain email capabilities up front than it is to do so later on down the road after damages from viruses and Trojan horses have occurred."[14] So, while users may be find frontline prevention measures inconvenient, they are imperative to ensure employees get the information they need in a timely fashion, within the confines of proper IG policy and by leveraging additional technology layers.

E-mail Security Myths

So, you have blocked executable files from opening and believe that will keep them from infecting systems? Not so fast—with technology-immersed Generation Gmail in the workforce, innovative work-arounds are springing up. If .exe or .msi files are blocked, users can simply change the name of the extension and send the message and attachment to a personal account (their own or that of a co-worker or friend). From there, they can open the file and change the extension back to the original.[15]

Today malware can be spread by clicking on a link to a website as well, so e-mail administrators and IG policymakers must be aware of this and include measures to counter possible attacks by this *drive-by* method. Sensational attacks on large companies like Sony, Google, and Bank of America make headlines, and smaller companies may feel they have security by obscurity, meaning they are not big enough for hackers to target. Certainly attacks on smaller, lesser-known companies are not as newsworthy, so they don't hit the media, but these small- and medium-sized businesses (SMBs) have smaller and less sophisticated IT staffs and technologies, making them even more vulnerable. When it comes to infiltration and infection of systems, "It actually happens more frequently to small- and medium-sized enterprises than it does to the big corporations."[16]

Many firms are outsourcing their e-mail administration and moving it to the cloud. It seems intuitive that moving e-mail outside of corporate firewalls exposes it to more security risks—after all, it is out of an organization's control. But providers of cloud-based e-mail have invested heavily in multiple layers of security—the type of investment that most SMBs cannot afford to make. So moving e-mail services to the cloud may actually be the *safest* bet for SMBs; cloud service providers have distributed data centers that can provide fail-safe backup in the event of a regional disaster.[17] For instance, in September 2011, a power outage hit southern California and knocked out electricity from just south of Los Angeles to all of San Diego, and even into the Baja peninsula in Mexico, for nearly a day. A cloud provider would typically have servers in the Midwest and on the East Coast, which could have provided continuous service to users who were still able to get online.

E-record Retention: Fundamentally a Legal Issue

Considering the massive volume of e-mail exchanged in business today, most e-mail messages do not rise to the level of being formal business records. But many of them do and are subject to IG, regulatory compliance, and legal requirements for maintaining and producing business records.

Although often it is lumped in with other information technology (IT) concerns, the retention of e-mail and other e-records is ultimately a legal issue. Other departments, including records management and business units, should certainly have input and should work to assist the legal team to record retention challenges and archiving solutions. But e-mail and e-record retention is "fundamentally a *legal* issue," particularly for public or highly regulated companies. According to Nancy Flynn of the ePolicy Institute, "It is essential for the organization's legal department to take the lead in determining *precisely* which types of email messages will be preserved, *exactly* how and where data will be stored, and *specifically when*—if ever—electronically stored information [ESI] will be deleted."[18]

> Managing e-records is primarily a legal issue, especially for public and heavily regulated companies.

Since they are often shot out in the heat of battle, e-mail messages are often evidence of a smoking gun in lawsuits and investigations and are the most requested type of evidence in civil litigation today. The content and timing of e-mail messages can also provide exonerating information, too.

In January 2010, a U.S. House of Representatives committee probing bailout deals subpoenaed the Federal Reserve Bank of New York for e-mail and other correspondence from Treasury Secretary Timothy Geithner (former president of the New York Federal Reserve Bank) and other officials. The House Oversight and Government Reform Committee was in the process of examining New York Fed decisions that funneled billions of dollars to big banks, including Goldman Sachs Group and Morgan Stanley.[19]

This is just one example of how crucial e-mail messages can be in legal investigations and how they play an important role in reconstructing events and motives for legal purposes.

Preserve E-mail Integrity and Admissibility with Automatic Archiving

Most users are not aware that e-mail contents and characteristics can be changed—"and rendered legally invalid"—by anyone with malicious motives, including those who are essentially "covering their tracks." Not only can the content be edited, but metadata that includes information like the time, date, and total number of characters in the message can also be changed retroactively.[20]

To offset this risk and ensure that spoliation does not occur, that is, the loss of proven authenticity of an e-mail, *all messages, both inbound and outbound, should be captured and archived automatically, and in real-time.* This preserves legal validity and forensic compliance. Additionally, e-mail should be indexed to facilitate the searching process and all messages should be secured in a single location.

E-mail Archiving Rationale: Compliance, Legal, and Business Reasons

There are good reasons to archive e-mail and retain it according to a specific retention schedule that follows your organization's IG policies. Having a handle on managing voluminous e-mail archives translates to being able to effectively and rapidly search and retrieve exactly the right messages, which can provide a significant legal advantage. It gives your legal team more and better information, and more time to figure out how to leverage it in legal strategy sessions. This means the odds are tipped in your organization's favor in the inevitable litigation arena. Your legal opponent may be driven to settle a weak claim when confronted with indisputable e-mail evidence, and in fact "email often produces supportive evidence that may help 'save the day' by providing valuable legal proof" of innocence.[21] This may stop frivolous lawsuits in their tracks. Further, reliable e-mail evidence—and bear in mind that e-mail is the most common type of information requested in civil lawsuits today—can also curtail lengthy and expensive lawsuits, and prevail. And if your company is public, Sarbanes-Oxley (SOX) regulations require the archiving of e-mail.

Don't Confuse E-mail Archiving with Backup

All backups are not created equal. *There is a big difference between traditional system backups and specialized e-mail archiving software.*

Backups are huge dumps to mass storage, where the data is stored sequentially and not compressed or indexed.[22] So it is impossible to search except by date, and even that would mean combing through troves of raw, non-indexed data.

The CEO may not be aware of it, but without true e-mail archiving, system administrators could spend long nights loading old tapes and churning out volumes of data and legal teams will bill hourly for manual searches through troves of data. This compromises your enterprise's legal position and increases not only raw costs but also leads to less capable and informed legal representation. According to one study, fully one-third of IT managers stated they would have difficulty producing an e-mail that is more than one year old. *"A backup system is no substitute for automatic archiving technology"* (italics added).[23]

No Personal Archiving in the Workplace

Employees are naturally going to want to back up their most important files, just as they probably do at home. But for an overall IG information-security program to be effective, personal archiving at work must be prohibited. This underground archiving results in hidden shadow files and is time-consuming and risky. According to Flynn, *"Self-managed email can result in the deletion of electronic records, alteration of email evidence, time-consuming searches for back-up tapes, and failure to comply with legal discovery demands"* (italics added). Also, users may compromise formal electronic records, or they may work from unofficial records, which therefore by definition might be inaccurate or out-of-date, posing compliance and legal ramifications.[24]

Are All E-mails Records?

This has been argued for years. *The short answer is no; not every e-mail message constitutes a record.* But how do you determine whether a message is a business record or not? The general answer is that a record documents a transaction or business-related event that may have legal ramifications or historic value. Most important are e-mails that document business activities that may relate to compliance requirements or those that could possibly come into dispute in litigation. Particular consideration should be given to financial transactions of any type.

Certainly evidence that required governance oversight or compliance activities have been completed needs to be documented and becomes a business record. Also, business transactions, where there is an exchange of money or the equivalent in goods or services, are also business records. Today, these transactions are often documented by a quick e-mail. And, of course, any contracts (and any progressively developed or edited versions thereof) that are exchanged through e-mail become business records.

The form or format of a potential record is irrelevant in determining whether it should be classified as a business record. For instance, if a meeting of the board of directors is recorded by a digital video recorder and saved to a DVD, it constitutes a record. If photographs are taken of a groundbreaking ceremony for a new manufacturing plant, the photos are records, too. If the company's founders tape-record a message to future generations of management on reel-to-reel tape, it is also a record, since it has historical value. But most records are going to be in paper, microfilm, or e-document form.

Some basic guidelines for determining whether an e-mail message should be considered a business record are:

1. The e-mail documents a transaction or the progress toward an ultimate transaction where anything of value is exchanged between two or more parties. All parts or characteristics of the transaction, including who (the parties to it), what, when, how much, and the composition of its components are parts of the transaction. Often seemingly minor parts of a transaction are found buried within an e-mail message with the pace of today's business environment. One example would be a last-minute discount offered by a supplier based on an order being placed or delivery being made within a specified timeframe.
2. The e-mail documents or provides support of business activity that pertains to internal corporate governance policies or compliance to externally mandated regulations.
3. *The e-mail documents other business activities that could possibly be disputed in the future*, whether it ultimately involves litigation or not (that is to say, most business disputes are actually resolved without litigation, provided proof of your organization's position can be shown). For instance, your supplier may dispute the amount of a discount, but once you forward the e-mail thread to them, they acquiesce.[25]

Destructive Retention of E-mail

Destructive retention is an approach to e-mail archiving where e-mail messages are retained for a limited time (e.g., 90 days or six months), "followed by its permanent deletion manually or automatically, from the company's network"[26]—if it is not declared a business record, in accordance with IG and records management policies. Implementing this as a policy may shield the enterprise from retaining potentially libelous or litigious e-mail that is not a formal business record—for example, off-color jokes or other personnel violations.

For heavily regulated industries, such as health care, energy, and financial services, organizations may need to archive e-mail for longer periods of time.

Chapter Summary: Key Points

- Nearly 80 percent of all employees send work e-mail messages to and from their personal e-mail accounts, which exposes critical information assets to uncontrolled security risks.
- Meeting e-mail retention and archival requirements becomes an impossible task when e-mail messages are routed in a haphazard manner via personal accounts.
- In developing e-mail policies, an important step is consulting with stakeholders.
- E-mail policies must not be too restrictive or tied to a specific technology. They should be flexible enough to accommodate changes in technology and should be reviewed and updated regularly.
- The latest and greatest security tools can create a false sense of security that causes IT staff and users to overlook the little things. A multilayered defense is essential.
- Opening executable and zip files pose the greatest risk in e-mail attachments.
- Hacker attacks occur more frequently to small- and medium-sized businesses (SMBs) than large corporations, but these smaller stories are not widely reported and sensationalized in the media.
- Encrypting e-mail messages is seen as cumbersome by users but it provides essential security. Social factors come into play with encryption, as well as technical factors.
- Not all e-mail messages constitute a business record.
- Not all e-mail rises to the level of admissible legal evidence. Certain conditions must be met.
- Automatic archiving protects the integrity of e-mail for legal purposes.

Notes

1. "Research Finds that Restrictive Email Policies Are Creating Hidden Security Risks for Businesses," *BusinessWire*, March 9, 2011, www.businesswire.com/news/home/20110309005960/en/Research-Finds-Restrictive-Email-Policies-Creating-Hidden, retrieved March 28, 2012.
2. Elizabeth Montalbano, "AntiSec Hacks Booz Allen, Posts Confidential Military Email," *InformationWeek*, July 12, 2011, www.informationweek.com/news/security/attacks/231001418?cid=nl_IW_daily_2011-07-12_html, retrieved March 28, 2012.
3. Ibid.
4. Mathew J. Schwartz, "AntiSec Hacks FBI Contractor" *InformationWeek*, July 11, 2011, www.informationweek.com/news/security/attacks/231001326, retrieved December 16, 2011.
5. "Research Finds that Restrictive Email Policies Are Creating Hidden Security Risks for Businesses," *BusinessWire*, March 9, 2011, www.businesswire.com/news/home/20110309005960/en/Research-Finds-Restrictive-Email-Policies-Creating-Hidden, retrieved March 28, 2012.
6. Ibid.
7. Paul Mah, "How to Reduce the Email Security Risks to Your Business," *The EmailAdmin*, March 10, 2011, www.theemailadmin.com/2011/03/how-to-reduce-the-email-security-risks-to-your-business/, retrieved December 16, 2011.
8. Kahn, Blair, *Information Nation: Seven Keys to Information Management Compliance*, AIIM International, 2004, pp. 98–99.
9. Ibid, pp. 95–96.
10. Ibid.
11. Shirley Gaw, Edward W. Felten, Patricia Fernandez-Kelly, Princeton University, www.cs.princeton.edu/~sgaw/publications/presentations/CHI2006-sgaw.pdf, retrieved August 9, 2011.
12. Jeff Orloff, "Understanding Email Encryption (Part 1)," *TheEmailAdmin.com,* August 9, 2011, www.theemailadmin.com/2011/08/understanding-email-encryption-part-1/, retrieved August 9, 2011.
13. Jeff Orloff, "5 Simple Mistakes When It Comes to Email Security," *TheEmailAdmin.com,* June 13, 2011, www.theemailadmin.com/2011/06/5-simple-mistakes-when-it-comes-to-email-security/, retrieved August 10, 2011.
14. Mike Rede, "Email Attacks," posted January 7, 2009, www.theemailadmin.com/2009/01/email-attacks/, retrieved January 13, 2012.
15. Jeff Orloff, "Misconceptions about Email Security," *TheEmailAdmin.com,* July 25, 2011, www.theemailadmin.com/2011/07/misconceptions-about-email-security/, retrieved December 16, 2011.
16. Ibid.

17. Ibid.
18. Nancy Flynn, *The E-Policy Handbook: Rules and Best Practices to Safely Manage Your Company's E-Mail, Blogs, Social Networking, and Other Electronic Communication Tools,* AMACOM, 2009, p. 20.
19. Hugh Son and Andrew Frye, "Geithner's E-mails, Phone Logs Sub-poenaed by House (update3)," www.bloomberg.com/apps/news?pid =newsarchive&sid=aGzbhrSxFlXw, January 13, 2010, retrieved December 16, 2011.
20. Nancy Flynn, *The E-Policy Handbook: Rules and Best Practices to Safely Manage Your Company's E-Mail, Blogs, Social Networking, and Other Electronic Communication Tools,* AMACOM, 2009, p. 37.
21. *Email Archiving and the Law,* Blake Lyons, bllaw.co.uk, March 27, 2007 and Nancy Flynn, *The E-Policy Handbook,* AMACOM, 2009, pp. 40–41.
22. Nancy Flynn and Randolph Kahn, *Email Rules, A Business Guide to Managing Policies, Security, and Legal Issues for E-Mail and Digital Communication,* AMACOM, 2003, p. 81-82.
23. Nancy Flynn, *The E-Policy Handbook,* p. 41.
24. Ibid., p. 43.
25. Robert F. Smallwood, *Taming the Email Tiger: Email Management for Compliance, Governance, & Litigation Readiness,* Bacchus Business Books, 2008.
26. Nancy Flynn, *The E-Policy Handbook,* p. 25.

CHAPTER 5

Information Governance and Security for Instant Messaging

I nstant messaging (IM) use in enterprises has proliferated—despite the fact that frequently—proper policies, controls, and security measures are not in place to prevent e-document and data loss. There are a variety of threats to IM use that enterprises must defend against to keep their information assets secure.

The first basic IM systems had real-time text capabilities for routing messages to users logged on to the same mainframe computer, which came into use in the mid-1960s. Early chat systems, like AOL Instant Messenger have been in use since the late 1980s, but true IM systems that included buddy list features appeared on the scene in the mid-1990s, followed by the release of Yahoo! and Microsoft IM systems. The use of these personal IM products in the workplace has created new security risks.[1]

There are also more secure enterprise instant messaging (EIM) products that can be formally deployed. Leading EIM installed systems include IBM Lotus Sametime, Microsoft Office Communications Server, Cisco Unified Presence, and Jabber XCP. In the financial sector, Bloomberg Messaging and Reuters Messaging are leading platforms.

By the year 2000 it was estimated that nearly 250 million people world-wide were making use of IM,[2] and today estimates reach over two billion users, with the addition of hundreds of millions of users in China.

As with many technologies, IM became popular first for personal use, then crept into the workplace—and exploded. IM is seen as a quicker and more efficient way to communicate short messages than engaging in a telephone conversation or going through rounds of sending and receiving endless e-mail messages. *The problem with IM is that many organizations are blind to the fact that their employees are going to use it one way or another*, sometimes for short personal conversations outside the organization, and if left unchecked, it exposes the organization to a myriad of risks and gives hackers another way to compromise confidential information assets.

Instant Messaging Security Threats

"IM networks provide the ability to not only transfer text messages, but also the transfer of files" (italics added), *which means that viruses, worms, Trojan horses, and other malware can infect the network and user desktop.*[3] Hackers do not have to scan through a sea of unknown IP addresses, but instead simply choose from an existing buddy list to find victims. They can do this covertly, through backdoor access, which allows them to avoid any firewall detections. Once they penetrate a computer, they have access to all files on a hard drive, through peer-to-peer communications.

Malware such as viruses and worms can be transferred easily through IM.

Stealing Information through Hijacking and Impersonation

Hackers can steal passwords using a keystroke logger or Trojan horse that is passed along through the open IM ports on a computer and then imperson-ate victimized users. The leading consumer IM systems do not encrypt chat sessions, so IM use is also vulnerable to *man-in-the-middle* attacks, where they intercept IM traffic and can impersonate a user. Using an EIM from a leading vendor will add additional enterprise security layers and tools.[4]

According to Neal Hindocha at Symantec, a leading Internet security provider:

> *Though more difficult, one can also highjack the entire connection by using a man-in-the middle attack. For example, a disconnect message, which appears to come from the server, can be sent to the victim from the hacker. This will cause the client to disconnect. The hacker can also use a simple denial of service exploit, or other unrelated exploits, to keep the client disconnected. Since the server keeps the connection open and does not know that the client has been disconnected, the hacker can then impersonate the victim user.*[5]

Denial-of-Service Attacks Freeze Access

Denial-of-service (DoS) attacks cut off access to a website or other comput-ing utility, and using IM can make an enterprise more vulnerable to DoS attempts. DoS can be accomplished by literally overloading a server with a flood-attack of requests. Successful DoS attacks can be merely a temporary annoyance that crashes the IM client, slows response time or makes IM unavailable, but they can also bring an enterprise to its knees, if it relies heavily on the computing resource that is targeted.[6]

Network Sniffers and Unauthorized Disclosure of Information Assets

A Trojan horse isn't the only tool hackers can use to spy on transmitted information. A network sniffer allows for (unencrypted) characters and data to be seen and monitored and can also be deployed maliciously to capture IM conversations. Using an EIM solution will reduce exposure, but enterprises must be aware that detailed conversations and confidential information assets can be exposed—even if no malware is found at the desktop or laptop level.[7]

Best Practices for Business IM Use

Employing best practices for enterprise IM use can help mitigate its security risks while helping to capitalize on the business agility and velocity benefits IM can provide. Best practices must be built in to information governance (IG) policies governing the use of IM although, "the specifics of these best practices must be tailored for each organization's unique needs."[8]

A methodology for forming IM-specific IG policies and implementing more secure use of IM must begin with surveying and documenting the proliferation of IM use in the organization. It should also discover how and why users are relying on IM—perhaps there is a shortcoming with their available IT tools and IM is a work-around.

> Documenting IM use in the organization is the first step in building IG policies to govern its use. Those policies must be tailored to the organization and its IM use.

Typically, executives will deny there is much use of IM, and that if it is being used, its impact is not worth worrying about. Also, getting users to come clean about their IM use may be difficult, since this may involve personal conversations and violations of corporate policy. A survey is a good place to start, but more sophisticated network monitoring tools need to be used to factually discover what IM systems are actually in use.

Once this discovery process has concluded, and the use of IM is mapped out, the IG team or steering committee must create or update policies to decide which IM systems it will allow to be used, how, when, and by whom; what restrictions or safeguards must be imposed; and guidelines as to appropriate use and content must be formulated. As a part of an overall IG effort, a well-written IM usage policy will:

- **Clearly and explicitly explain the organization's instant messaging objectives.** *Users should know why the organization permits IM and how it is expected to be used.*
- **Define expectations of privacy.** *Users should be made aware that the organization has the right to monitor and log all IM sessions for corporate compliance, safety, and security reasons.*
- **Detail acceptable and unacceptable uses.** *An exhaustive list of permitted and forbidden activities may not be necessary, but specific examples are helpful in establishing a framework of IM behavior for users.*
- **Detail content and contact restrictions (if any).** *Most organizations will want to limit the amount of idle IM chat that may occur with family, friends, and other non-business related contacts. There may also be additional issues related to information confidentiality and privacy. Some businesses may choose to block the distribution of certain types of information via live IM chat session or file transfer.*
- **Define consequences for violations of the policy.** *Users should be advised of the consequences of policy violations. Generally these should be aligned with the company's personnel and acceptable use policies.*[9]

The use of a standard disclaimer, to be inserted into all users' IM sessions, can remind employees of appropriate IM use and that all chat sessions are being monitored and archived, and can be used in court or compliance hearings.

The next major step is to work with the IT staff to find the best and most appropriate security and network-monitoring tools, given the computing environment. Alternatives must be researched, selected, and deployed. In this research and selection process, it is best to start with at least an informal survey of enterprises within the same industry to attempt to learn what has worked best for them.

The key to any compliance effort or legal action will be ensuring that IM records are true and authentic, so the exact, unaltered archiving of IM messages along with associated metadata should be implemented in real time. This is the only way to preserve business records that may be needed in the future. But also, a policy for deleting IM messages after a period of time, so long as they are not declared business records, must be formulated.

> Records of IM use must be captured in real time and preserved to ensure they are reliable and accurate.

IG requires that these policies and practices not be static, but rather that they be regularly revisited and updated to reflect changes in technology and legal requirements, and also to address any shortcoming or failure of the IG policies or technologies deployed.

Technology to Monitor IM

Today, it has been estimated that as much as 80 percent of all IM used by corporate employees comes from free IM providers like Yahoo!, MSN, or AOL. These programs are also the least secure. Messages using these IM platforms can fly around the Internet unprotected. So any monitoring technology implemented must have the capability to apply and enforce established IM use policies by constantly monitoring Internet traffic to discover IM conversations. Traffic containing certain key words can be monitored or blocked, and chat sessions between forbidden users (e.g., those who are party to a lawsuit) can be stopped before they start. But this all necessarily starts with IG and policy formulation.[10]

Tips for Safer IM

Organizations should assume that IM is being used, whether they have sanctioned it or not. And that may not be a bad thing—employees may have found a reasonable business use for which IM is expedient and effective. So management should not rush to ban its use in a knee-jerk reaction. Here are some tips for safer use of corporate IM:

- Just as e-mail attachments and embedded links are suspect and can contain malicious executable files, beware of IM attachments, too. The same rules governing e-mail use apply to IM, in that employees should never open attachments from people they do not know. Even if they do know them, with phishing and social-engineering scams, these attachments should first be scanned for malware using anti-virus tools.
- Do not divulge any more personal information than is necessary. This comes into play even when creating screen names—so the naming convention for IM screen names must be standardized for the enterprise.

Microsoft advises, "Your screen name should not provide or allude to personal information. For example, use a nickname such as SoccerFan instead of BaltimoreJenny."[11]

- Keep IM screen names private; treat them as another information asset that needs to be protected to reduce unwanted IM requests, phishing, or spam (actually *spim* in IM parlance).
- Prohibit transmission of confidential corporate information. It is fine to set up a meeting with auditors, but do not attach and route the latest financial report through unsecured IM.
- Restrict IM contacts to known business colleagues. If personal contacts are allowed for emergencies, limit personal use for everyday communication. In other words, do not get into a long personal IM conversation with a spouse or teenager while at work. Remember, these conversations are going to be monitored and archived.
- Use caution when displaying default messages when you are unavailable or away. Details such as where an employee is going to have lunch or where their child is being picked up from school may expose the organization to liability if a hacker takes the information and uses it for criminal purposes. This can mean that employees may be unknowingly putting themselves in harm's way by giving out too much personal information.
- Ensure that IM policies are being enforced by utilizing IM monitoring and filtering tools, and by archiving messages in real time for a future verifiable record, should it be needed.
- Conduct an IM usage policy review at least annually; more often in the early stages of policy development.

Chapter Summary: Key Points

- Instant messaging (IM) use in business and the public sector has become widespread, despite the fact that often few controls or security measures are in place.
- Typically as much as 80 percent of all IM use in corporations today is over one free public network, which heightens security concerns.
- IM networks provide the ability to transfer text messages as well as files, which can transfer worms and other malware, including backdoor Trojan horses.
- IM monitoring and management technology provides the crucial components that enable the organization to fully implement best practices for business IM.

- Enterprise IM (EIM) systems provide a greater level of security than IM from free services like Yahoo! and MSN.
- Regular analysis and modification (if necessary) of business IM policies and practices will help organizations leverage the maximum benefit from the technology.
- Records of IM use must be captured in real time and preserved to ensure they are reliable and accurate.

Notes

1. Quest Software, Inc., "Best Practices in Instant Messaging Management," October 2008, http://media.govtech.net/Digital_Communities/Quest%20Software/Best_Practices_in_Instant_Messaging_Management.pdf, p.5, retrieved August 10, 2011.
2. Ibid.
3. Neal Hindocha, "Instant Insecurity: Security Issues of Instant Messaging," January 13, 2003, updated November 2, 2010, www.symantec.com/connect/articles/instant-insecurity-security-issues-instant-messaging, retrieved December 19, 2011.
4. Ibid.
5. Ibid.
6. Ibid.
7. Ibid.
8. Quest Software, Inc., "Best Practices in Instant Messaging Management," October 2008, http://media.govtech.net/Digital_Communities/Quest%20Software/Best_Practices_in_Instant_Messaging_Management.pdf, retrieved August 10, 2011.
9. Ibid.
10. Debra Young, "Put IM Archiving on Your Compliance To-Do List," ZDNet, March 29, 2004, http://techupdate.zdnet.com/techupdate/stories/main/Put_IM_archiving_compliance_to_do_list.html, retrieved August 10, 2011.
11. M. Adeel Ansari, "10 Tips for Safer IM Instant Messaging," http://adeelansari.wordpress.com/tag/safer-im-instant-messaging/, retrieved February 4, 2012.

CHAPTER 6

Information Governance and Security for Social Media

S ocial media use has skyrocketed over the past several years. Organiza-tions are using social media and Web 2.0 platforms like blogs, podcasts, and wikis to connect people to corporate and government organizations, and to share information. In the government sector, agencies are able to directly provide information to the public, and can solicit responses on planned projects or policy changes in new, more collaborative, and per-sonal ways.[1] These new social media platforms are creating content that must be managed, monitored, and archived, and, in fact, some of the content supports key marketing or strategic business processes and may be classified as business records. *Often social media content is not man-aged by information governance (IG) policies and monitored with controls that ensure protection of critical information assets, and preservation of business records.*

Types of Social Media in Web 2.0

The term *Web 2.0* was coined to characterize the move from static websites on the Internet that passively provided information to consumers to more participative, interactive, collaborative, and user-oriented websites and web applications that allow for input, discussion, and sharing. Users actually can add content, increasing the value of the website or service. Examples may be blogs or podcasts (usually audio) where readers can post comments or pose questions; wikis that hyperlink to related information to create a knowledge base that shows interrelationships and that allow users to add content; and RSS (really simple syndication) feeds that provide a stream of fresh content to the user or consumer.

Web 2.0 does not literally mean a new revision level of the web but rather a newer approach that software developers have taken to allow consumers of web content to participate, collaborate, and add content. These development efforts reflect consumer needs and preferences that surfaced as a result of increased use of the web for daily information and communications.

Social media sites like Facebook, Twitter, and LinkedIn encourage social networking online by allowing users to create their own close network of friends or colleagues—essentially a hand-picked audience—and to post their own content in the form of comments, photos, videos, links, and so forth. Others in their social network may view, forward, share, organize, and comment on this content.[2]

Web 2.0 and social media platforms began as outward-facing, public web services that could link users from around the world. Subsequently, businesses discovered that social media technology could also be leveraged for internal use, such as by creating a directory and network of subject matter experts (SMEs) that users can search for special projects, or by sending out short microblog messages to keep their workforce informed. These internal social networks may be extended to include other stakeholders, like suppliers and customers, in a controlled environment. A number of platform and software options exist for enterprise social media development and use.

According to the U.S. National Archives and Records Administration (NARA):

Social media platforms can be grouped into the categories below. Some specific platforms may fit into more than one category depending on how the platform is used:

Web Publishing: *Platforms used to create, publish, and reuse content.*

- *Microblogging (Twitter, Plurk)*
- *Blogs (WordPress, Blogger)*
- *Wikis (Wikispaces, PBWiki)*
- *Mashups (Google Maps, popurls)*

Social Networking: *Platforms used to provide interactions and collaboration among users.*

- *Social Networking tools (Facebook, LinkedIn)*
- *Social Bookmarks (Delicious, Digg)*
- *Virtual Worlds (Second Life, OpenSim)*
- *Crowdsourcing/Social Voting (IdeaScale, Chaordix)*

File Sharing/Storage: *Platforms used to share files and host content storage.*

- *Photo Libraries (Flickr, Picasa)*
- *Video Sharing (YouTube, Vimeo)*
- *Storage (Google Docs, Drop.io)*
- *Content Management (SharePoint, Drupal)*

Agencies [and businesses] use a variety of software tools and platforms. The examples given above are not meant to be an exhaustive list.[3]

Social Media in the Enterprise

Consumer-facing social networks manage and interact with the subnetworks of millions of public users. Implementing tight security on these types of mass networks would likely slow response time, inhibit the user experience, and may not provide a sufficient level of security to warrant its investment.

In the business world, Facebook-like social networking software is offered for private, closed networks with a finite number of users. In this computing environment, implementing security is more manageable and practical. Some services are cloud-based, others operate internally behind the enterprise firewall, and some operate either way or in conjunction as a hybrid architecture. In addition, usage statistics that reflect trends, adoption rates, and areas of content interest can be provided to help feed the metrics needed to chart out the progress and effectiveness of the enterprise social network.[4]

Enterprise social networking is being adopted by business and public sector entities at a rapid rate. With the entry of Generation Gmail into the workforce, many of these initiatives take on an experimental, "cool" image, although it is crucial to establish social media business objectives, to define time-limited metrics, and to measure progress. But there does need to be some leeway, as calculating return on investment (ROI) for enterprise social networks is very new, and all the benefits have not been discovered or defined. Certainly the network load and required bandwidth for e-mail and attachments will decrease; instead of a 25MB PowerPoint file being sent back and forth among ten co-workers, it can sit in a common workspace for collaboration.

Another intangible benefit is the competitive value in being a market leader or industry innovator. Engaging in online conversations with customers and other stakeholders is one sign of a progressive-thinking organization. This can attract and retain prospective employees.

> Social media differs greatly from e-mail use. There are important rami-
> fications in these distinctions.

Key Ways Social Media Is Different from E-mail and Instant Messaging

Social media offers some of the same functionality as other messaging and collaboration systems like e-mail and instant messaging (IM), yet its architecture and underlying assumptions are quite different.

When implementing enterprise versions of social media applications, a company may exert more control over the computing and networking environment through in-house implementation rather than outsourcing. When the use of consumer-oriented social media applications like Facebook and Twitter springs up in the organization, application servers are outside of the enterprise and cannot be controlled. This creates IG and records management challenges, and poses legal risks.[5]

Obviously, social media is new, so standards, design, and architecture are in flux, whereas e-mail has been stable and established for 15 years or more. E-mail is a mature technology set, meaning it is unlikely to change much. There are standard e-mail communications protocols and the technology's use is pervasive and constant. So when e-mail IG policies are formed, there is less updating and fine-tuning required. With social media, new features are being added, standards do not exist, privacy settings change overnight, and the legalese in terms of service agreements continues to change to include these new features and settings.

E-mail, IM, and social media all are ways to share content and collaborate, but social media also features user interaction abilities, such as "Like" on Facebook or "re-tweet" (copying and posting a tweet on Twitter), which brings attention to the content in the user's network and can be construed as an endorsement or rejection of content, based on user opinions expressed and associated with the content.[6]

Further confounding the organization's ability to control the social media environment is the fact that the sites are ever-changing and dynamic, with comments and opinions being published in real time. This is not true with e-mail and IM systems, which are more stable and static.

Biggest Security Threats of Social Media

Social media is the Wild West of collaboration and communication. Vulnerabilities are still being exposed, and rules are still being established. Users are still often unsure of exactly who can see what they have posted. They may believe that they've posted a comment only for the eyes of a friend or colleague, not realizing it may have been posted publicly. "One of the biggest risks that social networking poses to organizations is that *employees may be exposing information that's not meant for public consumption*, especially in highly regulated environments like banking and healthcare, in industries that rely heavily on proprietary research and development, or even in the military" (italics added).[7]

Here are five of the biggest security threats when using social media, according to Chris Nerney of *Network World*:

1. **Malicious mobile apps.** The world of computing has changed drastically in the last several years. The mobility of the workforce has been fueled by improvements in network coverage and communication speed, and also computing improvements in mobile devices. They've become smaller, faster, more capable. Physical office facilities have been downsized, and employees are just as likely to be working from home or a coffee shop as they are from a desktop. Frequently, they may be flipping between enterprise applications and social media networks, providing updates or commenting on posts.[8] They may also download a software application from a social media site, where malware can be inserted into the source code.[9] This creates security risks to the enterprise software application.

   Google started with a policy for developers of its Android phone that was described as "wide open," in that they were not closely qualifying or scrutinizing the software apps. In March 2011, after learning that some apps were designed to steal personal information, imitate banking websites, wipe out stored data, Google was forced to remove more than 60 applications that contained malicious software, and to revise its policy for accepting apps.

2. **Social phishing.** This involves essentially duping a victim into providing personal information by making them believe they are giving it to a trusted source. Often, an e-mail will arrive that seems to be from their employer, bank, Internet service provider (ISP), or a friend or business associate, and the victim unwittingly supplies their social security number, birth date, password, personal identification number (PIN), or other sensitive information. A compromise to the employee's personal information can result in a compromise of enterprise information.

   Social media has further complicated the picture and made it even easier for rogue operators to steal personal information since often people publicize details of their location, plans, and activities to their circle of networked associates or "friends."

3. **Third-party code.** People are often unaware that when they start to play a game or enter a contest on a social networking site, third-party apps may be able to steal personal or corporate information, or infect their computer with malware. Hackers can disguise dangerous links as links to entry forms, games, and other innocent enticements. When curious users are encouraged to click a link or open a program, they allow malicious sites to access their systems or install a virus.[10]

4. **Employees—the accidental insider threat.** Sometimes an employee intends to do harm to an organization, but *most times* they do not realize the negative impact of their behavior in posting to social media sites. People might use social media to vent about a bad day at work, but the underlying message can damage the company's reputation and alienate coworkers and clients. Other times, a post that is seemingly unrelated to work can backfire and take a toll on business. We're all human and sometimes emotion gets the best of us, before we have rationally thought out the consequences. And that is especially true in the new world of social media, where it may be unclear exactly who can see a comment.

The dangers of social media are quite different than an isolated, off-color, or offensive verbal comment in the workplace, or even one errant e-mail. With social media it is possible that the whole world will be able to see a comment meant only for a limited and controlled audience. For example, consider Ketchum PR Vice President James Andrews, who in 2009 "fired off an infamous tweet trashing the city of Memphis, hometown of a little Ketchum client called FedEx, the day before he was to make a presentation to more than 150 FedEx employees (on digital media, no less!)." FedEx employees complained to Ketchum and their own executives, pointing out that while they suffered from salary reductions, money was being spent on Ketchum, which had been clearly disrespectful of FedEx. Andrews was forced to make a "very public and humiliating apology."[11]

This story shows that high-level executives must be just as careful as lower-level employees. Andrews was not only a corporate vice president, but also a PR, communications, and social media expert, well versed in the firm's policies and mission. He also had no ill intent. Knowing this, consider what a rogue employee intent on damaging the company might do. Such impact could be much worse. For instance, what if the CEO's assistant were to release details of strategic plans, litigation, or ethics investigations to the public? The impact could be quite costly.

5. **Lack of a social media policy**. Many organizations are just now discovering that social media has popped up in pockets of their organization. They may believe that their e-mail and communications policy

will pretty much cover social media use, and it is not worth the time and expense to update IG policies to include social media.

This invites complexities, vagaries, and potential disaster. A simple comment could invite litigation; "Our new project is almost ready, but I'm not sure about the widget assembly." It's out there. There is a record of it. Instant potential liability in 140 characters or less.

Social media can add value to an organization's efforts to reach out to customers and other stakeholders, but this must be weighed carefully with its risks.

The objectives of a social media initiative must be spelled out and metrics must be in place to measure progress. But more than that, *who can utilize social media on behalf of the company and what they can state needs to be established with clarity in IG policy.* If not, employees are essentially flying blindly without controls, and they are more likely to put the enterprise at risk.[12]

More than policy is needed. If your organization is going to embark on a social media program, it needs an executive sponsor to champion and drive the program, communicating policy to key leaders. You will also need to conduct training—on a consistent basis. Training is key, since social media is a moving target.

Legal Risks of Social Media Posts

With an estimated 200 million tweets (140-character posts) per day in 2011 to the microblogging site Twitter,[13] a number that continues to increase, surely some employees in your organization are utilizing it. The casual use of public comments can easily create liability for a company. With no IG policy, guidelines, or governance, legal risks of using social media increase significantly. This is an avoidable risk.

While many people are posting birthday wishes and pictures of what they had for dinner, others may be venting about specific companies and individuals within those companies. There's a difference between, "I can't stand Wall Street," and "Goldman is run by Satan, and his name is John Smith. We're going to sue his butt off." Instant liability.

Now, the specifics of where and how an employee tweeted a message may be the difference in whether a lawsuit against your company is successful. If a personal Twitter account is used, but it was posted after hours using a PC from home, the company *may* be off the hook. But if it was done using a company computer, or network, or from a company-authorized Twitter account, a defense will be difficult. Questions about the policy for posting tweets will be the first to be asked by opposing counsel. One thing is true, "Much of this remains unsettled ground."[14]

Just when compliance and records managers thought they had nailed down information governance for e-mail, IM, and electronic records—social media came on the scene creating new, dynamic challenges. "Tweets are no different from letters, e-mail, or text messages—they can be damaging and discoverable, which is especially problematic for companies that are required to preserve electronic records, such as the securities industry and federal contractors. Yet another compliance headache is born."[15]

Blogs are simply Web logs, a sort of online journal, if you will, that is focused on a particular topic. Blog readers can become followers and receive notices when new content is posted, as well as add their own comments, although comments may be moderated or restricted. It seems confounding, but with the explosion in the use of blogs, there have been actual incidents where employees have "disclosed trade secrets and insider trading information on their blogs. Blogs have also led to wrongful termination and harassment suits."[16]

So the liability and potential for leakage or erosion of information assets isn't just theoretical, it is *real*.

To safeguard the enterprise that sanctions and supports blog use, real-time archiving of blog posts should be implemented. Remember, these can be business records that are subject to legal holds, and authenticity and accuracy are crucial in supporting a legal case. So a true and original copy must be archived, and, this may, in fact, be a legal or regulatory requirement, depending on the industry.

Tools to Archive Facebook and Twitter

Since Facebook and Twitter did not initially provide archiving tools themselves, some third-party applications have popped up to perform the task. These may not provide a legally defensible audit trail in court, so choosing between the tools requires a critical analysis. Other alternatives, such as real-time content archiving tools and even in-house developed customizations, would also have to be considered.

TwInbox is a free MS Outlook plug-in that archives Twitter postings, and TweetTake is a utility that archives followers and tweet posts, and is also free of charge. TwInbox allows users to install a (Twitter) menu option to send tweets directly from Outlook; these tweets are archived into a standard Outlook folder. It can even be configured to capture those tweets that a user sends outside of Outlook, so that everything is stored in one folder.

TweetTake does not require a software download, and the archive can be stored as a zip file, and then imported into a spreadsheet like Excel. By the time this book goes to press there will be even more options, and the existing ones will have changed and (hopefully) improved.

So, if your organization uses Twitter and social media archiving is required by law, regulations, or your internal IG policies, begin your research with TwInbox, if you operate in a Microsoft Office environment, and also evaluate TweetTake, among any new entrants, or other options your organization may have.[17]

For archiving Facebook posts, there are several options. There are free plug-ins for Mozilla's Firefox browser. One comes directly from Mozilla, which archives everything but fan pages into a zip file. Another is a Firefox plug-in called ArchiveFacebook. Other tools, including SocialSafe, PageFreezer, and Wayback Machine, charge a small fee. All of these options and any new ones need to be evaluated when selecting an archiving solution for Facebook that meets your organization's requirements.

For archiving LinkedIn posts and information, SocialSafe, PageFreezer, and Wayback Machine can be used, and other tools will surface.

There are also options to create PDF documents out of social media posts, with PDF995 and PrimoPDF.[18] Nuance Software also provides PDFCreate.

There are more archiving tools being developed as the social media market matures. Bear in mind that third-party developed tools always carry some risk that tools directly from the software or service provider do not.

IG Considerations for Social Media

In her report, "How Federal Agencies Can Effectively Manage Records Created Using Social Media Tools," Dr. Patricia Franks addressed building an IG framework for social media. An IG model provides the overarching policies, guidelines, and boundaries for social media initiatives.[19]

An IG framework for social media should incorporate social media policy, controls, and operational guidelines. Best practices for social media are evolving and still being established, and they should also include vertical market considerations that are industry-specific. A cross section of functional groups within the enterprise should provide input into the policy-making process. At the very minimum, marketing, finance, information technology (IT), legal, human resources, and records management must be consulted, and business units should be represented. Clear roles and responsibilities must be spelled out, and controls establishing acceptable use—essentially what is allowed and what is not—and even writing style, logo format, branding, and other marketing considerations should be weighed. The enterprise's image and brand are at risk and prudent steps must be taken to protect this valuable, intangible asset. And most important, all legal and regulatory considerations must be folded into the new IG policy governing the use of social media.[20]

Chapter Summary: Key Points

- Organizations are using social media and Web 2.0 platforms to connect people to companies and government.
- One of the biggest risks that social networking poses to organizations is that employees may be exposing information that is not meant for public consumption.
- Social media use presents unique challenges because of key differences between them and other electronic communications systems, such as e-mail and instant messaging (IM).
- Enterprise social networking software has many of the features of consumer social applications such as Facebook, but with more oversight and control, and they come with analytics features to measure adoption and use.
- Various software tools have become available in recent years for archiving social media posts and followers for records management purposes in Twitter, Facebook, and others.
- An information governance (IG) framework provides the overarching policies, guidelines, and boundaries for social media initiatives, so that they may be controlled, monitored, and archived.

Notes

1. The U.S. National Archives and Records Administration, "NARA Bulletin 2011-02," October 20, 2010, www.archives.gov/records-mgmt/bulletins/2011/2011-02.html, retrieved March 30, 2012.
2. Ibid.
3. Ibid.
4. Andrew Conry-Murray, "Can Enterprise Social Networking Pay Off?" March 21, 2009, www.internetevolution.com/document.asp?doc_id=173854, retrieved January 17, 2012.
5. Patricia C. Franks, "How Federal Agencies Can Effectively Manage Records Created Using New Social Media Tools," IBM Center for The Business of Government, San Jose State University, 2010, www.actgov.org/sigcom/SIGs/SIGs/CTSIG/Documents/Best%20Practices%20in%20Collaborative%20Technology%20Retention%20Policies/All%20Related%20Studies/IBM-How%20Federal%20Agencies%20Can%20Effectively%20Manage%20Records.pdf, pp. 20–21, retrieved March 30, 2012.
6. Ibid.

7. Paul McDougall, "Social Networking Here to Stay Despite Security Risks," *Information Week*, May 12, 2011, www.informationweek.com /news/security/privacy/229500138, retrieved December 19, 2011.
8. Chris Nerney, "5 Top Social Media Security Threats," *Network World*, May 31, 2011, www.networkworld.com/news/2011/053111-social-media-security.html, retrieved December 19, 2011.
9. Ibid.
10. Ibid.
11. Ibid.
12. Ibid.
13. Twitter, "#numbers," *Twitter Blog,* March 14, 2011, http://blog.twitter .com/2011/03/numbers.html, retrieved March 14, 2011.
14. Sharon Nelson, John Simek, and Jason Foltin, "The Legal Implications of Social Networking," *Sensei Enterprises*, 2009, www.senseient.com/art icles/pdf/The_Legal_Implications_of_Social_Networking.pdf, retrieved February 4, 2012.
15. Ibid.
16. Ibid.
17. Andy Opsahl, "Backing Up Twitter and Facebook Posts Challenges Governments," Government Technology, January 20, 2010, www .govtech.com/policy-management/Backing-Up-Twitter-and-Facebook-Posts.html?utm_source=related&utm_medium=direct&utm_campaign =Backing-Up-Twitter-and-Facebook-Posts, retrieved August 15, 2011.
18. Ibid.
19. Patricia C. Franks, "How Federal Agencies Can Effectively Manage Records Created Using New Social Media Tools," IBM Center for The Business of Government, San Jose State University, 2010, www.actgov .org/sigcom/SIGs/SIGs/CTSIG/Documents/Best%20Practices%20in%20 Collaborative%20Technology%20Retention%20Policies/All%20Related% 20Studies/IBM-How%20Federal%20Agencies%20Can%20Effectively%20 Manage%20Records.pdf, p. 13, retrieved March 30, 2012.
20. Ibid.

CHAPTER 7

Information Governance and Security for Mobile Devices

Mobile computing has vastly accelerated in popularity over the last five years or so. Several factors have contributed to this: improved network coverage, physically smaller devices, improved processing power, better price points, a move to next-generation operating systems (OSs) (beyond Microsoft Windows), and a more mobile workforce have fueled the proliferation of mobile devices.

Mobile devices include laptops, netbooks, tablet PCs, personal digital assistants (PDAs) like Blackberry, and smartphones, such as Apple's iPhone and those based on Google's Android platform. What used to be simple cell phones are now small computers with nearly complete functionality and some unique communications capabilities. These devices all link to an entire spectrum of public and private networks.

With these new types of devices and operating environments, come new, unknown security risks.[1] "The plethora of mobile computing devices flooding into the market will be one of the biggest ongoing security challenges [moving forward]..." the Digital Systems Knowledge Transfer Network, a UK think tank found. "With mobile devices connecting to Wi-Fi and Bluetooth networks, there are suddenly many more opportunities [for hackers] to get in and steal personal information."[2]

The rapid shift toward mobile computing means that companies with mobile personnel like salespeople and service technicians need to be aware of, and vigilant toward, these impending security threats.

According to CTIA (The Wireless Association), approximately 303 million people within the United States were utilizing mobile phones as of December 2010—a 96 percent household penetration rate.[3] Citizens of China, India, and the European Union (EU) have even greater mobile phone usage than the United States.

The reality is that *most mobile devices are not designed with security in mind*; in fact, some compromises have been made to enable new smartphone operating systems to run on a variety of hardware, such as the Android O/S from Google. This is analogous to the trade-offs Microsoft made when developing the Windows operating system to run across a variety of hardware designs from many PC manufacturers.

Smartphone virus infections are particularly difficult to detect and thorny to remove. A user may be unaware that all his or her data is being monitored and captured and that a hacker may be waiting for just the right time to use it. Businesses can suffer economic and other damage, such as erosion of information assets, or even negative goodwill from a damaged image.

The smartphone market is rapidly expanding with new developments almost daily, each providing criminals with a new opportunity. A 2011 International Data Corporation (IDC) report indicated that "*smartphone sales outpaced PC sales for the first time ever in the fourth quarter of 2010*, with 100.9 million smartphones shipped versus 92.1 million PCs" (italics added).[4] The growth in smartphone sales and new services from banks—such as making deposits remotely by snapping a picture of a check—means that there are new and growing opportunities for fraud and identity theft.

Awareness and education are key. *The first line of defense is for users to better understand cybercriminal techniques and to become savvier in their use of information and communications technologies.*

A large part of the battle will be won when biometric authentication technologies (those that use retina, voice, and fingerprint recognition) are mature enough to positively identify a user to ensure the correct person is accessing financial or confidential accounts. Application suppliers are first concerned about functionality and widespread adoption, so security is not their top priority. Users must be aware and vigilant to protect themselves from theft and fraud. On a corporate level, organizations must step up their training efforts in addition to adding layers of security technology to safeguard critical electronic documents and data and to protect information assets.

Social engineering—using various ways of fooling the user into providing private data—is the most common approach criminal hackers use, and it is on the rise. Machines do their job, and software performs exactly as it is programmed to do, but human beings are the weakest link in the security chain, and as usage trends in the direction of a more mobile and remote workforce, people need to be trained as to what threats exist, and constantly updated on new criminal schemes and approaches. This training is all part of an overall information governance (IG) effort, controlling *who* has access to *what* information, *when,* and from *where.*

With more and more sensitive business information being pushed out to mobile devices (e.g., financial spreadsheets, business contracts, strategic plans, and the like) and advancing and evolving threats to the mobile realm, *IG becomes an imperative; and the most important part of IG is that it is done on an ongoing basis, consistently and regularly.* Policies must be reviewed when a new mobile device starts to be utilized, when new threats are uncovered, as employees use unsecured public WiFi networks more and more, and as business operations change to include more and more mobile strategies. IT divisions must ensure their mobile devices are protected from the latest security risks but users must regularly be apprised of changing security threats and new criminal approaches by hackers.

Mobile device management (MDM) is critical to secure confidential information assets. Some available technologies can wipe devices free of confidential documents and data remotely, even after they are lost or stolen. These types of utilities need to be deployed to protect an enterprise's information assets.

Current Trends in Mobile Computing

With the rapid pace of change in mobile computing, it is crucial to convey an understanding of trends, to better know what developments to anticipate and how to plan for them. When a new mobile device or operating system is released, the best thing may be to first wait to see what security threats pop up. It is important to understand the direction mobile computing usage and deployment are taking in order to plan and develop IG policies to protect information assets.

From CIOZone.com, here are the top trends in mobile computing:

1. ***Long term evolution (LTE).*** *The so-called fourth generation of mobile computing (4G) is expected to be rolled out across North America over the next three years [2012–15], making it possible for corporate users to run business applications on their devices simultaneously with Voice over IP (VoIP) capabilities.*

2. ***WiMax*** *[Worldwide Interoperability for Microwave Access]. As LTE and WiMax networks are deployed in the U.S. through 2012, expect to see more netbooks and laptops equipped with built-in radio frequency identification (RFID) and wireless support. [WiMax is protocol for communications that provides up to 40 Megabits/second speeds (much faster than WiFi) for fixed and mobile Internet access. The next IEEE 802.16m update will push the speed to up to 1 Giga-bit/second fixed speeds.]*

3. ***3G and 4G interoperability.*** *Sprint has developed a dual mode card which will enable mobile device users to work on both 3G and 4G networks. Other carriers are expected to follow suit.*

4. ***Smartphone applications.*** *Third-party software vendors will increasingly make enterprise applications available for smartphones, including inventory management, electronic medical records management, warehousing, distribution and even architectural and building inspection data for the construction industry.*

5. ***GPS.*** *Global Positioning Systems (GPS) will increasingly be used to identify end users by their whereabouts and also to analyze route optimization for delivery workers and service technicians.*

6. ***Security.*** *As new and different types of mobile devices are introduced, corporate IT departments will find it increasingly challenging to identify and authenticate individual end users. As such, expect to see a combination of improvements in both Virtual Private Network (VPN) software and hardware-based VPNs to support multiple device types.*

7. ***Anti-virus.*** *As more third-party business applications are made available on smartphones and other mobile devices, CIOs will also have to be cognizant about the potential for viruses and worms.*

8. ***Push-button applications.*** *Let's say a waste disposal truck arrives at an industrial site and is unable to empty a dumpster because a vehicle is blocking its path. Smartphones will increasingly have applications built into them that would make it possible for the disposal truck driver to photograph the impeding object and route the picture to a dispatcher to document and time-stamp the obstruction.*

9. ***Supplemental broadband.*** *As carriers implement LTE and WiMax networks, companies such as Sprint and Verizon are looking at potentially extending wireless broadband capabilities to small businesses which don't have fiber optic or copper connections on the ground. Under this scenario, a small packaging company in New Jersey could potentially be able to receive T-1 level (high speed) broadband capabilities in regions of the U.S. where it has offices but doesn't have wireline broadband connections.*

10. ***Solid state drives (SSD).*** *Corporate customers should expect to see continued improvements in the controllers and firmware built into SSDs in order to improve the longevity of the write cycles in notebooks.*[5]

Security Risks of Mobile Computing

Considering their small size, mobile computing devices store a tremendous amount of data and storage capacities are increasing with the continued shrinking of circuits and advancement in SSD technologies. Add to that the fact that they are highly portable and often unsecured and you have a vulnerable mix that criminals can target. Considering how often people lose or misplace their mobile devices daily, and what valuable targets they are for physical theft (this author had a laptop stolen in the Barcelona airport, right from under his nose), and it is clear that the use of mobile devices represents an inherent security risk.

But they don't have to be lost or stolen to be compromised, according to Stanford University's guidelines, intended to help mobile computing device users protect the information the devices contain, "... *intruders can sometimes gain all the access they need if the device is left alone and unprotected, or if data is 'sniffed out of the air' during wireless communications*" (italics added).[6] The devices can be compromised with the use of keystroke loggers which capture every single entry a user makes. This can be done without the user having any knowledge of it. That means company passwords, confidential databases, and financial data (including personal and corporate credit card numbers) are all at risk.

Securing Mobile Data

The first and best way to protect confidential information assets is to remove confidential, unnecessary, or unneeded data from the mobile device. Confidential data should not be stored on the device unless explicit permission is given by the IT department, business unit head, or the IG Board to do so. This includes price lists, strategic plans, competitive information, photo images of corporate buildings or co-workers, and financial data such as tax identification numbers, company credit card or banking details, and other confidential information.

If it is necessary for sensitive data to be stored on mobile devices, there are options to secure the data more tightly, like USB drives, flash drives, and hard drives that have integrated digital identity and cryptographic (encryption) capabilities.

IG for Mobile Computing

Stanford University's guidelines are a helpful foundation for IG of mobile devices. They are "relatively easy to implement and use and can protect your privacy" and safeguard data "in the event that the device becomes compromised, lost or stolen."

Smartphones and Tablets
- **Encrypt communications**. For phones that support encrypted communication (secure sockets layer [SSL], virtual private network [VPN], hypertext transfer protocol secure [https]) *always configure defaults to use encryption*.
- **Encrypt storage**. Phones approved to access confidential information assets must encrypt their bulk storage with hardware encryption.

- **Password protect**. Configure a password to gain access and or use the device. Passwords for devices that access confidential information assets should be at least seven characters in length, and use upper- and lowercase letters, as well as some numerical characters. Passcodes should be changed every 30 days.
- **Timeout**. Set the device so that it is locked after a period of idleness or timeout, perhaps as short as a few minutes.
- **Update**. Keep all system and application patches up to date, including mobile OS and installed applications. This allows for the latest security measures and patches to be installed to counter ongoing threats.
- **Protect from hacking**. Phones approved to access confidential and restricted data must not be jailbroken (hacked to gain privileged access on a smartphone using the Apple iOS) or rooted (typically refers to jailbreaking on a smartphone running the Android operating system). The process of rooting varies widely by device. It usually includes exploiting a security weakness in the firmware shipped from the factory. "'Jailbreaking' and 'rooting' removes the manufacturer's protection against malware."
- **Manage**. Phones approved to gain access to confidential information assets must be operating in a managed environment to maintain the most current security and privacy settings, and monitor use for possible attacks.[7]

Portable Storage Devices

These include thumb drives or memory sticks, removable hard drives, and even devices like iPods that are essentially mobile disk storage units with extra bells and whistles.

- Create a user name and password to protect the device from unauthorized access—especially if lost or stolen.
- Utilize encryption to protect data on devices used to store and/or transport confidential information assets.
- Use additional levels of authentication and management for accessing the device, where possible.
- Use biometric identification to authenticate users, where possible.

Laptops, Netbooks, Tablets, and Portable Computers

- **Password protect**. This is the most basic protection, yet it is often not used. Create a user name and password to protect the device from unauthorized access; require that they are entered each time the computer is used.
- **Timeout.** Require that the password is re-entered after a timeout period for the screensaver.

- **Encrypt.** Laptops, notebooks, or tablets used to access confidential information assets should be required to be encrypted with whole disk encryption (WDE).
- **Secure physically**. Physical locks should be used *"whenever the system is in a stationary location for extended periods of times."*[8]

Building Security into Mobile Applications

While it's a relatively new channel, mobile e-commerce is growing rapidly and new software applications or *apps* are emerging for consumers as well as business and public sector enterprises. These apps are reducing business process cycle times and making the organizations more agile, more efficient, and more productive. There are some key strategies that can be used to build secure apps.

As is the case with any new online delivery channel, security is at the forefront for organizations as they rush to deploy or enhance mobile business apps in the fast-growing smartphone market. Their priorities are different from those of the software developers churning out apps.

In the banking sector, initially many mobile apps limited customers to a walled off set of basic functions—checking account balances and transaction histories, finding a branch or ATM location, and initiating transfers—but "a new wave of apps is bringing person-to-person payments, remote deposit capture and bill pay to the mobile channel. Simply, the apps are getting smarter and more capable. *But with those capabilities comes the potential for greater threats*" (italics added).[9]

Security experts state that the majority of the challenges that could result from mobile fraud have not been seen before. Mobile e-commerce is relatively new and has not been heavily targeted—yet. But also industrial espionage and the theft of trade secrets by targeting mobile devices is going to be on the rise and the focus of rogue competitive intelligence-gathering organizations. So user organizations have to be even more proactive, systematic, and diligent in designing and deploying mobile apps than they did with web-based apps.

Software developers of mobile apps necessarily seek the widest audience possible, so they often deploy them across multiple platforms (e.g., Apple's iOS, Google's Android, Windows Phone, Research in Motion's BlackBerry, and others) and this forces some security trade-offs: *Enterprises have to build apps for the "strengths and weaknesses intrinsic to every device, which adds to the security challenges"* (italics added).[10]

A side effect of mobile app development from the user perspective is that it can reshape the way users interact with core information management (IM) applications within the enterprise.

The back-office IM systems such as accounting, customer relationship management (CRM), human resources, and other enterprise apps that are driving online and mobile are the same as before, but the big difference comes in how stakeholders including employees, customers, and suppliers, are interacting with the enterprise. In the past, when deploying basic online applications for browser access, there was much more control over the operating environment; whereas with newer mobile applications running on smartphones and tablets, that functionality has been pushed out to the end-user device.

Real Threats Are Poorly Understood

The list of threats to mobile apps is growing and existing threats are poorly understood, in general. They are just too new, because mobile commerce by downloadable app is a relatively new phenomenon—the Apple iTunes App Store and the Android Marketplace debuted in the second half of 2008. So the current list of threats is not complete or well understood. "But that doesn't mean the threat isn't real—even if the app itself is not the problem."[11] It could be the unsecure network users are on, or a device infection of some sort.

For mobile apps, antivirus protection is not the focus as it is in the PC world; the security effort mostly focuses on keeping malware off the device itself by addressing software development methods and network vulnerabilities. Surely, new types of attacks on mobile devices will continue to be introduced. That is the one thing that can be counted on.

There already have been some high-profile examples of mobile devices being compromised. For example, in 2010 "New York-based Citibank's iPhone app was found to be storing customers' [private] data on their phones, with obvious privacy implications [and exposing it to theft and fraud]. Meanwhile, Google (New York) has had to pull a number of apps from the Android Marketplace built by an anonymous [criminal] developer who was creating fake bank apps [with realistic and usable features] that attempted to exploit information on users' devices to commit banking and [credit] card fraud."[12]

There are many more examples, but these cited incidents make it imperative to understand the mobile app marketplace itself in order that effective IG policies and controls may be developed, deployed, and enforced. Simply knowing how Google has approached soliciting app development is key to developing an IG strategy for Android devices. Their relative open door approach initially meant that almost anyone could develop and deploy an app for Google Android. While the open door policy has evolved somewhat to protect Android users, it is still quite easy for any app developer—well-intentioned or malicious—to release an app to the Android Marketplace.

This in itself can pose a risk to end users, who sometimes cannot tell the difference between a real app released by a bank and a banking app built by a third party, which may be fraudulent. Apple has taken a more prudent and measured approach by enforcing a quality-controlled approval process for all apps released to its iTunes App Store. Sure, it slows development, but it also means apps will be more thoroughly tested and secure.

Both approaches, Android and Apple, have their positives and negatives for Google and Apple, and for their users. But clearly, Apple's curated and quality-controlled approach is better from a security risk standpoint.

Understanding the inherent strengths and, perhaps more important, weaknesses of specific mobile hardware devices and operating systems—and their interaction with each other—is key when entering the software design phase for mobile apps.

It's a different development environment altogether. Windows programmers will experience a learning curve. Mobile apps under Android or Apple operating systems operate in a more restricted and less transparent file management environment.

Bearing that in mind—regardless of the mobile OS—*first ensure that data is secured, and then check the security of the application itself.* That is, practice good information technology (IT) governance to ensure that the software source code is also secure. Malicious code can be inserted into the program and once it is deployed the hackers will have an easy time stealing confidential data or documents.[13]

Innovation versus Security: Choices and Trade-Offs

As organizations deploy mobile apps, they must make choices, given the limited or confined software development environment and the need to make agile, intuitive apps that run fast so users will adopt them. To ensure that a mobile offering is secure, many businesses are limiting their apps' functionality. So stakeholder users get mobile access that they didn't have before, and a new interface with new functionality, but it is not possible to offer as much functionality as in web apps. And more security means some sacrifices and choices will need to be made versus speed and innovative new features.

Some of the lessons learned in the deployment of online web apps still apply to mobile apps. Hackers are going to try social engineering like phishing (duping the user into providing access or private information) and assuming the identity of an account holder, bank, or business. They will also attempt man-in-the-middle attacks. (More on that topic soon).

With mobile applications, the most used mode of operation is operating the app directly on a mobile device such as a smart phone. *This is a key difference between apps and traditional PC-based interfaces that rely on browser access or using basic mobile phone text messaging.* Connecting to a business via app can be more secure than relying on a browser or texting platform, which require an additional layer of software (e.g., the browser, texting platform, or WiFi connection) to execute sensitive tasks. These security vulnerabilities can compromise the safety of information transmitted to a secure site. Thankfully, *if the app is developed in a secure environment, it can be entirely self-contained, and the opportunity to keep mobile data secure is greatest when using the app as opposed to a browser-based platform.*

This is because a mobile app provides a direct connection between the user's device and the business, governmental agency, or e-commerce provider. Some security experts believe that mobile apps potentially could be more secure because they can communicate on an app-to-app (or computer-to-computer) level, as opposed to browser-based access on a PC.

In fact, "a customer using a bank app on a mobile network might just be safer than a customer accessing online banking on a PC using an open Wi-Fi connection" that anyone can monitor.[14]

How do you combat this browser-based vulnerability if it is required to access an online interface? *The most effective and simplest way to counter security threats in the PC-based browser environment and to eliminate man-in-the-browser or man-in-the-middle attacks is to use two different devices*, rather than communicate over a standard Internet connection. This approach can be built into IG guidelines.

Consider this: Mobile apps can actually *bring about greater security.* For example, do you receive alerts from your bank when hitting a low balance threshold? Or a courtesy e-mail when a transaction is posted? Just by utilizing these types of alerts—and they can be applied to any type of software application beyond banking—tech-savvy users can serve as an added layer of protection themselves. If they receive an alert of account activity regularly, they may be able to identify fraudulent activity immediately and take action to counter it and stop it in its tracks, limiting the damage, and potential exposure of additional private data or confidential information assets.[15]

Best Practices to Secure Mobile Applications

Mobile computing is not going away, it is only going to increase in the future. Most businesses and governments are going to be forced to deploy mobile apps to compete and provide services customers will require. There is the potential for exposure of confidential data and e-documents, but this does not mean that organizations must shy away from deploying mobile apps.[16] There are some proven best practice approaches, which can help to ensure that mobile apps are secure.

There are some steps that can be taken to improve security—although there can never be any guarantees—and some of these should be folded into IG guidelines in the policy development process. *BankTech* magazine identified six best practices that can shape an organization's app development process:

1. *Make sure your organization or outside development firm uses seasoned application developers who have had secure-coding training and use a* secure software development life cycle *(SDLC).*
2. *[Developed for banking apps, this approach can be applied to other vertical apps, too.] Follow the guidance suggested by the Federal Deposit Insurance Corp. (FDIC FIL-103-2005) regarding authentication in an Internet banking environment. The guidance describes* enhanced authentication methods, *such as multifactor authentication, that regulators expect banks to use when authenticating the identity of customers using the bank's online products and services.*
3. *Make sure that the customer (or employee) is* required to re-enter his or her credentials after a certain time period *to prevent someone other than the mobile device's owner from obtaining access to private account information.*
4. Hire an information security expert *to assess the security around your mobile application servers. Unfortunately,* an organization's servers are often overlooked *during a risk assessment, as they require a specialized skill set to test them.*
5. Encrypt sensitive data *that is stored on a mobile device and account data that travels from the handset across the Internet. Ensure that the encryption is implemented properly.*
6. *Hire a security expert* to test the security of a mobile application *before you implement it across your customer base.* [all emphasis added].[17]

Chapter Summary: Key Points

- The plethora of mobile computing devices flooding into the market will be one of the biggest ongoing security challenges moving forward.
- A 2011 International Data Corporation (IDC) report indicated that smartphone sales outpaced PC sales for the first time ever in the fourth quarter of 2010.
- As businesses work to deploy mobile apps, they walk a fine line between innovation and risk. To ensure that a mobile offering is secure, many businesses are limiting their apps' functionality.

(continued)

(*continued*)

- Human beings remain the weakest link in security, particularly with the increasing use of mobile devices. Information governance policies must be established and employees must be trained to be aware of security and privacy risks.
- Connecting to a business directly via an app can be more secure than relying on a browser or texting platform, which require an additional layer of software.
- Over the next several years North America will be upgrading to 4G networks, faster WiMax will be deployed, and there will be 3G and 4G interoperability.
- There will be new enhanced security and anti-virus products developed to combat the increasing threat of cyber-attacks.
- Mobile computing security challenges require that organizations follow best practices when developing and deploying apps. Some keys are: encrypting sensitive data, using the secure software development lifecycle (SDLC) methodology and enhanced authentication methods, and hiring a security expert to test new apps.

Notes

1. "Current Mobile Computing Calls for Security as Powerful as Titanium," http://techreview.blogpool.co.uk/2011/02/10/modern-day-mobile-computing-calls-for-security-as-powerful-as-titanium, retrieved March 30, 2012.
2. Warwick Ashford, "Mobility Among the Top IT Security Threats in 2011, Says UK Think Tank," *Computer Weekly*, January 7, 2011, www.computerweekly.com/Articles/2011/01/07/244797/Mobility-among-the-top-IT-security-threats-in-2011-says-UK-think.htm, retrieved March 30, 2012.
3. CTIA, "Wireless Quick Facts," www.ctia.org/advocacy/research/index.cfm/aid/10323, retrieved August 16, 2011.
4. Matt Gunn, "How to Build a Secure Mobile App," Bank Systems and Technology, July 6, 2011, www.banktech.com/risk-management/231001058?itc=edit_stub, retrieved December 19, 2011.
5. "Top Ten Trends in Mobile Computing," CIO Zone, www.ciozone.com/index.php/Editorial-Research/Top-Ten-Trends-in-Mobile-Computing/2.html, retrieved December 19, 2011.

6. Stanford University, "Guidelines for Securing Mobile Computing Devices," www.stanford.edu/group/security/securecomputing/mobile_devices.html#Risks, retrieved December 19, 2011.
7. Ibid.
8. Ibid.
9. Matt Gunn, "How to Build a Secure Mobile App," Bank Systems and Technology, July 6, 2011, www.banktech.com/risk-management/231001058?itc=edit_stub, retrieved March 30, 2012.
10. Ibid.
11. Ibid.
12. Ibid.
13. Ibid.
14. Ibid.
15. Ibid.
16. Beau Woods, "6 Ways to Secure Mobile Apps," Bank Systems and Technology, May 26, 2011, www.banktech.com/architecture-infrastructure/229700033, retrieved March 30, 2012.
17. Ibid.

CHAPTER 8

Information Governance and Security for Cloud Computing Use

Cloud computing represents one of the most significant paradigm shifts in information technology (IT) in history. Sure, it is similar in concept to sharing an application hosting provider, which has been around for a half-century and was common in highly regulated vertical industries, such as banks and healthcare institutions. But it has evolved into something very different, with advances in IT.

Cloud computing provides economies of scale by spreading costs across clients and matching client computing needs to consumption, in a flexible, (near) real-time way. Cloud computing can be considered as a sort of utility that is vastly scalable and can be modulated. This approach has great potential, promising on-demand computing power, off-site backups, heavy security, and "innovations we cannot yet imagine."[1]

When executives hear of the cost savings and elimination of capital outlays associated with cloud computing, their ears perk up. Users are glad to have some autonomy and independence from their information technology department, and IT departments are enthused to have instant resources at their disposal and to shed some of the responsibilities for infrastructure so they can focus on applications. Most of all, they are enthused by the agility offered by the on-demand provisioning of computing and the ability to align IT with business strategies more nimbly and readily.

But for all the hoopla and excitement, *there are also grave concerns about security risks and loss of direct control*, while still holding ultimate responsibility for which they are held accountable.

Organizations need to understand the security risks of cloud computing, and they must have information governance (IG) policies and controls in place to safeguard critical e-documents.

Defining Cloud Computing

The definition of cloud computing is rather, well, *cloudy*, if you will. The flurry of developments in cloud computing make it difficult for managers and policymakers to define it clearly and succinctly, and to evaluate available options. There are many misconceptions and vagaries surrounding cloud computing. Some misconceptions and questions include:

- *"That hosting thing is like SaaS"*
- *"Cloud, SaaS, all the same, we don't own anything"*
- *"OnDemand is Cloud Computing"*
- *"ASP, Hosting, SaaS seems all the same"*
- *"It all costs the same so what does it matter to me?"*
- *"Why should I care if it's multi-tenant or not?"*
- *"What's this private cloud versus public cloud?"*[2]

Cloud computing is a shared resource that provides dynamic access to computing services that may range from raw computing power, to basic infrastructure, to fully operational and supported applications. It is a set of newer information technologies that provides for on-demand, modulated, shared use of computing services remotely. This is accomplished by telecommunications via the Internet or a virtual private network (VPN, which provides more security). It eliminates the need to purchase hardware and deploy IT infrastructure to support computing resources and gives users access to applications, data, and storage within their own business unit environments or networks.[3] Best of all, services can be turned on or off, increased or decreased, depending on user needs.

> "Cloud computing encompasses any subscription-based or pay-per-use service that, in real time over the Internet, extends IT's existing capabilities."[4]

There are a range of interpretations and definitions, some of which are not completely accurate. Some merely define it as renting storage space or applications on a host organization's servers; others center definitions around web-based applications like social media and hosted application services.

Someone has to be the official referee, especially in the public sector. The National Institute of Standards and Technology (NIST) is the official federal arbiter of definitions, standards, and guidelines for cloud computing. NIST defines cloud computing as *a model for enabling convenient, on-demand network access to a shared pool of configurable computing resources (e.g., networks, servers, storage, applications, and services) that can be rapidly provisioned and released with minimal management effort or service provider interaction.*[5]

> Cloud computing enables convenient, on-demand network access to a shared pool of configurable computing resources that can be rapidly provisioned.

Given the changing nature of IT, especially for newer developments, NIST has stated that the definition of cloud computing "is evolving." To find the latest official definition, one should consult the most current definition available from NIST's website at www.nist.gov (and other resources).

Key Characteristics of Cloud Computing

NIST also identifies five essential characteristics of cloud computing:

1. **On-demand self-service.** *A [computing] consumer can unilaterally provision computing capabilities, such as server time and network storage, as needed automatically without requiring human interaction with each service's provider.*
2. **Broad network access.** *Capabilities are available over the network and accessed through standard mechanisms that promote use by heterogeneous thin or thick client platforms (e.g., mobile phones, laptops, and PDAs).*
3. **Resource pooling.** *The [hosting] provider's computing resources are pooled to serve multiple consumers using a multi-tenant model, with different physical and virtual resources dynamically assigned and reassigned according to consumer demand. There is a sense of location independence in that the customer generally has no control or knowledge over the exact location of the provided resources but may be able to specify location at a higher level of abstraction (e.g., country, state, or datacenter). Examples of resources include storage, processing, memory, network bandwidth, and virtual machines.*
4. **Rapid elasticity.** *Capabilities can be rapidly and elastically provisioned, in some cases automatically, to quickly scale out and rapidly released to quickly scale in. To the consumer, the capabilities available for provisioning often appear to be unlimited and can be purchased in any quantity at any time.*

5. ***Measured service.*** *Cloud systems automatically control and opti-mize resource use by leveraging a metering capability at some level of abstraction appropriate to the type of service (e.g., storage, process-ing, bandwidth, and active user accounts). Resource usage can be monitored, controlled, and reported providing transparency for both the provider and consumer of the utilized service.*[6]

What Cloud Computing Really Means

It's fast. It's cheap. It's efficient. Yes, cloud computing is all the rage. NIST has offered its official definition, but "the problem is that (as with Web 2.0) everyone seems to have a different definition."[7]

> Among metatrends, "Cloud Computing is the hardest one to argue with in the long term."[8]

The phrase "the cloud" has entered the mainstream—it is promoted on primetime TV—but its meaning and description are in flux: that is, if you ask 10 different people to define it, you will likely get 10 different answers. According to Eric Knorr and Galen Gruman in *InfoWorld,* it's really just "a metaphor for the Internet" but when you throw in "computing" alongside it "the meaning gets bigger and fuzzier." Cloud computing provides "a way to increase capacity [e.g., computing power, network connections, storage] or add capabilities dynamically on the fly without investing in new infrastructure, training new personnel, or licensing new software. Cloud computing encompasses any subscription-based or pay-per-use service that, in (near) real time over the Internet, extends IT's existing capabilities."[9]

> The idea of loosely coupled services running on an agile, scalable in-frastructure should eventually "make every enterprise a node in the cloud."[10]

The use of *service-oriented architecture (SOA)*—which separates infras-tructure, applications, and data into layers—permeates enterprise applica-tions, and the idea of loosely coupled services running on an agile, scalable infrastructure may eventually "make every enterprise a node in the cloud." That is the direction the trend is headed. "*It's a long-running trend with a far-out horizon. But among big metatrends, cloud computing is the hardest one to argue with in the long term*" (italics added).[11]

Cloud Deployment Models

Depending upon user needs and other considerations, cloud computing services are typically deployed using one of the following four models, as defined by NIST:

1. ***Private cloud****. This is dedicated to and operated by a single enterprise. This is a particularly prudent approach when privacy and security are key issues, such as in the health care and financial services industries, and also for sensitive government or military applications and data. A private cloud may be managed by the organization or a third party and may exist on-premise or off-premise.*
2. ***Community cloud.*** *Think co-ops, nonprofit organizations, and non-governmental organizations (NGOs). In this deployment, the cloud infrastructure is* shared by several organizations *and supports a specific community that has shared concerns (e.g., mission, security requirements, policy, and compliance considerations). It may be managed by the organizations or a third party and may exist on-premise or off-premise.*
3. ***Public cloud.*** *Open to the public, this cloud can be maintained by a user group, or even a fan club. In this case, "the cloud infrastructure is made available to the general public or a large industry group and is owned by an organization selling cloud services."*
4. ***Hybrid cloud.*** *This utilizes a combined approach, using parts of the aforementioned deployment models: private, community, and/or public. The cloud infrastructure is a* "composition of two or more clouds, *(private, community, or public) that remain unique entities but are bound together by standardized or proprietary technology that enables data and application portability (e.g., cloud bursting for load-balancing between clouds)"* [all emphasis added].[12]

Greatest Security Threats to Cloud Computing

Cloud computing comes with serious security risks—some of which have not yet been uncovered—but the business benefits largely outweigh the security threats for the vast majority of enterprises, so long as they are planned for, and preventive action is taken. In planning and IG policy development, these risks must be borne in mind and dealt with through controls and counter measures. Controls must be tested and audited, although the actual enforcement must be carried out by management. The following are key cloud computing security threats, with specific examples, and remedial fix measures that can be taken. The majority of this information is courtesy of the Cloud Security Alliance.

Document and Data Breaches

Many times damage to e-documents and data is malicious, at other times it is unintentional. Lack of training and awareness, for example, can cause an information user to accidentally compromise sensitive data. Organizations must have proactive IG policies that combat either type of breach. The loss of data, documents, and records is always a threat and can occur whether cloud computing is utilized or not.

When officially declared business records are deleted or altered without a backup of the original record or content, they may be lost forever. A record can also be lost by unlinking it from its indexes, deleting its identifying meta-data, or losing its encoding key, which may render it unrecoverable. Another way data/document loss can occur is by storing it on unreliable media.[13] And as with any architecture—not just cloud computing—unauthorized parties must be prevented from hacking into the system and gaining access to sensitive data. In general, providers of cloud services have more resources at their disposal than their individual clients typically have.

But the threat of data compromise inherently increases when using cloud computing, due to "the number of and interactions between risks and challenges which are either unique to cloud, or more dangerous because of the architectural or operational characteristics of the cloud environment."[14]

Examples
- Lack of document lifecycle security (DLS) technologies, such as data loss prevention (DLP) and information rights management (IRM) technologies.
- Insufficient *authentication, authorization, and audit (AAA)* controls to govern login access.
- Ineffective encryption and software keys, including lost keys or inconsistent encryption.
- Basic operational failures, such as server or disk drive crashes.
- Security challenges related to persistent data or ineffective disposal methods.
- Inability to verify disposal at the end of a business record's lifecycle.
- Risk of association with any larger failures of the cloud provider.
- Jurisdiction and political issues that may arise due to the fact that the cloud provider likely resides outside of the geographic region of the client.
- Data center reliability, backup, and disaster recovery/business continuity issues.

The Fix
- IG policies and controls to protect the most sensitive documents and data.

- DLS implementation where needed to protect documents from creation to their final disposition.
- More robust and secure application programming interface (API) access control.
- Strong e-mail and e-document encryption to protect sensitive data at rest, in use, and in transit.
- IG policies for data and document security during the software application design phase, as well as testing and auditing the controls for those policies during live operation.
- Strong encryption generation, as well as secure storage, management, and document destruction practices.
- Contractual agreement by cloud service providers to completely delete data before storage media are reused by other clients.
- Agreement by cloud provider to follow standard operating procedures for data backup, archiving, and retention.

The Enemy Within: Insider Threats

Since the advent of the WikiLeaks scandal and the slew of other examples in the corporate world, the threat of the malicious insider is well known. *"This threat is amplified for consumers of cloud services by the convergence of IT services and customers under a single management domain, combined with a general lack of transparency into provider process and procedure"* (italics added).[15] For example, question a cloud provider on its security procedures—for not only the applications and services, but also for their employees: How are they screened? Are background checks performed? How is physical access to the building and data center granted and monitored? What are its remedial procedures for non-compliance?

When these security, privacy, and support issues are not fully investigated, it creates an opportunity for hackers, industrial spies, and even "nation-state sponsored intrusion. The level of access granted could enable such an adversary to harvest confidential data or gain complete control over the cloud services with little or no risk of detection."[16]

Examples
- An internal company employee steals information to give or sell to a competitor.
- A cloud provider's employee steals information to give or sell to one of your company's competitors.
- Inadequate screening processes (by your company or a cloud provider) can result in the hiring of people with criminal records, granting them access to sensitive information.

- A cloud provider's employee allows unauthorized access to data that your company believes is secure in the cloud. The physical cloud storage facility lacks security, so anyone can enter the building and access information.

The Fix
- IG policies and controls to secure information assets.
- Implementation of DLP and IRM technologies and related technology sets at all stages of DLS.
- Assessment of suppliers' practices and complete supply chain.
- Screening and hiring requirements (e.g., background checks) as part of contract with cloud provider.
- Transparent policies regarding information security, data management, compliance, and reporting, as approved by the client.
- Clear delineation of the process for notifying the client of a security breach or data loss.[17]

Hacking and Rogue Intrusions

Although cloud computing providers, as a rule, invest heavily in security, they can also be the target of attacks, and those attacks can affect many client enterprises. Providers of cloud infrastructure service (e.g., network management, computing power, databases, storage) offer their customers the illusion of unlimited infrastructure expansion in the form of computing, network resources, and storage capacity. This is often coupled with a very easy sign-up process, free trials (even for anonymous users), and simple activation with a credit card. This is a boon to hackers who can assume multiple identities.[18] Using these anonymous accounts to their advantage, hackers and spammers can engage in criminal operations while remaining elusive.

Examples
- Cloud services providers have often unknowingly hosted malicious code, including Trojan horses, keystroke loggers, bot applications, and other programs that facilitate data theft. Recent examples include the Zeus botnet and InfoStealer.
- Malware can masquerade as downloads for Microsoft Office, Adobe PDFs, or other innocuous files.
- Botnets can infect a cloud provider to gain access to a wide range of data, while leveraging the cloud provider's control capabilities.
- Spam is a perennial problem—each new countermeasure is met with new ways to sneak spam through filters to phish for sensitive data.

The Fix
- IG policies and monitoring controls must require tighter initial registration and thorough user verification processes.

- IG policies and technologies to combat credit card fraud.
- Total network monitoring, including deep content inspection.
- Requirement that the cloud provider regularly monitor public blacklists to check for exploitation.

Insecure Points of Cloud Connection

APIs are a way of standardizing the connection between two software applications. They are essentially standard hooks that an application uses to connect to another software application—in this case, the cloud. System actions like provisioning, management, orchestration, and monitoring are all performed using these API interfaces.

It comes down to this: A chain is only as strong as its weakest link, so APIs must be more thoroughly tested to ensure that all connections abide by established policy. This will thwart hackers seeking workarounds for ill intent, as well as valid users who have made a mistake. It is possible for third parties to piggyback value-added services on APIs, resulting in a layered interface that is more vulnerable to security breaches.

Examples
- Weak APIs provide opportunities for data compromise.
- Anonymous logins and reusable passwords can undermine the security of an entire cloud community.
- Unencrypted transmission or storage and unencrypted verification allow successful man-in-the-middle data theft.
- Rigid basic access controls or false authorizations pose a threat.
- Poor management, monitoring, and recording of cloud logins and activity make it difficult to detect malicious behavior.
- Dependency on unregulated API interfaces, especially third-party add-ons can allow critical information to be stolen as necessary connections are made.

The Fix
- An understanding of the security model of cloud provider APIs and interfaces, including any third-party or organization-created dependencies.
- Utilization of multiple logon authentication steps and strong access controls.
- Encryption of sensitive data during transmission.
- Understanding how the API impacts associated cloud usage.

Issues with Multi-tenancy and Technology Sharing

The foundations of many cloud services providers were not developed to support multiple tenants on a single piece of hardware, or to isolate each tenant on its own system. Basic cloud infrastructure is designed to leverage scale through the sharing of components. Despite this, many component manufacturers have not caught up, and their products have not been designed to function in a multi-tenant system. Surely, newer architectures will evolve to address this issue.

In the meantime, virtual computing is often used, allowing for multiple instances of an operating system (and applications) to be walled off from others that are running on the same computer. Essentially, each instance of the operating system (OS) runs independently as if it were the only one on the computer. A "virtualization hypervisor mediates access between guest operating systems and the physical compute resources" (like CPU processing power). Yet flaws have been found in these hypervisors "that have enabled guest operating systems to gain inappropriate levels of control or influence on the underlying platform"—and therefore indirectly impact the other guest operating systems running on the machine. To combat this, "security enforcement and monitoring" of all shared computing resources must be employed. Solid partitions between the guest operating systems—known as compartmentalization—should be employed to ensure that one client's activities do not interfere with others running on the same cloud provider. Customers should *never* have access to any other tenant's "actual or residual data, network traffic," or other proprietary data.[19]

Examples

- Joanna Rutkowska's Blue Pill root technique, which describes how an unauthorized user could intercept data by using virtual hardware called a hypervisor. The Blue Pill would be undetectable as long as the host system was functioning properly. Rutkowska also developed a Red Pill, which could detect a Blue Pill hypervisor, allowing the owner to eliminate it.
- Kostya Kortchinksy's CloudBurst is another example of hypervisor exploitation.

The Fix

- Security IG that leverages best practices for installation, configuration, monitoring, testing, and auditing of cloud computing resources.
- Requirements for monitoring the computing environment for any rogue intrusions or misuse of cloud resources.
- Control and verify access. Promote a more secure two-factor authentication procedure.
- Enforceable service-level agreements (SLAs) for patching software bugs, addressing data breaches, and fixing vulnerabilities.
- An IG policy that requires regular audits and evaluations to detect weaknesses in cloud security and configuration.[20]

Hacking, Hijacking, and Unauthorized Access

Hacking into accounts to assume the identity of a victim has been happening almost since personal e-mail existed. It can be as simple as stealing passwords with a keystroke logger. Attack methods such as social engineering (e.g., phishing), fraud by identity theft, and exploitation of software vulnerabilities are still effective at compromising systems. Most people recycle a few passwords and reuse them for multiple accounts, so once one is breached, criminals can gain access to additional accounts, including client databases and sensitive documents. If login credentials are compromised, a hacker can monitor nearly everything your organization is doing: A less passive hacker might alter or destroy sensitive documents, create false information, or replace your links with fraudulent ones that direct users to sites harboring malware or phishing scams. Once they have control, it can look like *your organization* is the origin of the malicious downloads or information capture. From here, the attackers can assume the good name and reputation of an organization to further their attacks.

Examples
- Examples are widespread in the general population; however, no clear instances of this occurring with cloud services providers are known (as this book goes to press).

The Fix
- IG policies should clearly state that users and providers should never reveal their account information to anyone.
- An IG policy should require more secure two-factor authentication techniques to verify login identity, where possible.
- Require your cloud services provider to actively monitor and log all activity in order to quickly identify users engaging in fraudulent actions or those that otherwise fail to comply with the client's IG policy.
- Understand, analyze, and evaluate the cloud provider's contract, especially regarding security protocols. Negotiate improved terms in SLAs to improve or enhance security and privacy.[21]

Who Are Your Neighbors?

The primary selling point of cloud computing is that enterprises are freed up to focus on their core business, rather than being focused on providing IT services. Modulating computer hardware and software resources without making capital expenditures is another key advantage. Both of these business benefits allow companies to invest more heavily in line-of-business activities and focus on their core products, services, and operations. The security risks must be weighed against the financial and operational advantages—and projected estimates for costs are often understated, which throws off the entire cost-justification analysis. Further complicating things is the fact that cloud deployments are often enthusiastically driven by overzealous cost-cutters who focus inordinately on potential benefits, and do not factor in risk and security issues.

An analysis of an organization's exposure to risk *must* include checking on software versions and revision levels, overall security design, and general IG practices. This includes updating software, tools, and policy, as needed.

Knowing your neighbors—those who are sharing the same infrastructure with you—is also important and, as we all know, good fences make good neighbors. If the cloud services provider will not or cannot be forthcoming about who else is sharing their infrastructure services with your organization and this becomes a significant issue, then moving to a private cloud architecture may be the best option.

Examples

- Amazon's Elastic Compute Cloud (EC2) service was utilized by the Internal Revenue Service (IRS) When the IRS asked Amazon for a certification and accreditation (C&A) report, Amazon declined. Note: The C&A process was developed to help ensure compliance with NIST standards and mandated by the Office of Management and Budget, which oversees Federal Information Security Management Act of 2002 (FISMA) compliance.

- Heartland, a payment processing corporation, suffered a data breach in 2008. Hackers stole account details for over 100 million credit and debit cards. This data was stored on Heartland's network, which the hackers broke into using information (pertaining to employees, corporate structure, company networks, and related systems) it had stolen in the weeks leading up to the major breach.

The Fix

- An IG policy that requires full disclosure of activity and usage logs, and related information. Audit the policy for compliance.

- Investigate the architecture of your cloud services provider (e.g., version levels, network operating systems, firewalls, etc.).

- Robust and vigilant supervision, logs, and reporting of all system activity, particularly that requesting expansive and detailed reports on the handling of sensitive information.[22]

IG Guidelines: Managing Documents and Records in the Cloud

The following guidelines have been established by the National Archives and Records Administration (NARA) for creating standards and policies for managing an organization's e-documents records that are created, used, or stored in cloud computing environments:

1. *Include the Chief Records Management Officer and/or lead RM staff in the planning, development, deployment, and use of cloud computing solutions.*
2. *Define which copy of records will be declared as the organization's record copy and manage these in accordance with information governance policies and regulations (e.g. for federal agencies, 36 CFR Part 1222). Remember, the value of records in the cloud may be greater than the value of any other set because of indexing or other reasons. In such instances, this added value may require designation of the copies as records.*
3. *Include instructions for determining if records in a cloud environment are covered under an existing records retention schedule.*
4. *Include instructions on how all records will be captured, managed, retained, made available to authorized users, and retention periods applied.*
5. *Include instructions on conducting a records analysis, developing and submitting records retention schedules to an organization's central records department for unscheduled records in a cloud environment, These instructions should include scheduling system documentation, metadata, and related records.*
6. *Include instructions to periodically test transfers of records to other environments, including departmental servers, to ensure the records remain portable.*
7. *Include instructions on how data will be migrated to new formats, operating systems, etc., so that records are readable throughout their entire life cycles. Include in your migration planning provisions for transferring permanent records in the cloud to central records.*
8. *Resolve portability and accessibility issues through good records management policies and other data governance practices. Data governance typically addresses interoperability of computing systems, portability of data (able to move from one system to another), and information security and access. However, such policies by themselves will not address an organization's compliance and information governance demands and requirements.*[23]

Managing E-Docs and Records in the Cloud: A Practical Approach

The risks and security vulnerabilities of cloud computing have been reviewed in this chapter—so much so that perhaps some readers are thinking,

"Is it really worth it?" The answer is a *qualified* yes—it can be, based on your organization's business needs and computing resource capabilities.

Formal business records are the most valuable documents in an organization. For recordkeeping purposes, records held within the cloud are subject to a higher risk of loss and inaccessibility, which can cause the organization to be non-compliant, lose in litigation, be fined, and experience other negative results. So what is the solution to managing these critical records? [24]

Sometimes people overthink and overcomplicate things. Perhaps the solution is a simple approach: Research and define organizational business requirements and then, "*only allow those documents and records into the cloud that need to be shared across collaborative teams that do not require significant time for retention or are at low risk for litigation*" (italics added). [25]

What is a *significant* retention time period? As a practical matter, anything that needs to be retained for over two years probably should not be put into the cloud. Your organization will have to conduct its own business-specific analysis and develop IG policies for records management in the cloud that are best suited, and most appropriate. A thorough records inventory, retention schedule, and risk analysis in relation to business requirements should be conducted, which includes examining security and compliance concerns such as privacy, in addition to high-risk litigation issues. [26]

Another possible approach for utilizing cloud services for managing records is to *maintain hard copies of records held in the cloud*. If the information suddenly disappears, then the hard copy is available as a backup. *But that may be even more problematic*—you have to determine which copy is the *official* record, as well as analyze and identify which hard copies to keep, how to keep the paper and electronic copies synchronized, how and where to store paper copies, what file organization system to use, how to document it, and how and when hard copy records can be accessed. The other thorny issue is that printing out all electronic records is contrary to what most records management experts advise, and eco-conscious organizations will especially want to avoid this. All organizations have been moving toward the paperless office, becoming more sustainable, and reducing their carbon footprint. [27]

Chapter Summary: Key Points

- Organizations are rapidly moving applications and storage to the cloud. Cloud computing allows users to access and use shared data and computing services via the Internet or a VPN.

- Organizations need to understand cloud computing's security risks and formulate IG policies and controls before deploying.
- Five key characteristics of cloud computing are: 1) on-demand self-service; 2) broad network access; 3) resource pooling; 4) rapid elasticity; and 5) measured service.
- Cloud computing services are typically deployed using one of four models: 1) private cloud, 2) public cloud, 3) community cloud, and 4) hybrid cloud.
- Utilizing cloud computing carries significant security risks, which can be offset by establishing IG policies and preventive measures so that the business benefits of agility and reduced cost may be exploited.
- Cloud applications may lack the capability to implement records disposition schedules and to prove that every instance of a record was destroyed after its final disposition, so that defensible disposition practices can be argued in court.
- Carefully determine which types of documents should be stored in the cloud. The most likely candidates are those that are unlikely to pose a litigation risk, do not have retention requirements of more than two years, and are shared for collaborative projects.

Notes

1. Cloud Security Alliance, "Top Threats to Cloud Computing V1.0," March 2010, https://cloudsecurityalliance.org/topthreats/csathreats.v1.0.pdf, p.6, retrieved March30, 2012.
2. R. "Ray" Wang, "Tuesday's Tip: Understanding the Many Flavors of Cloud Computing and SaaS," March 22, 2010, http://blog.softwareinsider.org/2010/03/22/tuesdays-tip-understanding-the-many-flavors-of-cloud-computing-and-saas/, retrieved December 21, 2011.
3. "NARA Bulletin 2010-05," September 8, 2010, www.archives.gov/records-mgmt/bulletins/2010/2010-05.html, retrieved August 15, 2011.
4. Eric Knorr, Galen Gruman, "What Cloud Computing Really Means" *InfoWorld*, July 2010, www.infoworld.com/d/cloud-computing/what-cloud-computing-really-means-031, retrievedMarch 30, 2012.
5. NIST Definition of Cloud Computing, Version 15, 10-07-2009, nist.gov, retrieved March 30, 2012.
6. Ibid.
7. Eric Knorr, Galen Gruman.
8. Ibid.
9. Ibid.

10. Ibid.

11. Ibid.

12. All definitions are from NIST Definition of Cloud Computing, Version 15, 10-07-2009, retrieved August 15, 2011.

13. Cloud Security Alliance, "Top Threats to Cloud Computing V1.0," March 2010, https://cloudsecurityalliance.org/topthreats/csathreats.v1.0.pdf, retrieved March 30, 2012

14. Ibid.

15. Ibid.

16. Ibid.

17. Ibid.

18. Ibid.

19. Ibid.

20. Ibid.

21. Ibid.

22. Ibid.

23. "NARA Bulletin 2010-05," September 8, 2010, www.archives.gov/records-mgmt/bulletins/2010/2010-05.html, retrieved August 15, 2011.

24. "Records Management and the Cloud," Rhizome Digital, March 9, 2010, http://rhizomedigital.wordpress.com/2010/03/09/records-management-the-cloud/, retrieved December 21, 2011.

25. Ibid.

26. Ibid.

27. Ibid.

PART III

E-Records Considerations

CHAPTER 9

Information Governance and Security for Vital Records

The most critical information assets an organization has are vital records. Without them, the organization cannot continue to function. They must be secured with the utmost of care and caution as part of an overall program to secure information assets.

Defining Vital Records

Vital records are *mission-critical records* that are necessary for an organization to continue to operate in the event of disruption or disaster, and cannot be re-created from any other source. They are the most important records to be protected, and a plan for *disaster recovery (DR)/business continuity (BC)* must be in place to safeguard these records.

> Vital records are mission-critical records that are necessary for an organization to continue to operate in the event of a disaster.

According to one source:

Vital records must be protected from destruction because they offer direct evidence of legal status, ownership, accounts receivable, and the particulars of obligations incurred by government agencies [and businesses]. These records are critical because they contain information required to continue functioning during a disaster, or to reestablish operations after a calamity has ended. Vital records are irreplaceable, and in some instances must be maintained in their original form to be legally admissible as evidence.[1]

Vital records include records that maintain and protect the rights of stakeholders and are needed[2] to continue or re-start operations in the event of a disaster or other business interruption.[3]

In the past, enterprises have underinvested in security and protections for vital records. Often management seeks to minimize costs by holding off on investing in a DR/BC plan and associated safeguarding tools, such as disaster insurance, fireproof safes, sprinkler systems, backup power and communications systems. This can be tempting, especially if an enterprise has never experienced a disaster and operates under a false sense of security.

The tragedies of the 9-11 attack in 2001 and Hurricane Katrina in 2005 emphasize the importance of DR/BC planning and preparation. *Vital records management is a cost-justifiable strategy because it safeguards critical assets and provides insurance that preserves stakeholder and public trust.*

Managing vital records involves

- *Inventorying:* identifying and documenting vital records;
- *Securing:* protecting them through electronic and physical security; and
- *Recovering*: following a disaster or business interruption, having the capability to quickly obtain access to them (or working copies) and putting them into operation.

The information governance (IG) policies, procedures, and controls, when developed and implemented, provide assurance that business operations can survive a disaster and resume in a timely manner. Failure to plan can destroy the business—nearly three-quarters of organizations go out of business after having vital records destroyed by a disaster.

A vital records program is an essential component of a *counter-disaster program,* which aims to minimize the impact of disasters and enable the organization *to execute a business continuity plan* for quick recovery and resumption of operations.[4]

In DR/BC planning, varied considerations need to be given for short versus long business interruptions. Business disruption may be temporary, as in the event of a fire alarm or bomb scare, or long-term, which may be caused by a flood, hurricane, tornado, fire, or even a terrorist attack. Different responses need to be fashioned and executed for various scenarios. In each case, the preservation and acquisition (or regeneration) of vital records must be the paramount consideration.

Effective vital records program policies and procedures can protect against continuity disruptions and provide insurance against information damage incurred by disasters.

Types of Vital Records

Often vital records are thought of in a public sector sense, that is, birth and death certificates, marriage licenses, and other official records. These are vital records for governments, and it is critical for them to maintain historical records, but *every formal organization—business, nonprofit, or government—has vital records.*

In government, and in most every business, personnel and payroll records are vital records, as employees cannot be paid accurately without them. After Hurricane Katrina, employees of the local school district and universities could not be paid correctly once power was restored, since the details of their withholdings and deductions were not available. So the temporary workaround was to run a plain vanilla payroll check for employees without accurate deductions and to reconcile them later.

In most every organization, active contracts are also vital records. In health care, medical records are vital records; pharmaceutical firms cannot operate without their research and drug compound records; in banking and financial services firms, customer information files are vital records; in a university, student academic records are vital records; a law or consulting firm needs its client files to operate; a publisher must have book files; and a manufacturing firm needs current material safety data sheets (MSDS) to continue manufacturing operations safely.

Not all records are vital, in fact; typically *only about three to five percent of an organization's total records are vital records.*

> Users have a tendency to blur the lines between important records and vital records. Only about three to five percent of records are vital.

Although each department or business unit will have a tendency to blur the lines between important records and vital records, it is the duty of the vital records team, (which may include representatives from records management, information technology [IT], legal, compliance, risk management, and operations), to determine which crucial (and small) subset of important records are, in reality, *vital* records. This is important because the extra investment in IG, auditing procedures, testing, hardware, software, secure filing equipment, backup facilities and other required components of a vital records program are costly, and in fact, *pay no return unless there is an actual disaster.*

A relatively new option, another tool in the toolkit of a vital records program, is the use of secure cloud computing (see Chapter 8) for storing vital records off site and out of the reach of a local or regional disaster. Cloud computing has various levels of functionality, from basic infrastructure to fully functioning applications, and in its fundamental software-as-a-service (SaaS) offering for collaboration, it is using the Internet or a virtual private network (VPN) and remote servers to store or process electronic files, documents, software application programs, e-mail, and other potential vital records. Some organizations use cloud computing to process e-mail, store large or critical files, or to operate key information management software applications.

Cloud computing is relatively new and immature but may be a good option for storing third or fourth copies of vital records, or backups of backup copies, that can be accessed quickly in the event of a disaster or business interruption.

Vital records are not determined by their media, or their status (e.g., active or inactive; in use, at rest, or in transit). They can be paper, microfilm, audio/video tape, or electronic records. They can be digital or analog. They are not always permanent or active records, and may not even be original records, but critical copies. They may be only temporarily considered vital, and then their status can change, such as when an organization is in the midst of a critical transaction.

Impact of Losing Vital Records

The impact of the loss of vital records should not be underestimated. In the event of major disasters, the loss of the building or equipment generally matters less than the loss of vital records; after all, hard capital assets like buildings and equipment can be replaced through lease, repair, or purchase. According to the University of Edinburgh, more than 70 percent of organizations go out of business within three years of suffering a fire that causes loss of paperwork and software.[5]

According to United Nations guidelines, key points for managing risks and protecting vital records include:

1. *Small subset:* Your vital records will be small in number—only about two to four percent of all business records are vital.
2. *Inventory and secure:* Identify and protect them using IG policies, technologies, and physical security measures.
3. *Keep updated:* Remember to exchange older security copies for current versions as necessary. Also, official copies of vital records need to be tested periodically to ensure they are readable and on the most current and prevalent electronic formats.
4. *Test the plan:* Have a plan for accessing the security copies in the event of an emergency—and practice it.[6]

Creating, Implementing, and Maintaining a Vital Records Program

The U.N. describes a vital records program as "a management regimen for vital records which includes preventative and protection measures and procedures, retention requirements and locations, staff and service provider contact details together with documentation."[7]

A vital records program requires IG, which means not only protecting vital records from natural or man-made disasters, but also assuring *record integrity*, that is, the accuracy, authenticity, and validity of records. *Vital records, and most especially electronic vital records, are subject to theft, unauthorized alteration, or misuse.* So, for instance, a bank or credit reporting company must protect its vital customer records so that they are not used for identity theft or other fraudulent purposes.

Essential Steps to Implementing a Vital Records Program

A vital records program includes all of the following:

- *Sponsorship*: Announcement, planning, and development of the vital records program by senior management.
- *Policy creation:* Establishment of IG policies for vital records.
- *Inventorying:* Survey, identification, and inventory maintenance of vital records.
- *Assessing risk:* Determination of key threats and potential losses if vital records are lost, damaged, altered, or stolen.
- *Securing:* Evaluation and implementation of appropriate protective, prevention, and recovery measures, including utilization of external services, archiving of safe copies, physical security, and secure cloud computing.
- *Educating:* Training and communicating with employees about vital records issues on an ongoing basis.
- *Auditing:* Ensuring vital records program procedures are being followed.
- *Testing:* Engaging in actual live testing and mock disaster exercises.

Senior management sets the tone for vital records program governance and compliance.

TABLE 9.1   Critical Identifiers for Vital Records

1. Vital Records

Records without which an organization cannot function. These records are essential to the core business of the organization.	Examples: Records which give evidence of organizational legal status; ■ Current financial and tax records; ■ Records which protect the assets and interests of the organization; ■ Current and recent contracts; ■ Software source code; ■ Research information; ■ Records which are subject to a legal retention requirement; ■ Minutes of board meetings dealing with major policy issues; ■ Historical records if needed for evidential or other legal purposes; ■ Business plan

2. Important Records

These records are important to the continued operation of the organization. They can be reproduced or recreated from original sources, but only at considerable time and expense.	Examples: Procedures; Training manuals; Business timetables; Minutes of some meetings; Business contact information; Emails with potential legal implications

3. Useful Records

Loss of these records would cause temporary inconvenience to the organization, but they are replaceable.	Examples: Most correspondence; Management emails; Records of historical transactions; Marketing plans

4. Non-Essential Records

These records have no value beyond the immediate purpose for which they were created.	Examples: E-Mails and materials about one-off events which are now completed; Advertisements

Source: Adapted from The University of Edinburgh, "Vital Records version 8," March 22, 2011, www.recordsmanagement.ed.ac.uk/InfoStaff/RMstaff/VitalRecords/VitalRecords.htm.

Critical Identifiers for Vital Records

All vital records must contain critical identifying information:

- Record series title.
- Rationale for vital record designation, that is, what mission-critical business functions are dependent on these specific records.
- Description of the record series' business role, function and its medium(s).
- Department responsible for producing and maintaining the vital records.
- Department responsible for protecting and preserving the vital records.
- Protective measures prescribed for safety, preservation, reproduction.

When identifying which of your records are vital, it may be helpful to divide them into the following categories: 1) vital, 2) important, 3) useful, and 4) non-essential as shown in Table 9.1, adapted from the vital records policy of the University of Edinburgh in Scotland. [8] Please note that the examples are not exhaustive and will vary from organization to organization.

U.S. National Archives Approach to Identify Vital Records

The U.S. National Archives has created guidelines that federal agencies should follow when identifying critical information and creating document inventories:

- *Consult with the official responsible for emergency coordination,*
- *Review agency statutory and regulatory responsibilities and existing emergency plans for insights into the functions and records that may be included in the vital records inventory,*
- *Review documentation created for the contingency planning and risk assessment phase of emergency preparedness. The offices performing those functions are obvious focuses of an inventory,*
- *Review current file plans of offices that are responsible for performing critical functions or may be responsible for preserving rights, and,*
- *Review the agency records manual or records schedule to determine which records series potentially qualify as vital.*

Agencies must exercise caution in designating records as vital and in conducting the vital records inventory. A review of the available literature suggests that from 1 to 7 percent of an agency's records may be vital records. Only those records series or electronic information systems (or portions of them) most critical to emergency operations or the preservation of legal or financial rights should be so designated. Agencies must make difficult and judicious decisions in this regard.

The inventory of vital records should include:

- *The name of the office responsible for the records series or electronic information system containing vital information*
- *The title of each records series or information system containing vital information*
- *Identification of each series or system that contains emergency-operating vital records or vital records relating to rights*
- *The medium on which the records are recorded*
- *The physical location for offsite storage of copies of the records series or system*
- *The frequency with which the records are to be cycled (updated).* [9]

Implementing Protective Procedures

Once vital records have been identified, practical steps to preserve and protect them must be taken. A range of events could occur, disrupting your work and endangering your vital records.[10] These include, but are not limited to:

- *Power surges and outages:* Fluctuations or temporary outages that cause hardware downtime at the desktop, shared network hard drive, or server level.
- *Hardware failures:* Server crash resulting in inability to access e-records for a few hours, or even days.
- *Fire alarm or bomb threat:* Forced evacuation prohibiting building access for a few hours or days.
- *Non-malicious insider:* Loss or damage through carelessness.
- *Malicious attacks:* Theft or destruction of information assets including vital records.
- *Physical exposure or deterioration:* Excessive humidity, heat, or sunlight, and biological factors (e.g., mold, rats, mice, insects), can deteriorate or destroy physical and electronic vital records.
- *Natural and man-made disasters:* Fire, flood, tornado, hurricane, tsunami, acts of terrorism, and so on can lead to document loss and destruction.

As required by 36 CFR 1236, U.S. governmental agencies must include vital records management procedures in their business continuity plan in the event of disaster or prolonged business interruption.

Public corporations are also obligated to protect vital records, under multiple laws and statutes. The Sarbanes-Oxley Act of 2002 (SOX) sets regulatory requirements for the disclosure of financial records and statements, accounting practices, and related communications in an attempt to root out fraud. SOX does not specify "*how* a [public corporate] business should store its records; rather, it defines *which* records are to be stored and for *how long*" (italics added).[11]

The SOX legislation not only impacts financial reporting, it also impacts the records management, compliance, legal, and IT departments—those charged with maintaining the corporation's electronic records. It also affects those who audit public corporations. *The Sarbanes-Oxley Act states that all business records, including e-records, e-mail and other electronic messages, must be saved for "not less than five years."*

The consequences for non-compliance are serious and can include monetary fines, imprisonment of executives, or both. Since SOX, executives of public corporations have increasingly taken an active role in dictating IG and records management policies, and the records management and compliance functions have gained elevated visibility and importance. Cost-effectively achieving transparency and compliance in records management functions has been a great challenge over the past decade, and it requires new policies, new technologies, and new governance, risk management and compliance (GRC) tools.

Private corporations are subject to much less scrutiny, so much so that some public enterprises have made the move to turn private. But private corporations are also regulated under the Foreign Corrupt Practices Act (FCPA) of 1977 (amended 1988, 1998), which affects private corporations, limited liability corporations (LLCs) and partnerships. The FCPA was originally intended to prevent the destruction of business records to hide bribery or other crimes. Substantial penalties are imposed for failure to keep proper financial records.

Additional recordkeeping regulations affect specific vertical industries. The Healthcare Insurance Portability and Accountability Act (HIPAA) requires application data backup and business continuity plans for electronic data and records kept by health care providers. 45 CFR 164.30 requires healthcare organizations to "protect against any reasonably anticipated threats or hazards to the security and integrity of such information," and business continuity plans are required "to create and maintain retrievable exact copies of electronic protected health information."

The Federal Deposit Insurance Corporation (FDIC) requires banks to have business continuity/disaster recovery plans in place for computing facilities. These plans are reviewed by the Federal Financial Institutions Examination Council (FFIEC).

E-records are easier to protect than paper or other physical records.

There are a range of levels of investment that an organization may make in safeguarding its vital records, from inexpensively storing paper records in sturdy cardboard boxes, to portable file cabinets that can be rolled out of an area should the need arise, to costly fireproofed rooms. The medium and format of the records along with the level and speed of access needed will dictate which choices of protection are suitable. Other factors include budgetary constraints, operating environment, and whether or not a copy exists safely off-site. The most expensive options should be selected for vital records which cannot be recreated or have lasting historical value. Only chose the highest security alternatives when absolutely required, such as for classified government operations.

Protective and preventative measures must be undertaken to safeguard your organization's *vital e-records*. These safeguards must first provide for physical security, using means like control for physical access (e.g., smart-cards for file room access; a fireproof safe) and for online access (passwords; access and authentication security measures) and records preservation over the long term.

In general, electronic records are easier to protect from disaster than physical (paper) records, due to their portability and ease of copying for backups. Copying a vital e-record may be as simple as a few keystrokes to burn it to CD or DVD, or even a thumb drive or memory stick, all of which are fast and inexpensive. *Protecting those e-records from unauthorized copying or use is more difficult than if they were paper records locked in a storage safe.*

How do you flag records as vital and therefore note their importance, and invoke a set of IG policies that apply to them? It is as simple as including the word "vital" in the document or folder title, as this will make them easier to search and retrieve—and also it means that their handling must be dictated by IG policies and guidelines that are specific to vital records.

Vital records should not be stored on individual PCs, laptops, or tablets, but rather, on networked servers that make regular backups, and are managed by formal procedures.[12]

Instant Continuous Backup

Organizations may protect themselves by employing software and methods to back up their data and vital records in real time, instantly, on a continuous basis. This can be as basic as disk mirroring or using a redundant array of independent disks (RAID) which writes all data in two places at once. Or, it can be as complex as backing up the data in two or more remote sites, instantaneously. Organizations such as banks and hospitals and critical military units that cannot allow downtime may use this approach to ensure continuity of operations.

Off-site Continuity Options

An organization may make arrangements to switch its computing operations over to an alternate backup site for complete redundancy or for backup operations in the event of a business disruption. This may be accomplished through a remote unit of the same organization, a sister organization, or a third-party data center. *There are three basic types of backup sites: hot sites, warm sites, and cold sites.*

A hot site is one that has identical or nearly identical hardware and operating system configurations, and copies of application software, and receives live, real-time backup data from business operations. In the event of a business interruption, the IT and electronic vital records operations can be switched over automatically, providing uninterrupted service. *This is the most expensive option.* It may be offered by corporate data centers, service bureaus, hardware manufacturers, and specialized disaster recovery service organizations.

A warm site may have all (or mostly all) identical hardware and operating systems, such as a hot site does, and software licenses for the same applications, and needs only to have data loaded to resume normal operations. Internal IT staff may have to retrieve magnetic tapes, optical disks, or other storage media containing the most recent backup data, and some data may be lost if the backup is not real-time and continuous.

A cold site is simply an empty computer facility or data center that is ready with air-conditioning, raised floors, telecommunication lines, and electric power. Backup hardware and software will have to be purchased and shipped in quickly to resume operations. Arrangements can be made with suppliers for rapid delivery in the event of a disaster. *A cold site is the least expensive option, but will take the longest for the organization to get running again.* The site may be shared among multiple business units, or even organizations, to spread the cost.

Auditing the Vital Records Program

Regular, periodic audits, some internal and some by a trusted third party, will ensure that IG policies and legal compliance requirements are being met. Audits can take a sampling or subset of vital records and follow them through the entire vital records program process to see that each critical step is taken. The vital records program audit may be coordinated with, or a component of, an overall governance audit, compliance audit, or even an accounting audit, to reduce costs and duplication of effort while providing a complete view of the organization's governance and compliance status.

Some of the questions that must be answered are included in this checklist, based on recommendations from the U.S. National Archives:

1. *Has the agency [or business unit] prepared and disseminated written information to appropriate agency staff, describing the vital records program, including the responsibilities of various agency officials?*
2. *Has the agency [or business unit] assigned an official responsibility for managing the vital records program and coordinating it with other appropriate officials?*
3. *Have liaison officers been delegated responsibility for implementing the program in the agency's [or business unit] field offices?*
4. *Has the agency [or business unit] identified its vital records, i.e., its emergency operating records and records needed to protect legal and financial rights?*
5. *Does the agency [or business unit] make copies of the vital records for offsite storage?*
6. *Does the agency [or business unit] store duplicates at a remote location not subject to the same fire or other risks (such as high-risk geographic areas prone to flooding or earthquakes) present in storage areas where original records are kept?*
7. *Are agency [or business unit] personnel trained in their vital records responsibilities?*
8. *Does the agency [or business unit] conduct a periodic review of its vital records plan and update it to ensure that it is current, complete, and usable in case of emergency?*
9. *If special records (such as electronic information systems or microform records) are designated as vital records, have provisions been made for access to the equipment needed to use the records in the event of an emergency?*[13]

Creating a checklist that is specific to your organization can begin with these questions and then be revised and expanded appropriately until it is complete. Planning and testing are key elements of any program to recover business operations in the event of a disruption and to secure vital records in the event of a disaster.

Chapter Summary: Key Points

- Vital records are mission-critical records that are necessary for an organization to continue to operate.
- Typically only about three to five percent of an organization's total records are vital records.
- A vital records program is a management regimen for vital records which includes preventative and protection measures and procedures, retention requirements and locations, and staff and service provider contact details, as well as with documentation.
- Managing vital records involves: 1) identifying and documenting vital records; 2) protecting them through electronic and physical security; and 3) recovering them quickly and putting them into operation after a business interruption or disaster.
- An organization may make arrangements to switch its computing operations over to an alternate backup site. There are three basic types of backup sites: hot sites, warm sites, and cold sites.
- Regular, periodic audits, some internal and some by a trusted third party, will ensure that IG policies and legal compliance requirements are being met in a vital records program.

Notes

1. State of Delaware, "Vital Records Management," January 5, 2010, http://archives.delaware.gov/govsvcs/records_policies/vital%20records%20management.shtml, retrieved March 30, 2012.
2. The University of Edinburgh, "Vital Records," March 22, 2011, www.recordsmanagement.ed.ac.uk/InfoStaff/RMstaff/VitalRecords/VitalRecords.htm, retrieved March 30, 2012.
3. NSW Government, "State Records," www.records.nsw.gov.au/recordkeeping/dirks-manual/doing-a-dirks-project/manage-your-vital-records, retrieved December 21, 2011.
4. NSW Government, "State Records," www.records.nsw.gov.au/recordkeeping/dirks-manual/doing-a-dirks-project/manage-your-vital-records, retrieved October 21, 2011.
5. The University of Edinburgh, "Vital Records.
6. United Nations, Archives and Records Management, "Section 15—Managing Risks and Protecting Vital Records," http://archives.un.org/unarms/en/unrecordsmgmt/unrecordsresources/managingrisksandprotectingvitalrecords.htm#main, retrieved December 21, 2011.

7. Ibid.
8. The University of Edinburgh, "Vital Records."
9. The U.S. National Archives and Records Administration, "Vital Records and Records Disaster Mitigation and Recovery: An Instructional Guide," 1999, www.archives.gov/records-mgmt/vital-records/#Vital, retrieved December 21, 2011.
10. The University of Edinburgh, "Vital Records."
11. SearchCIO.com, "Sarbanes-Oxley Act (SOX)", retrieved December 21, 2011.
12. The University of Edinburgh, "Vital Records."
13. The U.S. National Archives and Records Administration, "Vital Records and Records Disaster Mitigation and Recovery.

CHAPTER 10

Long-Term Preservation of E-Records

Organizations today are creating increasingly voluminous amounts of digital data—some of which are formal business records, some of which are confidential information assets—and the larger this mountain of digital archives becomes; the greater the threat of it being compromised, eroded, or lost. *Long-term digital preservation (LTDP) attempts to address these archival storage, preservation, and retrieval challenges.*[1]

Defining Long-Term Digital Preservation

LTDP provides a path for storing digital information so that it may be retrieved exactly as it was stored, accurately and authentically, for use in the future—despite the known obsolescence over the long term of key elements: computer hardware, storage media, retrieval software, business processes, digital formats, and even those who are custodians of the stored data themselves. Over the long term, "LTDP is particularly challenging when preserving large amounts of heterogeneous data for very long periods of time of tens or even hundreds of years."[2]

> Long-term digital preservation ensures that e-documents may be retrieved in the future exactly as they were stored, despite known obsolescence of computing and storage components.

Business records must be preserved, cared for, and tested to ensure they are authentic, complete, and unaltered over the long term, for those records requiring long-term retention. Preserving these records is a component of an overall program to secure confidential information assets.

The term *preservation* implies permanence, yet electronic documents and the media they are stored on are inherently unstable. The definition of *long term* will vary by industry and organization, but generally refers to records that need to be retained longer than five to seven years. For instance, retention requirements for personal health records in the health care industry may stretch to decades. During the course of routine business, thousands or millions of electronic records are generated. Most are useful for only a short period of time, but some may need to be retained for long periods or permanently. For those records, organizations will need to plan for their preservation in order to ensure that they remain accessible, trustworthy, and useful over time.[3]

Key Factors in LTDP

Long-term access does not just happen. There must be a plan in place. Records are like any other asset. For as long as they have value, they need to be maintained and then disposed of when they no longer have value to the organization. All records require management, but because different types of records require different levels of care, *it is essential at the outset to identify records as high-risk and low-risk.*

Low-risk records may require less maintenance, while high-risk records will need to be maintained regularly to ensure they are preserved and remain retrievable, understandable, and authentic for as long as they need to be retained—twenty, fifty, or a even a hundred years from now.

The first step is using an integrated, cross-functional approach to establish an information governance (IG) team. A chief corporate archivist, if one exists in the organization, should be primarily responsible for this effort. Records management leaders are a key part of that team, and may drive the effort forward, with input from compliance, legal, and information technology (IT) departments. Identify who will be involved and who will have responsibility for developing and carrying out the long-term preservation plan. The overall objectives of governance activities are to understand the issues and the strategic importance of IG, to ensure that the organization can sustain its operations, and determine if it can implement the strategies required to extend preservation activities into the future.[4]

An assessment of records management practices provides a diagnostic analysis of an organization's long-term preservation program strengths and weaknesses, and will identify the needs and difficulties within the organization, including staff and training needs, the need for additional space, to consolidate records, to dispose of obsolete records, and for security and accessibility. The International Standard: ISO 15489 Information and Documentation—Records Management, or the Generally Accepted Record-keeping Principles® (GARP) can be used to guide organizations through this process.

It is important that the culture of the organization reinforce the value and importance of good recordkeeping. Organizations often encounter resistance to change. This is normal and developing a change management program can help to mitigate resistance.

A training program ensures that the functions and benefits of managing records are widely understood. *Training is most effective when it is tailored to the needs of particular groups* and, in some cases, to individual staff members. This will make changes in an employee's area easier when programs are adopted throughout the organization.

In order to manage records, organizations must know their business processes, what the records are, where they are located, in what formats, and what their access, security, and retention requirements are. Records are representations of the activity and transactions of the business.

Analyze recordkeeping requirements to understand their business, regulatory, and social context. This is crucial to understanding the risks and requirements, and to establish business rules to manage records. Remember that one size does not fit all. *Different records will have different requirements for retention, disposition, and preservation.*

To determine retention requirements, first consider any legal requirements, and then assess the *value* of the organization's records. The value appraisal will justify the investment in technology, over the short and the long terms.

As technology changes, hardware and software will become obsolete, and then management may face some hard choices. The challenge is to preserve the usefulness and trustworthiness of the organization's information in an efficient and cost-effective way.

Have a preservation plan. Include an organizational needs analysis, an analysis of the costs, benefits, and risks involved with each of the options. Do not let the preservation plan gather dust on a shelf. It should become a reference document and road map for all preservation activities. Keep it up to date as changes occur—changes in user needs, hardware, software, media, security and access requirements, retention periods, and legal mandates.

Records should be created, maintained, and managed systematically. Records creation and management practices should be incorporated into the design and operation of both records systems and business systems. Records systems should have accurately documented policies, assigned responsibilities, and procedures. Destroy, delete, or throw away obsolete and valueless records that have met their retention requirements. Ensure that the records targeted for preservation have enduring value and can be accessed as long as they need to exist.[5]

Electronic Records Preservation Processes

Preserving e-documents that rise to the level of being declared as formal business records presents unique challenges. Due to the nature of the digital medium, the stored bits and bytes of an electronic record are transformed into a presentation form that is readable to the user, yet there are substantial differences between the digital representation of the stored record and the form presented for use. So, "empirically, it is not possible to preserve an electronic record: it is only possible to preserve the ability to reproduce the record. That is because it is not possible to store an electronic record in the documentary form in which it is capable of serving as a record."[6]

This assembly of bits into a meaningful and readable form is always needed, and this necessary software translation from digital bits into the final, intended documentary form is always required. This transformation is caused when a record presented for use introduces some level of risk: The stored digital bits could be altered or inaccurate when they are converted into a user interface that is readable and recognizable for humans—regardless of how well the digital data was secured in storage. This introduces complexities not found when preserving hard-copy records, and, *the process of preserving an electronic record goes well beyond keeping it safely in storage.* The process of digital preservation begins with the initial act of storage and extends through reproduction of the record" (italics added).[7]

At some point, as IT advances in the decades to come, it can be reasonably expected that computers will be able to store the human readable form of records. But still, while the digital display of a record—a scanned text document, for instance—may look like a replica of the paper version, the digital version is derived from and presented on a fundamentally different medium, and *the myriad of factors introduced in the digital medium may mean the record is exposed to alteration.*

Controlling the Process of Preserving Records

At least three key factors control the process of preserving electronic records. First, external legal and regulatory requirements dictate the need to retain certain records, and these requirements must be known and adhered to. Records must be preserved as authentic, and in accordance with legal, regulatory, and IG considerations. *Legal requirements trump all others.* Second, internal IG considerations that dictate internal governance guidelines must be adhered to by the organization preserving the records themselves. And third, control of the preservation process is constrained by the current state of the art of IT; that is, the latest technologies form the outer limit of what digital techniques are possible to apply to the preservation of the record.[8]

While the state of the art of IT determines what is possible and not possible to do, the technology infrastructure of the organization itself also constrains what is possible. This infrastructure includes the computer hardware, digital imaging-specific software, and physical storage media used to store and process the digital components of electronic records. These IT mechanisms are used in all records preservation activities.

"Records are preserved because they have been determined to have enduring value."[9] That value is determined by a document's importance to the organization when used, or conversely, how it would be negatively impacted if the record were lost, altered, or stolen.

There are other derived outputs of the preservation process: A *certificate of authenticity* is produced when tangible evidence of authenticity is required, and it *attests to the authenticity of a reproduced record.* Also produced is information that attests to the integrity and reliability of the overall preservation process. Often, in court or regulatory proceedings information about overall IG processes, controls in the preservation process, and the technologies employed is required "in response to a challenge to their adequacy or appropriateness for preserving authentic records."[10]

When the IG or records management team have determined a group of records to be worthy of preservation, the LTDP preservation management process determines *how, where,* and *on which medium* to store the digital records, given their technical characteristics and the current limits of IT. "For each body of records thus selected for preservation, managing the preservation process requires articulating a preservation strategy."[11]

The preservation strategy is a subset of IG strategy and policy, and "rolls up" to become a part of it. It includes all the established rules, guidelines, and processes for preserving those records, and at each step a defined completion criteria must be met to ensure proper execution. The specific technological methods that will be used to preserve the records must be articulated from storage to retrieval to actual reproduction. So a long-term preservation strategy will necessarily include those little steps—all of the subprocesses involved in the preservation process.

The approach to preservation will vary, depending on the type digital components, that is, the processes for storing and retrieving a digital video or voice file will differ from storing a static text document. The latest proven technologies and methods should be applied, and a technological path over the long term should be plotted.

In addition to methods and technologies, a "preservation strategy also defines specific *actions* that should be taken with respect to the body of records," and these actions—processes—are set to take place at specific intervals, or when certain conditions occur (such as degradation in the accuracy of storage, requiring a move to another medium).[12]

Articulating a LTDP strategy is a part of an overall program for securing confidential information assets over the long term.

Chapter Summary: Key Points

- Long-term digital preservation (LTDP) provides a path for storing digital information so that it may be retrieved exactly as it was stored, accurately and authentically, for use in the future—despite the known obsolescence of key elements over the long term.
- Some electronic records may need to be retained for long periods or permanently. For those records, organizations will need to plan for their preservation to ensure that they remain accessible, trustworthy, and useful.
- Electronic records are digital representations of hard-copy records; in the process of presenting the documented form of the record for the user, there are possibilities that the bits and bytes could have been altered—a characteristic unique to e-records.
- The first step is using an integrated approach to establish an information governance (IG) team. Identify who will be involved and who will have responsibility for developing and carrying out the long-term preservation plan.
- It is important that the culture of the organization reinforces the value and importance of good recordkeeping.
- Records are preserved because they have been determined to have enduring value.
- Different records and record types will have different requirements for retention, disposition, and preservation.
- The process of preserving an electronic record goes well beyond keeping it safely in storage.
- A records preservation strategy also defines specific actions that should be taken and will entail requirements for specific information technology infrastructure needed in order to implement the strategy.

Notes

1. IBM, "Long Term Digital Preservation," www.research.ibm.com/haifa/ projects/storage/ltdp/index.shtml, retrieved December 22, 2011.
2. Ibid.
3. Charmaine Brooks, CRM, via e-mail to the author, August 21, 2011.
4. Ibid.
5. Ibid.
6. InterPARES, "Preservation Task Force Report," www.interpares.org/ book/interpares_book_f_part3.pdf, p. 5, retrieved March 30, 2012.
7. Ibid.
8. InterPARES, "Preservation Task Force Report.
9. Ibid.
10. Ibid.
11. Ibid.
12. Ibid.

PART IV

Information Technology Considerations

CHAPTER 11

Technologies That Can Help Secure E-Documents

An information governance (IG) program for securing confidential information assets cannot be a successful effort without the proper technology tools to monitor, enforce, and control information policies, and to provide security. There are some specific technologies that organizations must become familiar with to have the technological literacy to be able to construct a program for securing confidential information assets. This chapter introduces and discusses these enabling technologies.

Challenge of Securing E-Documents

Today's various document and content management systems (as described in Chapter 3) were not initially designed to allow for secure document sharing and collaboration, while also preventing document leakage. These software applications were mostly designed before the invention and adoption of newer business technologies that have extended the computing environment. The introduction of cloud computing, mobile PC devices, smartphones, social media, and online collaboration tools all came after most of today's document and content management systems were developed and brought to market.

This has exposed vulnerabilities that need to be addressed with other, complementary technologies. One needs to look no further than the WikiLeaks incident and the myriad of other major security breaches resulting in document and data leakage to see that there are serious information security issues in both the public and private sectors.

Technology is the tool, but without proper IG policies, and a culture of compliance that supports the knowledge workers following them, any effort to secure confidential information assets will fail. An old information technology (IT) adage is that *the perfect technology will fail without user commitment.*

Protecting E-Documents: Limitations of Repository-Based Approaches

Organizations invest billions of dollars in IT solutions that manage e-documents and records in terms of security, auditing, search, records retention and disposition, version control, and so on. These information management solutions are predominantly repository-based, including enterprise content management (ECM) systems and collaborative workspaces (for unstructured information, such as *e-documents*). With content or document repositories, the focus has always been on perimeter security, that is, keeping intruders out of the network. But that provides only partial protection. Once intruders are in, they are *in,* and have full access to confidential e-documents. For those who are authorized to access the content, there are no protections, so they may freely copy, forward, print, or even edit and alter the information.[1]

The glaring vulnerability in the security architecture of ECM systems is that few protections exist once the information is legitimately accessed.

These confidential information assets, which may include military plans, price lists, patented designs, blueprints, drawings, and financial reports, can often be printed, e-mailed, or faxed to unauthorized parties without any security attached.[2]

> The glaring vulnerability in the security architecture of ECM systems is that few protections exist once the information is legitimately accessed.

Also, in the course of their normal work processes, knowledge workers—as most everyone—tend to keep an extra copy of the electronic documents they are working on stored at their desktop, or they download and copy them to a tablet or laptop to work at home or while traveling. *This creates a situation where multiple copies of these e-documents are scattered about on various devices and media, which creates a security problem, since they are outside of the repository and no longer secured, managed, controlled, or audited.*

It also creates records management issues in terms of the various versions that might be out there and determining which one is the official business record.

> Technologies like firewalls, access controls, and gateway filters can grant or deny access but can't provide granular enforcement of acceptable-use policies that define what users can and cannot do with confidential data and documents.

Limitations of Current E-Document Security

Traditionally, *electronic document security (EDS)* has been primarily perimeter security—securing the firewalls and perimeters within which e-documents are stored, attempting to keep intruders out, rather than securing e-documents directly upon their creation. *The basic access security mechanisms implemented, like passwords, two-factor authentication, and identity verification, are rendered totally ineffective once the e-documents or records are legitimately accessed by an authorized employee.* The documents are bare and unsecured. This poses tremendous challenges if the employee is suddenly terminated, if they are a rogue intent on doing harm, or if outside hackers are able to penetrate the secured perimeter. And, of course, it is common knowledge that they do it all the time. *So the focus should rightly be on securing the documents themselves.*

Restricting access is the goal of conventional perimeter security, but it does not directly protect the information inside. Perimeter security protects information the same way a safe protects valuables; if safecrackers get in, the contents are theirs. There are no protections once the safe is opened. Similarly, if hackers penetrate the perimeter security, they have complete access to the information inside, which they can steal, alter, or misuse.[3] The perimeter security approach has several fundamental limitations:

- *Limited effectiveness.* Perimeter protection stops dead at the firewall, even though sensitive information is sent past it, and circulates around the web, unsecured. Today's extended computing model, and the trend toward global business means that business enterprises and government agencies frequently share sensitive information externally with other stakeholders, including business partners, customers, suppliers, and constituents.
- *Haphazard protections.* In the normal course of business, knowledge workers send, work on, and store copies of the same information outside the organization's established perimeter. Even if the information's new digital environment is secured by other perimeters, each one utilizes different access controls or sometimes no access control at all (e.g., copying a price list from a sales folder to a marketing folder; an attorney copying a case brief or litigation strategy document from their paralegal's case folder).
- *Too complex.* With this multi-perimeter scenario, there are simply too many perimeters to manage, and oftentimes they are out of the direct control of the organization.
- *No direct protections.* Attempts to create boundaries or portals protected by perimeter security within which stakeholders (partners,

suppliers, shareholders, or customers) can share information causes more complexity and administrative overhead, while it fails to protect the e-documents and data directly.[4]

Despite all the current investment in electronic document security, it is astounding that once information is shared today, it is largely unknown who will be accessing it tomorrow.

Apply Better Technology for Better Enforcement in the Extended Enterprise

The discussion of key technologies to secure confidential information assets begins with showing basic security functions in the Microsoft Office and XP desktop environments, and how to print documents more securely. Then, it moves on to the process of controlling login access to the e-documents themselves, and finally to the basics of securing documents, files, and e-mail. An overview of the document security problems that organizations need to address is presented, along with how these issues have arisen based on the repository model utilized by systems that have traditionally managed e-documents.

Protecting E-Documents in the Extended Enterprise

Sharing e-documents and collaborating are essential in today's increasingly mobile and global world. Businesses are operating in a more distributed model than ever before, and they are increasingly sharing and collaborating with not only co-workers but also suppliers, customers, and even at times competitors (e.g., in pharmaceutical research). This reality presents a challenge to organizations dealing in sensitive and confidential information.[5]

Basic Security for the Microsoft Windows Office Desktop

The first level of protection for e-documents begins with basic protections at the desktop level. Microsoft Office provides ways to password-protect Microsoft Office files, such as those created in Word and Excel, quickly and easily. Many corporations and government agencies around the world use these basic protections. A key flaw or caveat is that *passwords used in protecting documents cannot be retrieved if they are forgotten or lost*.

Where Do Deleted Files Go?

When you delete a file it is gone, right? Actually, it is not (with the possible exception of solid state hard drives). For example, after a file is deleted in Windows, a simple undelete DOS command can bring back the file, if it has not been overwritten. That is because when files are deleted, they are not really deleted, but that space where they reside is now marked for re-use and it can be overwritten. If it is not yet overwritten, the file is still there. The same process occurs as drafts of documents are created, and temp (for *temporary*) files are stored. The portions of a hard drive where deleted or temp files are stored can be overwritten. This is called unallocated space. *Most users are unaware that deleted files and fragments of documents and drafts are stored temporarily on their computer's unallocated space.* So it must be wiped clean and completely erased to be sure that any confidential documents or drafts are completely removed from the hard drive.

A part of an IG program to secure confidential information assets includes the highest security measures, which means to have a policy that includes deleting sensitive materials from a computer's unallocated space, and to test it periodically.

Lock Down: Stop All External Access to Confidential E-Docs

There are other approaches that organizations are taking to stop document and data leakage: physically restricting access to a computer by disconnecting it from any network connections and forbidding or even blocking use of any ports. Although cumbersome, this is effective in highly classified or restricted areas where confidential e-documents are held. Access is controlled by utilizing multiple advanced identity verification methods, such as biometric means.

Secure Printing

Organizations normally expend a good amount of effort making sure that computers, documents, and private information are protected and secure. However, if your computer is hooked up to a network printer (shared by multiple knowledge workers) all of that effort might have been wasted.[6]

However, there are basic measures that can be taken to protect confidential documents from being compromised as they are printed. You simply invoke some standard Microsoft Office protections, which allow you to print the documents once you arrive in the copy room or at the networked printer. This process varies slightly, depending on the manufacturer of the printer (you may have to refer to the documentation for the printer itself).

In Microsoft Office, there is an option in the Print Dialog Box to accomplish delayed printing of documents.

How to Print Securely Using Microsoft Office

Secure print to a Xerox printer

1. On the File menu, click Print.
2. Click Properties, and then click Advanced.
3. Under Job type, select Secure Print.
4. It will ask the user to type in a four digit code twice.

After arriving at the network printer, select the job and then type in the same four digit code.

Note: The procedure documented above is a general one; the actual procedure may differ for specific models of Xerox printers.

Secure print to an HP printer

1. On the File menu, click Print.
2. Click Properties, and then click the Destination tab.
3. Under Destination features, select Job Retention and then click Options.
4. In the next dialog box, under Job Retention Mode, select Private Job.
5. Enter your name, assign a name to the job you're about to print, and then type a four digit code.

Once you go to the printer, you select the job and then type in the same four digit code.

Note: The procedure documented above is a general one; the actual procedure may differ for the specific model of HP printer.

Source: Annik Stahl, "Secure printing: No more mad dashes to the copy room," Microsoft, http://office.microsoft.com/en-us/help/secure-printing-no-more-mad -dashes-to-the-copy-room-HA001227631.aspx, retrieved August 22, 2011.

Serious Security Issues with Large Print Files of Confidential Data

According to Canadian output and print technology expert William Broddy, in a company's data center, a print file of, for instance, investment account statements or bank statements, contains all the rich information that a hacker or malicious insider needs. "It is distilled information down to the most important core data about customers, which has been referred to as 'data syrup' since it has been boiled down and contains no mountains of extraneous data, only the culled, cleaned, essential data that gives criminals exactly what they need."[7]

What most managers are not aware of is that entire print files, and sometimes remnants of them, stay on the hard drives of high-speed printers and are vulnerable to security breaches. Data center security personnel closely monitor calls to their database. To extract as much data a hacker needs requires hundreds or even thousands of calls to the database, which sets off alerts by system monitoring tools. But, to retrieve a print file would take only one intrusion and it may go entirely unnoticed. The files are sitting there so that even a rogue service technician or field engineer could retrieve them on a routine service call.

> A print file contains all the distilled customer information a hacker might want. Retrieving a print file takes only one intrusion and may go entirely unnoticed.

To help secure print files, there are hardware devices that sit between the print server and the network and cloak server, so print files are only visible to those who have a cloaking device on the other end.

Organizations must practice good IG and have specific procedures to erase sensitive print files once they have been utilized. For instance, in the example of preparing statements to mail to clients, there are at least six points in the process (starting with print file preparation and ending with the actual mailing) where the file is exposed to possible intrusions. These points must be tightly monitored and controlled. Typically, an organization will retain the print file for about 14 days, though some keep files long enough for customers to receive statements in the mail and review them. *Organizations must make sure that print files or their remnants are secured and then completely erased when the printing job is finished.*

> There are at least six points between print file preparation and final hard-copy mailing where the file is exposed to possible intrusions.

Controlling Access to Documents Using Identity Access Management

Identity access management (IAM) software can provide an important piece of the security solution, *as a first level of defense*. It aims to prevent unauthorized people from accessing a system, and to ensure that only authorized individuals engage with information, including critical e-documents.

Today's business environment operates in a more extended and mobile model, often including stakeholders that are outside of the organization. With this more complex and fluctuating group of users accessing information management applications, the idea of identity management has gained increased importance.

The response to the growing number of software applications using inconsistent or incompatible security models is strong identity management enforcement software. These scattered applications offer opportunities for not only identity theft, but also identity drag, where the maintenance of identities does not keep up with the changing identities, especially in organizations with a large workforce. This can result in theft of confidential information assets by unauthorized or out-of-date access, and even failure to meet regulatory compliance, which can result in fines and imprisonment.[8]

> "IAM addresses 'access creep' where employees move to a different department of business unit and their rights to access information fail to get updated."[9]

IAM—along with sharp IG policies—"manages and governs user access to information through an automated, continuous process."[10] Implemented properly, good IAM does keep access limited to authorized users, while increasing security, reducing IT complexity, and increasing operating efficiencies.

Critically, *"IAM addresses 'access creep' where employees move to a different department of business unit and their rights to access information fail to get updated"* (italics added).[11]

In France in 2007, a rogue stock trader at Société Générale had in-depth knowledge of the bank's access control procedures from his job at the middle office.[12] He used that information to defraud the bank and its clients out of over €7 billion (over US$10 billion). If the bank had implemented an IAM solution the crime may not have been possible.

A robust and effective IAM solution will provide for:

1. **Auditing.** Detailed audit trails of *who* attempted to access *which information*, and *when*. Stolen identities can be uncovered if, for instance, an authorized user attempts to log in from more than one computer at a time.
2. **Constant updating**. Regular reviews of access rights assigned to individuals, including review and certification for user access, an automated

re-certification process (*attestation*), and enforcement of IG access policies that govern the way users access information in respect to segregation of duties (SoD).

3. **Evolving roles**. Role lifecycle management should be maintained on a continuous basis, to mine and manage roles and their associated access rights and policies.
4. **Risk reduction**. Remediation regarding access to critical documents and information.

Enforcing IG: Protect Files with Rules and Permissions

One of the first tasks often needed when developing an IG program that secures confidential information assets is to define roles and responsibilities for those charged with implementing, maintaining, and enforcing IG policies. Corollaries that spring from that effort get down to the nitty-gritty of controlling information access by rules and permissions.

Rules and permissions specify *who* (by roles) is allowed access to *which* documents and information, and even contextually, *from where* (office, home, travel), and *at what times* (work hours, or extended hours). Using the old policy of the *need-to-know* basis is a good rule of thumb to apply when setting up these access policies, that is, only those who are at a certain level of the organization or are directly involved in certain projects are allowed access to confidential and sensitive information. The roles are relatively easy to define in a traditional hierarchical structure, but today's flatter and more collaborative enterprises present challenges.

To effectively wall off and secure information by management level, many companies and governments have put in place an information security framework, which is a model that delineates which levels of the organization have access to specific documents and databases as a part of implemented IG policy. This framework shows a hierarchy of the company's management distributed across a range of defined levels of information access. "The U.S. Government Protection Profile for Authorization Server for Basic Robustness Environments" is an example of such a framework.

Data Governance Software to Manage Information Access

There are other technological tools that use advanced techniques to control access to confidential documents and sensitive data. With data governance software, *users* are grouped by job function in directories, and unstructured data (e.g., e-documents, e-mail) is grouped in folders on file servers. *The two become linked and are recorded when a document, report, or spreadsheet is accessed, or a file is deleted* (an "access event").[13] These events are recorded on the file servers.

Some conclusions can be derived from the analysis of the information access behavior of users in specific groups, that is, under *rightful use* conditions, members of a particular group in the organization frequently access the same document types and data sets (e.g., the financial department accesses accounting data; the legal group accesses legal documents). These group information access patterns inherently reveal them to be a group. This fact, when expressed as a matrix of activity, establishes the basis for a mathematical model by which to derive *business context*.

Data governance software which manages information access analyzes user, data, and access event information to compute relationships and to show exactly who has appropriate group membership and who does not. Anomalies are detected and stand out. This is a "simple and elegant premise," which is executed by very complex statistical modeling technology.[14]

E-Mail Encryption

Encrypting (scrambling using advanced algorithms) sensitive e-mail messages is an effective step to securing confidential information assets while in transit. Encryption can also be applied to desktop folders and files, and even entire disk drives (full disk encryption, or FDE). All confidential or sensitive data and e-documents that are exposed to third parties or transferred over public networks should be secured with file-level encryption, at a minimum.[15]

Secure Communications Using Record-Free E-Mail

What types of tools can you use to encourage the free flow of ideas in collaborative efforts without compromising your confidential information assets or risking litigation or compliance sanctions?

Stream messaging is an innovation that became commercially viable around 2006. It is similar in impact to information rights management (IRM) software, which limits the recipients' ability to forward, print, or alter data in an e-mail message (or reports, spreadsheets, etc.), *but goes further by leaving no record on any computer or server*.

> With stream messaging no record or trace of communication is left.

Stream messaging is a simple, safe, secure electronic communications system ideal for ensuring that sensitive internal information is kept confidential and not publicly released. Stream messaging is not intended to be a replacement for enterprise e-mail, but is a complement to it. If you need an electronic record, e-mail it; if not, use stream messaging.[16]

What makes stream messaging unique is its recordless-ness. Streamed messages cannot be forwarded, edited, or saved. A copy cannot be printed as is possible with e-mail. That is because *stream messaging separates the sender's and receiver's names and the date from the body of the message, never allowing them to be seen together.* Even if the sender or receiver were to attempt to make a copy using the print-screen function, these elements are never captured together.[17]

The instant a stream message is sent, it is placed in a temporary storage buffer space. When the recipient logs in to read the message, it is removed from the buffer space. By the time the recipient opens it, the complete stream message no longer exists on the server or any other computer.

This new communications approach is web-based, meaning that no hardware or software purchases are required. It also works with existing e-mail systems and e-mail addresses and is completely immune to spam and viruses. Other solutions (both past and present) have been offered, but these have taken the approach of encrypting e-mail or generating e-mail that disappears after a pre-set time. Neither of these approaches is truly record-less.

Stream messaging is unique because its technology effectively eliminates the ability to print, cut, paste, forward, or save a message. It may be the only electronic communications system that separates the header information—date, name of sender, name of recipient—from the body of the message. This eliminates a traceable record of the communication. Soon, many other renditions of secure messaging will be developed.

In addition, stream messaging offers the added protection of being an indiscriminate web-based service, meaning that the messages and headers are never hosted on the subscribing companies' networks. This eliminates the risk that employers, competitors, or hackers could intercept stream messages, which is a great security benefit for end-users.[18]

Digital Signatures

Digital signatures are more than just digitized autographs—they carry detailed audit information used to *"detect unauthorized modifications"* to e-documents and to *"authenticate the identity of the signatory."* (italics added)[19]

Online transactions can be conducted with full trust that they are legal, proper, and binding. They prove that the person whose signature is on the e-document did, in fact, authorize it. A digital signature provides evidence in demonstrating to a third party that the signature was genuine, true, and authentic, which is known as *non-repudiation*. To repudiate is to dispute, and with digital signatures, a signatory is unable to claim that the signature is forged.

Digital signatures can be implemented a variety of ways—not just through software but also through firmware (programmed microchips), computer hardware, or a combination of the three. Generally, hardware- and firmware-based implementations are more difficult to hack, since their instructions are hardwired.

> There is a big difference between digital and electronic signatures. Digital signatures contain additional authenticating information.

Here is a key point: For those who are unfamiliar with the technology, *there is a big difference between electronic signatures and digital signatures.*[20]

An "electronic signature is likely to be a bit-map image, either from a scanned image, a fax copy or a picture of someone's signature, or may even be a typed acknowledgement or acceptance." *A digital signature contains "extra data appended to a message which identifies and authenticates the sender and message data using public-key encryption."*[21]

So digital signatures are the only type that offers any real security advantages.

Digital signatures are verified by the combination of applying a signatory's private signing key and the public key which comes from their personal ID certificate. After that, only the public key ID certificate is required for future verifications. "*In addition, a checksum mechanism confirms that there have been no modifications to the content.*" (italics added)[22]

A formal, trusted *certificate authority (CA)* issues the certificate associated with the public-private key. It is possible to generate self-certified public keys, but these do not verify and authenticate the recipient's identity, and are therefore flawed from a security standpoint. The interchange of verified signatures is possible on a global scale, as "digital signature standards are mature and converging internationally."[23]

> Requiring a physical signature can disrupt and slow business processes. Digital signatures speed that up and add a layer of security.

After more than 30 years of predictions, the paperless office is almost here. Business process cycles have been reduced and great efficiencies have been gained since the majority of documents today are created digitally and spend most of their lifecycle in digital form, and they can be routed through work steps using business process management (BPM) and workflow software. *However, the requirement for a physical signature can frequently disrupt and hold up these business processes.* Documents have to be printed out, physically routed, and physically signed—and often they are scanned back into a document or records management (or contract management) system—which defeats the efficiencies sought.

Often *multiple* signatures are required in an approval process, and some organizations require that each page is initialed, which makes the process slow and cumbersome when it is executed without the benefit of digital signatures. Also, multiple copies are generated—as many as 20—so digital signature capability injected into a business process can account for significant time and cost savings.[24]

Document Encryption

There is some overlap and sometimes confusion between digital signatures and document encryption. Suffice it to say, they work differently, in that document encryption secures a document for those who share a secret key, and digital signatures prove that the document has not been altered and the signature is authentic.

There are e-records management implications of employing document encryption:

> *Unless it is absolutely essential, full document encryption is often advised against for use within electronic records management systems as it prevents full-text indexing, and requires that the decryption keys (and application) are available for any future access. Furthermore, if the decryption key is lost or an employee leaves without passing it on, encrypted documents and records will in effect be electronically shredded as no one will be able to read them.*

> *Correctly certified digital signatures do not prevent unauthorized persons reading a document nor are they intended to. They do confirm that the person who signed it is who they say they are, and that the document has not been altered since they signed it. Within a records management system a digital signature is often considered to be an important part of the metadata of a document, confirming both its heritage and its integrity.*[25]

Data Loss Prevention Technology

The aforementioned document security challenges have given rise to an emerging but critical set of capabilities by a new breed of IT companies that provide data loss prevention (DLP) (also called data *leak* prevention). DLP providers create software and hardware appliances that thoroughly inspect all e-documents and e-mail messages before they leave the organization's perimeter, and attempt to stop sensitive data from exiting the firewall.

This filtering is based on several factors, but mostly using specified critical content keywords that are flagged by the implementing organization. DLP can also stop the exit of information assets by document types, origin, time-of-day and other factors.

DLP systems are designed to detect and prevent unauthorized use and transmission of confidential information.[26] In more detail, DLP is a computer security term referring to systems that identify, monitor, and protect data/documents in all three states: 1) *in use* (endpoint actions); 2) *in motion* (network actions); and, 3) *at rest* (data/document storage). DLP accomplishes this by deep content inspection, contextual security analysis of transaction data (e.g., attributes of the originator, the data object, medium, timing, recipient/destination, etc.) with a centralized management framework.

What DLP Does Well (and Not-So-Well)

DLP has been deployed successfully as a tool used to map the flow of data inside and exiting the organization to determine the paths that content takes, so that more sophisticated information mapping, monitoring, and content security can take place.

This use as a traffic monitor for analysis purposes has been much more successful than relying on DLP as the sole enforcement tool for compliance and to secure information assets. Today's technology is simply not fast enough to catch everything and if it does, it catches many e-mail messages and documents that users are authorized to send, which slows the network and the business down. This also adds unnecessary overhead, as someone has to go back and release each and every one of the e-mails or documents that were wrongly stopped.

Another downside: *Since DLP relies on content inspection, it cannot detect and monitor encrypted e-mail or documents.*

Basic DLP Methods

DLP solutions typically apply one of the following methods:

1. Scanning traffic for keywords or regular expressions, such as customer credit card or social security numbers.
2. Classifying documents and content based on a pre-defined set to determine what is likely to be confidential and what isn't.

3. Tainting (in the case of agent-based solutions), whereby documents are tagged and then monitored to determine how to classify derivative documents. For example, if someone copies a portion of a sensitive document into a different document, this document receives the same security clearance as the original document.[27]

All these methods involve the network administrator setting up a policy clearly defining what is allowed to send out and what should be kept in confidence. This is extremely difficult: Defining a policy that's *too broad* means accidentally letting sensitive information get out, and defining a policy that is *too narrow* means getting a significant amount of false positives, and stopping the flow of normal business communications.

While network security management is well established, defining these types of IG policies is extremely difficult for a network administrator, and leaving it to them means there will be no collaboration with business units, no standardization, and no real forethought. As a result, many installations are plagued with false positives that are flagged and stopped, which can stifle and frustrate knowledge workers. *The majority of DLP deployments simply use DLP for monitoring and auditing purposes.*

Examining the issue of the dissolving perimeter more closely, a deeper problem is revealed: DLP is binary; it's black or white. Either a certain e-document or e-mail can leave the organization's boundaries or it can't. This process has been referred to as outbound content compliance (OCC).

But this is not how the real world works today. Now there is an increasing need for collaboration and for the information to be shared or reside outside the organization on mobile devices or in the cloud.

Today's DLP technology is mostly not capable of addressing these complex issues on its own. Often, additional technology layers are needed.

The Missing Piece: Information Rights Management

Another technology tool for securing information assets is information rights management (IRM) software (also referred to as enterprise rights management [ERM] and previously as enterprise digital rights management [E-DRM].) *For purposes of this book, we use IRM when referring to this technology set, so as not to be confused with electronic records management. Major software companies like Microsoft, Oracle, and Documentum/EMC also use the term IRM.*

IRM technology provides a sort of "security wrapper" around documents and protects sensitive information assets from unauthorized access.[28] We know that DLP can search for key terms and stop the exit of sensitive data from the organization by inspecting its content. But it can also prevent confidential data from being copied to external media or sent by e-mail if the person is not authorized to do so. If IRM is deployed, files and documents are protected wherever they may be, with persistent security. *The ability to apply security to an e-document in any state* (in use, in motion, and at rest), across media types, inside or outside of the organization *is called persistent security*. This is a key characteristic of IRM technology and it is all done transparently without user intervention.[29]

> The ability to secure data at any time, in any state, is called persistent protection.

IRM has the ability to protect e-documents and data wherever they may reside, and however they may be used, and in all three data states (at rest, in use, and in transit).[30]

IRM allows for e-documents to be remote controlled, meaning that security protections can be enforced even if the document leaves the perimeter of the organization. This means that e-documents (and their control mechanisms) can be separately created, viewed, edited, and distributed.

IRM provides persistent, ever-present security and manages access to sensitive e-documents and data. IRM provides embedded file-level protections that travel with the document or data, regardless of media type.[31] These protections prevent unauthorized viewing, editing, printing, copying, forwarding, or faxing. So, even if files are somehow copied to a thumb drive and taken out of the organization, e-document protections and usage are still controlled.

The major applications for IRM services include cross-protection of e-mails and attachments, dynamic content protection on web portals, secure web-based training, secure web publishing, and secure content storage and e-mail repositories, while meeting Sarbanes-Oxley, HIPAA, and other compliance requirements. Organizations can comply with regulations for securing and maintaining the integrity of digital records, and IRM will restrict and track access to spreadsheets and other financial data, too.

In investment banking, research communications must be monitored, according to NASD regulation 2711, and IRM can help support compliance efforts. In consumer finance, personal financial information collected on paper forms and transmitted by fax (e.g., auto dealers faxing credit applications) or other low-security media can be secured using IRM, directly from a scanner or copier. Importers and exporters can use IRM to ensure data security and prevent the loss of cargo from theft or even terrorist activities, and they also can comply with U.S. Customs and trade regulations by deploying IRM software. Public-sector data-security needs are numerous, including intelligence gathering and distribution, espionage, and Homeland Security initiatives. Firms that generate intellectual property (IP), such as research and consulting groups, can control and protect access to IP with it, and in the highly collaborative pharmaceutical industry, IRM can secure research and testing data.

IRM protections can be added to nearly all e-document types including e-mail, word-processing files, spreadsheets, graphic presentations, computer-aided design (CAD) plans, and blueprints. This security can be enforced globally on all documents or granularly down to the smallest level, protecting sensitive fields of information from prying eyes. This is true even if there are multiple copies of the e-documents scattered about on servers in varying geographic locations. Also, the protections can be applied permanently or within controlled timeframes. For instance, a person may be granted access to a secure e-document for a day, a week, or year.

Key IRM Characteristics

Oracle recommends the following requirements to ensure effective IRM:

1. Security *is foremost; documents, communications, and licenses should be encrypted, and documents should require authorization before being altered;*
2. The system can't be any harder to use *than working with unprotected documents;*
3. It must be easy to deploy and manage, *scale to enterprise proportions, and work with a variety of common desktop applications.* [emphasis added].[32]

IRM software enforces and manages document access policies and use rights (view, edit, print, copy, e-mail forward) of electronic documents and data. Controlled information can be text documents, spreadsheets, financial statements, e-mail messages, policy and procedure manuals, research, customer and project data, personnel files, medical records, Intranet pages, and other sensitive information. IRM provides persistent enforcement of IG and access policies to allow an organization to control access to information that needs to be secured for privacy, competitive, or compliance reasons. *Persistent content security is a necessary part of an end-to-end enterprise security architecture.*

Well, it sounds like fabulous technology, but is IRM really so new? No, it has been has been around for a decade or more, and continues to mature and improve. It has essentially entered the mainstream since the 2004–2005 timeframe (when this author began tracking its development and publishing researched articles on the topic.)

IRM software is currently used for persistent file protection by thousands of organizations throughout the world. Its success depends on the quality and consistency of the deployment, which includes detailed policy-making efforts. *Difficulties in policy maintenance and lack of real support for external sharing and mobile devices have kept first-wave IRM deployments from becoming widespread, but this aspect is being addressed by a second wave of new IRM technology companies.*

Other Key Characteristics of IRM

POLICY CREATION AND MANAGEMENT   IRM allows for policies governing access and use of sensitive or confidential e-documents to be created and enforced. The organization's IG team sets the policies for access based on role and organizational level, determining what employees can and cannot do with the secured e-documents.[33] The IG policy defined for a document type includes the following controls:

1. Viewing
2. Editing
3. Copy/paste (including screen capture)
4. Printing
5. Forwarding e-mail containing secured e-documents

Access to sensitive e-documents may be revoked at any time, no matter where they are located or what media they are on, since each time a user tries to access a document, access rights are verified with a server or cloud IRM application. This can be done remotely—that is, when an attempt is made to open the document, an authorization must take place. In cloud-based implementations, it is a matter of simply denying access.

DECENTRALIZED ADMINISTRATION   One of the key challenges of e-document security traditionally is that a system administrator had access to documents and reports that were meant only for executives and senior managers. With IRM, the security of the data is administered by the e-document owner, which considerably reduces the risk of a document theft, alteration, or misuse.

AUDITING   This provides the smoking-gun evidence in the event of a true security breach. Good IRM software provides an audit trail of how all documents secured by it are used, and some go further, providing more detailed document analytics of usage.

INTEGRATION To be viable, IRM must integrate with other enterprise-wide systems like ECM, customer relationship management (CRM), product lifecycle management (PLM), enterprise resource planning (ERP), e-mail management, message archiving, e-discovery, and a myriad of cloud-based systems. This is a characteristic of today's newer wave of IRM software.

This ability to integrate with enterprise-based systems does not mean that IRM has to be deployed at an enterprise level. *The best approach is to target one critical department or area with a strong business need and to keep the scope of the project narrow to gain an early success before expanding the implementation into other departments.*

Chapter Summary: Key Points

- Today's ECM and document management solutions rely mostly on perimeter security and were not designed to allow for secure document sharing and collaboration.
- Businesses are operating in a more distributed model than ever before, and they are increasingly sharing and collaborating—exposing confidential documents.
- There are basic password-level protections that can be used to secure Microsoft Office documents and items created in the XP operating environment.
- Secure document printing reduces the chance that files can be compromised during or after printing. There are various methods to secure the print stream, depending on the print manufacturer. Copies or remnants of large print files often exist unsecured on the hard drives of high-speed printers. These files must be completely wiped to ensure security.
- Identity access management (IAM) software governs user access to information through an automated, continuous process which addresses access creep, whereby employees move to a different business unit and their access rights are not updated.
- Data governance software is another tool that looks at who is accessing which documents and creates a matrix of roles and access along behavioral lines.

(continued)

(*continued*)

- Encrypting sensitive e-mail messages is an effective step to securing confidential information assets while in transit. Encryption can be applied to desktop folders and files.
- For e-mail communication with no trace or record, stream messaging is a solution.
- Digital signatures authenticate the identity of the signatory and prove that the signature was, in fact, generated by the claimed signatory. This is known as non-repudiation.
- Data loss prevention (DLP) technology performs a "deep content inspection" of all e-documents and e-mails before they leave the organization's perimeter to stop sensitive data from exiting the firewall.
- DLP can be used to discover the flow of information within an organization. Additional security tools can then be applied. This may be the best use for DLP.
- Information rights management (IRM) software enforces and manages use rights of electronic documents. IRM provides a sort of "security wrapper" around documents and protects sensitive information assets from unauthorized use or copying. IRM is also known as enterprise rights management (ERM).

Notes

1. "Oracle Information Rights Management 11g—Managing information everywhere it is stored and used, an Oracle White Paper, March 2010, www.oracle.com/technetwork/middleware/webcenter/content/irm-tec hnical-whitepaper-134345.pdf, p. 4, retrieved December 23, 2011.
2. Robert Smallwood, "E-DRM Plugs ECM Security Gap," *KM World,* April 1, 2008, www.kmworld.com/Articles/News/News-Analysis/E-DRM -plugs-ECM-security-gap-41333.aspx, retrieved March 30, 2012.
3. Oracle Information Rights Management 11g—Managing Information Everywhere It Is Stored and Used".
4. Ibid.
5. Adi Ruppin, March 20, 2011, via e-mail to author.
6. Annik Stahl, "Secure Printing: No More Mad Dashes to the Copy Room," http://office.microsoft.com/en-us/help/secure-printing-no-more-mad-d ashes-to-the-copy-room-HA001227631.aspx, retrieved August 22, 2011.
7. Telephone interview of William Broddy by author, August 7, 2011.

8. HCL, "Identity and Access Management Services," www.hclisd.com/identity-and-access-management.aspx, retrieved September 2, 2011.
9. Ibid.
10. Ibid.
11. Ibid.
12. Nicola Clark, "Fraud Costs Bank 7.1 Billion," January 25, 2008, www.nytimes.com/2008/01/25/business/worldbusiness/25bank-web.html?hp, retrieved September 2, 2011.
13. Global Secure Systems, Varonis, www.gss.co.uk/products/index/Identity_and_Security/Varonis/Varonis_Data_Governance_Suite/?, retrieved December 22, 2011.
14. Ibid.
15. Bill Blake, "WikiLeaks, the Pearl Harbor of the 21st Century," eDocument Sciences LLC, December 6, 2010, http://edocumentsciences.com/wikileaks-the-pearl-harbor-of-the-21st-century.
16. VaporStream Recordless Messaging, www.vaporstream.com, retrieved February 2011.
17. Ibid.
18. Ibid.
19. NIST, "Federal Information Processing Standards Publication," FIPS PUB 186-3, issued June 2009, http://csrc.nist.gov/publications/fips/fips186-3/fips_186-3.pdf, retrieved August 15, 2011.
20. Doug Miles, "Digital Signatures for Document Workflow and SharePoint," AIIM whitepaper, 2010, www.arx.com/files/DOCUMENTS/Digital-Signatures-for-Document-Workflow-and-SharePoint-Survey.pdf, retrieved August 15, 2011.
21. Computer Desktop Encyclopedia, www.computerlanguage.com, retrieved March 30, 2012.
22. Doug Miles, "Digital Signatures for Document Workflow and SharePoint," AIIM white paper, 2010, www.arx.com/files/DOCUMENTS/Digital-Signatures-for-Document-Workflow-and-SharePoint-Survey.pdf, retrieved August 15, 2011.
23. Ibid.
24. Ibid.
25. Ibid.
26. Ari Ruppin, March 20, 2011, via e-mail.
27. Ibid.
28. Ibid.
29. Peter Abatan, "Who Should Be Blamed for a Data Breach?" Enterprise Digital Rights Management, www.enterprisedrm.info/post/1087100940/who-should-be-blamed-for-a-data-breach, retrieved February 2011.

30. Peter Abatan, "Understanding Enterprise Rights Management," Enterprise Digital Rights Management, www.enterprisedrm.info/page/2, retrieved August 3, 2011.

31. Robert Smallwood, "Securing Documents in the WikiLeaks Era," May 28, 2011, www.kmworld.com/Articles/Editorial/Feature/Securing-documents-in-the-WikiLeaks-era-75642.aspx, retrieved August 1, 2011.

32. Oracle, *IRM Technical White Paper*, Oracle.com, February 2008.

33. Peter Abatan, "Understanding Enterprise Rights Management."

CHAPTER 12

Safeguarding Confidential Information Assets

To reframe the issue of corporate security, IBM says, "Imagine if someone tried to break into your house. Now imagine it happening 60,000 times a day. That's how many times the average large company's IT infrastructure is attacked."[1] There were an estimated 354 million privacy breaches from 2005 to 2010 in the United States alone. One especially detrimental breach in January 2009 resulted in the theft of data for 130 million credit cards.[2] In a separate incident in 2007, retail giant TJX (TJ Maxx, Marshalls, etc.) set aside $197 million in reserves to deal with the online theft of 94 million credit card records.[3]

> There were an estimated 350 million privacy breaches in a recent 5-year period in the United States alone. Corporate breaches can cost firms hundreds of millions of dollars.

Cyber Attacks Proliferate

Online attacks and snooping continue at an increasing rate. Organizations must be vigilant about securing their internal, confidential documents, and e-mail messages. In 2011, security experts at Intel/McAfee "discovered an unprecedented series of cyber-attacks on the networks of 72 organizations globally, including the United Nations, governments and corporations, over a five-year period."[4] Dmitri Alperovitch of McAfee described the incident as *"the biggest transfer of wealth in terms of intellectual property in history"* (italics added).[5] The level of intrusion is ominous.

The targeted victims included governments, including the United States, Canada, India, and others; and corporations, including high-tech companies and defense contractors; the International Olympic Committee; and the United Nations. "In the case of the United Nations, the hackers broke into the computer system of its secretariat in Geneva in 2008, hid there for nearly two years, and quietly combed through reams of secret data, according to McAfee."[6] *So attacks can be occurring in organizations for years before they are uncovered—if they are discovered at all.* This means that an organization may be covertly monitored by criminals or competitors for extended periods of time.

> Attacks can continue in organizations for years before they are uncovered—if they are discovered at all.

Where this stolen information is going and how it will be used is yet to be seen. But it is clear that possessing this competitive intelligence could give a government or company a huge advantage, economically, competitively, diplomatically, and militarily.

> Information assets are invaded and eroded daily, often without detection. This compromises competitive position and has real financial impact.

The information assets of companies and government agencies are at risk globally and some are invaded and eroded daily, without detection. The victims are losing economic advantage and national secrets to unscrupulous rivals, so it is imperative that information governance (IG) policies are formed, followed, enforced, tested, and audited. It is also imperative to use the best available technology to counter or avoid such attacks.[7]

The Insider Threat: Malicious or Not

Ibas, a global supplier of data recovery and computer forensics, conducted a survey of 400 business professionals about their attitudes toward intellectual property theft (in 2004). Here are the results:

- Nearly 70 percent of employees have engaged in intellectual property (IP) theft, taking corporate property upon (voluntary or involuntary) termination.
- Almost one-third have taken valuable customer contact information, databases, or other client data.

- Most employees send e-documents to their personal e-mail accounts when pilfering the information.
- Almost 60 percent of surveyed employees believe such actions are acceptable.
- Those who steal IP often feel that they are entitled to partial ownership rights, especially if they had a hand in creating the files.[8]

These survey statistics are alarming, and by all accounts the trend is even worse today. Clearly, organizations have serious cultural challenges to combat prevailing attitudes toward IP theft. A strong and continuous program of IG aimed at securing confidential information assets can educate employees, raise their IP security awareness, and train them on techniques to help secure valuable IP. And the change needs to be driven from the top: from the CEO and boardroom. However, the magnitude of the problem in any organization cannot be accurately known or measured, as without the necessary IG monitoring and enforcement tools. Executives cannot ever know the extent of the erosion of information assets and the real cost in cash and intangible terms over the long term.

Countering the Insider Threat

Frequently ignored, the insider has been increasingly becoming the main threat—more than the external threats outside of the perimeter. According to CERT's 2011 "CyberSecurity Watch Survey," 67 percent of respondents stated that *insider threat breaches are more costly than outsider breaches.* Most of the insider incidents go unnoticed or unreported, and still the survey showed *the majority of incidents to be insider incidents.*[9]

> Security professionals state that insider threat breaches are more costly than outsider ones.

Companies have been spending a lot of time and effort protecting their perimeters from outside attacks. In recent years, most companies have realized that the insider threat is something that needs to be taken more seriously.

The Malicious Insider

Malicious insiders and saboteurs in fact comprise a very small minority of employees. A disgruntled employee or sometimes an outright spy can cause a lot of damage. Malicious insiders have many methods at their disposal to harm the organization by destroying equipment, gaining unsanctioned access to IP, or removing sensitive information by USB drive, e-mail, or other methods.

The Non-Malicious Insider

Fifty-eight percent of Wall Street workers say they have already taken data from their company, according to a recent survey by security firm CyberArk. Frequently, this is without malice. The majority of users indicated having sent out documents *accidentally* via e-mail. So, clearly it is easy to leak documents without meaning to do any harm, and that is the cause of most leaks.

The Solution

Trust and regulation is not enough. In the case of a non-malicious user, companies should invest in security, risk education, and IG training. A solid IG program can reduce IP leaks through education, training, monitoring, and enforcement.

In the case of the malicious user, companies need to take a hard look and see whether they have any effective IG enforcement and document lifecycle security (DLS) technology in place. Most often, the answer is no.[10]

Critical Technologies for Securing Confidential Documents

A firewall, sophisticated as it can get, is a gateway device. This means it resides between the trusted internal network and the public network. As such, even if it has some content filtering or data loss prevention (DLP) capabilities, it cannot, by definition, protect all enterprise data. This data, as previously discussed, can leak from anywhere, inside and outside the firewall. And, in fact, *some leaks are permitted as part of everyday collaboration and some are actual leaks.* Obviously, firewalls are totally incapable of making these distinctions, or doing anything about them. Advanced firewalls and other common security techniques may in fact give users a false sense of security when it comes to their documents and data.

Is Encryption Enough?

Many of the early solutions for locking down data involved encryption in one form or another:

- E-mail encryption
- File encryption
- Full disk encryption (FDE)
- Enterprise-wide encryption

These encryption solutions can be divided into two categories: encryption *in transit* (e.g., e-mail encryption) and encryption *at rest* (e.g., FDE).

The various encryption solutions mitigate some risks. In the case of data in transit, these risks could include an eavesdropper attempting to discern e-mail or network traffic. In the case of at-rest data, risks include loss of a laptop or unauthorized access to an employee's machine. The most advanced solutions are capable of applying a policy across the organization and encrypting files, e-mails, and even databases. However, encryption has its caveats.

Most simple encryption techniques necessarily involve the decryption of documents so they can be viewed or edited. At these points, the files are essentially exposed. Malware (e.g., Trojan horse, keystroke logger) installed on a computer may use the opportunity to send out the plain-text file to unauthorized parties. Alternatively, an employee may copy the contents of these files and remove them from the enterprise.

First-to-Market Enterprise Digital Rights Management Solutions

What was first called enterprise digital rights management (enterprise DRM), and then simply enterprise rights management (ERM), is now often referred to as information rights management (IRM), which is the term used in this book.

IRM embeds protection into the data (using encryption technology) allowing files to protect themselves. IRM may be the best available security technology for the new mobile computing world of the permeable perimeter.[11]

> Information rights management (IRM) technology protects e-documents and data directly, rather than relying on perimeter security.

With IRM technology, a document owner can selectively prevent others from viewing, editing, copying, or printing it. Despite its promise, most enterprises do not use IRM, and if they do, they do not use it on an enterprise-wide basis. This is due to the high complexity, rigidity, and cost of legacy IRM solutions.

It is clearly more difficult to use documents protected with IRM—especially when policy-making and maintenance is not designed by role but rather by individual. Some early implementations of IRM by first-to-market software development firms had as many as 200,000 different policies to maintain (for 200,000 employees). These have since been replaced by newer, second-wave IRM vendors, who have reduced that number to a mere 200 policies, which is much more manageable. Older IRM installations require intrusive plug-in installation; they are limited in the platforms they support and they largely prevent the use of newer platforms such as smartphones, iPads, and other tablets. This is a real problem in a world where almost all executives carry a smartphone, and use of tablets (especially the iPad) is growing.

Moreover, due to their basic design, first-wave or legacy IRM is not a good fit for organizations aiming to protect documents shared outside company boundaries. These now outdated IRM solutions were designed and developed in a world where organizations were more concerned with keeping information inside the perimeter versus protecting information beyond the perimeter.

Most initial providers of IRM focused on internal sharing and are heavily dependent on Microsoft Active Directory (AD) and lightweight directory access protocol (LDAP) for authentication. Also, the delivery model of older IRM solutions involves the deployment and management of multiple servers, SQL databases, AD/LDAP integration, and a great deal of configuration. This makes them expensive and cumbersome to implement and maintain. Furthermore, these older IRM solutions do not take advantage of or operate well in a cloud computing environment.

While encryption and legacy IRM solutions have certain benefits, it's clear that they are extremely unwieldy and complex and offer limited benefits in today's technical and business environment. Newer IRM solutions are needed to provide more complete document lifecycle security (DLS).

The Promise of Data Loss Prevention

DLP Experts reports that the Data Loss Prevention (DLP) market reached an estimated $400 million in 2011 and "with adoption of DLP technologies moving quickly down to the small to medium enterprise, DLP is no longer an unknown quantity." Although the DLP market has matured, it suffers from confusion about how DLP best fits into the new mix of security approaches, how it is best utilized (endpoint or gateway), and even the definition of DLP itself.[12]

Data loss is very much on managers' and executives' minds today. The series of WikiLeaks incidents exposed hundreds of thousands of sensitive government and military documents. According to the Ponemon Institute (as reported by DLP Experts), data leaks increased 33 percent in 2010 and continue to increase today. Billions of dollars are lost every year as a result of data leaks, with the cost of each breach ranging from an average of $700,000 to $31 million. Some interesting statistics from the study include:

- Almost half of breaches happen while an enterprise's data was in the hands of a third party.
- Over one-third of breaches involved lost or stolen mobile devices.
- The cost per stolen record is approximately $200–$225.

- One-quarter of breaches were conducted by criminals or with malicious intent.
- More than 80 percent of breaches compromised over 1,000 records.[13]

Data Loss Prevention: Limitations

DLP has been hyped in the past few years and resulted in several large acquisitions by major security players—especially those in the IRM market. Much like firewalls, DLP started in the form of network gateways that searched e-mail, web traffic, and other forms of information traveling out of the organization for data that was defined as internal. When it found such data, the DLP blocked transmission or monitored its use.

Soon agent-based solutions were also introduced, performing the same actions locally on users' computers. The next step brought a consolidation of many agent- and network-based solutions to offer a comprehensive solution.

IG policy issues are key. What is the policy? All these methods depend on management setting up a policy that clearly defines what is acceptable to send out and what should be kept in confidence. This is extremely challenging. Defining a policy that is too broad means accidentally letting sensitive information get out, and defining a policy that is too narrow means getting a significant number of false positives, slowing or impeding knowledge workers from getting their jobs done.

While network security management is well established, defining such policies is extremely difficult for a network administrator. As a result, many installations are plagued with false positives—stopping documents and data that are perfectly fine to transmit—or use DLP strictly for monitoring and auditing purposes. Looking closely at the issue of the dissolving perimeter, a deeper DLP issue is revealed: DLP is binary. It can allow or block, but it cannot use discretion.

With DLP, a certain document can either leave the organization's boundaries or it can't. But this is not how the real world works. In today's world, there is an increasing need for information to be shared or reside outside the organization on mobile devices or in the cloud. Simply put, *DLP is not capable of addressing this issue on its own, but it is a helpful piece of the overall technology solution*.

Device Control Methods

Another method that is related to DLP is *device control*. Many vendors offer software or hardware that prevents users from copying data via the USB port to portable drives and removing them from the organization in this manner. These solutions are typically as simple as blocking the ports; however some DLP solutions, when installed on the client side, have the capability to selectively prevent the copying of certain documents.[14]

Thin Clients

One last method worth mentioning is the use of thin clients to prevent data leaks. These provide a so-called walled garden containing only the applications users require to do their work via a diskless terminal. This prevents users from copying any data onto portable media; however, if they have e-mail or web access applications, it will still be possible for them to send information out via e-mail, blogs, or social networks.

A Note about Database Security

While they are outside the scope of this book, it's important to mention database and web security solutions. These have been developed over the past few years and can prevent leakage of structured data from databases and web services due to SQL injections and other vulnerabilities. That is a topic for another book. The focus of this book is mainly on unstructured data, or in other words *e-documents, e-records, and e-mail—which make up over 90% of an organization's total information.*

The Compliance Aspect

Compliance has been key in driving companies to invest in improving their security measures, such as firewalls, anti-virus software, and DLP systems. More than 400 regulations exist worldwide, mandating a plethora of information and data security requirements. One example is PCI-DSS, which is one of the strictest regulations for credit card processors. Companies that fail to comply with these regulations are subject to stiff penalties of up to $500,000 per month for lost financial data or credit card information. Forrester Research estimated the per-record cost of a breach is $90 to $305.[15] But do compliance activities always result in adequate protection of your sensitive data? In many cases the answer is no. It is important to keep in mind that *being formally compliant does not mean the organization is actually secure.* In fact, compliance is sometimes used as a fig leaf, covering a lack of real document security. One needs to look no further than the recent series of major document leakage incidents to understand this. Those all came from highly secure and regulated entities, like banks, hospitals, and the military.

A Hybrid Approach: Combining DLP and IRM Technologies

An idea being promoted of late is to make IRM an enforcement mechanism for platforms like DLP. Together, DLP and IRM accomplish what they independently cannot. Enterprises may be able to use their DLP tools to discover data flows, map them out, and detect transmissions of sensitive information. They can then apply their IRM or encryption protection to enforce their confidentiality and information integrity goals.[16]

Several vendors in the fields of DLP, encryption, and IRM have already announced integrated products. However, at this point in time most IRM solutions are by no means ready for primetime when it comes to this use. Only a select few select second-wave IRM software providers are able to offer comprehensive, streamlined, persistent security across many platforms.

As the enterprise perimeter dissolves, document and data security should become the focus of the Internet security field. However, most legacy solutions such as encryption and legacy IRM are complex, expensive, and provide only a partial solution to the key problems. Combining several methods offers effective countermeasures, but an ultimate solution has not yet arrived.

Securing Trade Secrets after Layoffs and Terminations

In today's global economy—which has shifted labor demands—huge layoffs are not uncommon in the corporate and public sectors. The act of terminating an employee creates document security and IP challenges, while raising the question: How does the organization retrieve and retain its IP and confidential data? An IG program to secure information assets must also deal with everyday resignations of employees who are in possession of sensitive documents and information.[17]

According to Peter Abatan, author of the Enterprise Digital Rights Management blog, "As a general rule *all organizations should classify all their documents with the aim of identifying the ones that need persistent protection*" (italics added).[18] That is to say, documents are protected at all times, regardless of where they travel and who is using them, while the organization still retains control of usage rights. There are two basic technological approaches to this:

1. The first (as discussed earlier in this chapter) is *combining IRM with DLP*; using DLP to conduct deep content inspection and identify all documents that may contain "sensitive corporate information and [then, the DLP agent] notifies the enterprise [information] rights management engine that sensitive information is about to be copied to external media or outside the firewall and therefore needs to be encrypted."
2. The second is using a form of *context-sensitive IRM* "in which all documents that contain sensitive data defined in the [global] data dictionary [are] automatically encrypted."[19]

These two technological approaches must necessarily be fostered by an IG program. They can have significant positive impact in protecting sensitive information, no matter where it is located, and can help document owners withdraw access to its sensitive documents at any time.

Organizations must educate their employees to increase awareness of the financial and competitive impact of breaches and to clarify that sensitive documents are the property of the organization. If those handling sensitive documents are informed of the benefits of IRM and related technologies they will be more vigilant in their efforts to keep information assets secure.[20]

Persistently Protecting Blueprints and CAD Documents

Certain IRM software providers have focused on securing large-format engineering and design documents, and they have made great strides in the protection of computer-aided design (CAD) files. *As much as 95 percent of CAD files are proprietary designs and represent valuable, proprietary IP of businesses worldwide.* And CAD files are just as vulnerable as any other electronic document in that, when unprotected they "can be emailed or transferred to another party without the knowledge of the owner of the content."[21]

> Up to 95 percent of CAD files are proprietary designs and represent valuable intellectual property.

In today's global economy, it is commonplace to conduct manufacturing operations in markets where labor is inexpensive and regulations are lax. Many designs are sent to countries like China, Indonesia, and India for manufacturing. They usually are accompanied by "confidential disclosure contracts [that are] binding on the manufacturer," but these agreements are often difficult to enforce, especially given the disparity in cultures and laws. And what happens if a rogue employee in possession of designs and trade secrets absconds with them and sells them to a competitor? Or starts their own competing business? There are a number of examples of this happening.

Owners of valuable proprietary IP like CAD documents must vigilantly protect them, for the very survival of the business may depend on it. Monitoring and securing IP wherever it might travel is now a business imperative.

Theft of IP and confidential information represent a clear and present danger to all types of businesses, especially global brands dependent on proprietary designs for a competitive advantage. Immediate IG action by executive management is required to identify possible leaks and plug the holes. The very livelihood of the business may depend on it. Not safe-guarding IP and confidential or sensitive documents puts the organization's competitive position, strategic plans, revenue stream, and very future at risk.

Securing Internal Price Lists

In 2010, it was reported that confidential information about the advertising expenditures of some of Google's major accounts was leaked to the public.[22] This may not seem like a significant breach but, in fact, with this information, Google's customers can determine if they are getting a preferred price schedule and competitors can easily undercut Google's pricing for major customers. According to document security blogger Peter Abatan, "[It is clear] why this information is so critical to Google that this information is tightly secured."[23]

So is your company's price list secured at all times? Price lists are confidential information assets, and if they are revealed publicly, major customers could demand steeper discounts and business relationships could suffer irreparable damage, especially if customers find out they are paying more for a product or service than their competitors.

A company's price list is critical to an organization because it impacts all aspects of the business, from the ability to generate revenue to private dealings with customers and suppliers. IRM should be used for price lists to protect them and printing of these valuable lists must be monitored and controlled using secure printing methods and document analytics.[24]

Confidential information like price lists should be persistently protected throughout their document lifecycle, in all three states (at rest, in motion, and in use) *so that if they are compromised or stolen, they are still protected and controlled by the owning organization.*[25]

Approaches for Securing Data Once It Leaves the Organization

It is obvious with today's trends that, as Andrew Jaquith of Forrester Research states, "the enterprise security perimeter is quickly dissolving." A lot of valuable information is routed outside the owning organization through unsecured e-mail. A breach can compromise competitive position, especially in cases dealing with personnel files, and marketing plans, or merger details. Consider for a moment that even proprietary software and company financial statements are sent out. Exposure of this data can have real financial impact. Without additional protections such as IRM and e-mail encryption, these valuable information assets are often out of the control of the IT department of the owning organization.[26]

Third-party possession or control of enterprise data is a critical point of vulnerability and many organizations realize that securing data outside the organizational perimeter is a high priority. But a new concept has cropped up of late that bucks unconventional wisdom: *"control does not require ownership."*

So instead of focusing on securing devices where confidential data is accessed, the new thinking focuses on securing the data and documents directly. With this new mindset, security can be planned under the assumption that the enterprise owns its data, but none of the devices that access it. As Jaquith simply states, *"treat all endpoints as hostile"* (italics added). Forrester Research refers to this concept as the "zero-trust model of information security." Zero trust, according to Jaquith, is "centered on the idea that security must become ubiquitous" throughout an organization's infrastructure.

Forrester has developed a new network architecture that builds security into the DNA of a network, using a mixture of five data security design patterns:

1. *Thin client*—Access information online only, with no local operations, using a diskless terminal that cannot store data, documents, or programs so confidential information stays stored and secured centrally. For additional security, "IT can restrict host copy-and-paste operations, limit data transfers, and require strong or two-factor authentication using SecurID or other tokens."[27]

2. *Thin device*—Devices such as smartphones, which have limited computing resources, web surfing, e-mail, and basic web apps, yet, locally, conduct no real "information processing" are categorized as "thin devices." In practice, these devices do not hold original documents but merely copies, so the official business record or master copy cannot be altered or deleted. A nice feature of many smartphones is the ability to erase or wipe data remotely, in the event the device is lost. This is a little added insurance, and it makes them "truly 'disposable,' unlike PCs," according to Jaquith.[28]

3. *Protected process*—This approach allows local processing with a PC where confidential e-documents and data are stored and processed in a partition which is highly secure and controlled. This can occur even if the PC is not owned and controlled by the organization. "The protected process pattern has many advantages: local execution, offline operation, central management, and a high degree of granular security control, including remote wipe [erase]." A mitigating factor to consider here is most business PCs today are Windows-based and the world is rapidly moving to other, more nimble platforms.[29]

4. *Protected data*—Deploying IRM and embedding security into the documents (or data) provides complete document lifecycle security. The newer wave of more sophisticated, easier-to-use IRM vendors have role-based policy implementation and such features as "contextual" enforcement, where document rights are dependent on the *context*—that is, *where* and *when* a user attempts access. For instance, allow access to documents on workers' desktops, but not on their laptops; or, provide access to printing confidential documents at the facility during office hours, but not after. *"Of all the patterns in the Zero Trust data security strategy, protected data is the most fine-grained and effective because it focuses on the information, not its containers."*[30]

5. *Eye-in-the-sky*—This design pattern uses technologies such as data loss prevention (DLP) to scan network traffic content and halt confidential documents or sensitive data at the perimeter. Deployed properly, DLP is "ideal for understanding the velocity and direction of information flow and for detecting potential breaches, outliers, or anomalous transmissions."[31]

It should be noted that DLP does not provide complete protection. To do so would mean that many legitimate and sanctioned e-mails and documents will be held up for inspection, thus slowing the business process. As stated earlier, DLP is best for discovering information flows and monitoring network traffic. Another negative is that you cannot always require your partner organizations and suppliers to install DLP on their computers. So this is a complementary technology and not a complete solution to securing confidential information assets.[32]

By throwing out the "age-old conflation of ownership and control, enterprises will be able to build data protection programs that encompass all possible ownership scenarios, including Tech Populism, offshoring, and outsourcing."[33]

Document Labeling

Document labeling is "an easy way to *increase user awareness about the sensitivity of information* in a document."(italics added)[34] What is it? It is the process of attaching a label to classify a document. For instance, who would not know that a document labeled *confidential* is indeed confidential? If the label appears prominently at the top of a document, it makes it difficult for the persons accessing it to claim they didn't know it was sensitive.

The challenge is to *standardize and formalize the process* of *getting the label onto the document—enterprise-wide*. This issue would be addressed in an IG effort focused on securing confidential e-documents, or may also be a part of a classification and taxonomy design effort. It cannot simply be left up to the users to type in labels themselves, or it will not be sufficiently executed, and will end up leaving a mishmash of labeled documents without any formal classification.

Another great challenge is classifying legacy or archived documents, which are the lion's share of an organization's information assets. How do you go back and label those? One by one? Nope. Not practical.

Some content repositories or portals such as Microsoft SharePoint provide some functionality toward addressing the document labeling challenge. SharePoint is the most popular platform for sharing documents today.

SharePoint has an information management policy tool called Labels, which can be used to add document labels, such as *Confidential*, to the top of documents.

There are several options available for administrators to customize the labels, including the ability to:

1. *Prompt users to add the label when they save or print, rather than relying on the user to click the Label button in the ribbon;*
2. *Specify labels containing static text and/or variables such as Project Name;*
3. *Control the appearance of the labels, such as font, size, and justification.*[35]

The labels are easily added from within Microsoft Office Word, Power-Point, and Excel. One method that can be used is for the user to click the *Label* button on the *Insert* ribbon group, and another method is to add the label through a prompt that appears when a user saves or prints a document (if the administrator has configured this option).

The labeling capabilities in document and content management systems such as SharePoint are a good start for increasing user awareness and improving the handling of sensitive documents. However, *the document-labeling capabilities of SharePoint are basic and limited.*[36] It may provide a partial or temporary solution, although organizations aiming for a high level of security and confidentiality for their documents will need to search for supplemental technologies from third-party software providers. For instance, to find the capabilities to label documents in bulk rather than one-by-one, add watermarks, or to force users to save or print documents with a standard document label that cannot be altered, may require looking at alternatives. There are software vendors who have enhanced the SharePoint document labeling capability and may provide the complete solution.

Document Analytics

Some software providers also provide document analytics capabilities that monitor the access, use, and printing of documents and create real-time graphical reports of document use activities. This is a *very* valuable tool.

Document analytics allows a compliance officer or system administrator to view exactly how many documents a user accesses in a day, and how many documents the user accesses *on average*. Using this information, analytics monitors can look for spikes or anomalies in use. It is also possible to establish baselines and compare usage with that of an employee's peers as well as his or her past document usage. If, for instance, a user normally accesses an average of 25 documents a day and that suddenly spikes to 200, then the system sends an alert, and perhaps it is time to pay a visit to that person's office. Or if an employee normally prints 50 pages per day, then one day prints 250 pages, a flag is raised. Document analytics capabilities can go so far as to calculate the average time a user spends reading a document, and significant time fluctuations can also be flagged as potentially suspicious activity.

Confidential Stream Messaging

E-mail is dangerous. It contains much of an organization's confidential information, and 99 percent of the time it is sent out unsecured. It has been estimated that as many as 20 percent of e-mail messages transmitted pose a legal, financial, or regulatory threat to the organization. Specifically, "34% of employers investigated a leak of confidential business information via email, and an additional 26% of organizations suffered the exposure of embarrassing or sensitive information during the course of a year," according to Nancy Flynn. These numbers are rising, giving managers and business owners cause to look for confidential messaging solutions.[??]

Since stream messaging separates the header and identifying information from the message, sends them separately, and leaves no record or trace, it is a good option for executives and managers, particularly when engaged in sensitive negotiations, litigation, or other highly confidential activities. Whereas e-mail leaves behind an indelible fingerprint that lives forever on multiple servers and systems, stream messaging does not.

Business records, IP and trade secrets, and confidential executive communications can be protected by implementing stream messaging. It can be implemented alongside and in concert with a regular e-mail system, but clear rules on the use of stream messaging must be established, and access to it must be tightly restricted to a small circle of key executives and managers.

The ePolicy Institute offers seven steps to controlling stream messaging:

1. *Work with your legal counsel to define "business record" for your organization on a companywide basis. Establish written records retention policies, disposition and destruction schedules. And litigation hold rules. Support the email retention policy with a bona fide email archiving solution to facilitate the indexing, preservation and production of legally authentic records. Implement a formal electronic records management system to manage all records.*
2. *Work with your legal counsel to determine when, how, why, and with whom confidential stream messaging is the most appropriate, effective—and legally compliant—way to hold recordless, confidential business discussions* when permanent records are not required.
3. *In order to preserve attorney-client privilege, a phone call or confidential electronic messaging may be preferable to email. Have corporate counsel spell out the manner in which executives and employees should communicate with lawyers when discussing business, seeking legal advice, or asking questions related to specific litigation.*
4. *Define key terms for employees. Don't assume employees understand what management means when using terms like "confidential," "proprietary," or "private" or "intellectual property," etc. Employees must clearly understand definitions if they are to comply with confidentiality rules.*
5. *Implement written rules and policies governing the use of email and confidential stream messaging. E-policies should be written clearly and should be easy for employees to access, and understand. Make them "short and sweet" as possible. Do not leave anything up to interpretation.*
6. *Distribute a hard copy of the new confidential messaging policy, email policy and other electronic communications (e.g. social media, blogs). Insist that each and every employee signs and dates the policy, acknowledging that they understand and accept it and that disciplinary action including termination may result from violation of the organization's established policies.*
7. *Educate, educate, educate. Ensure that all employees who need to know the difference between email which leaves a potential business record and stream messaging which does not, and is confidential.*[38]

Securing confidential information assets effectively requires an eclectic, multifaceted approach. It takes clear and enforced IG policies, a collection of technologies, and regular testing and audits, both internally, and by a trusted third-party.

Chapter Summary: Key Points

- Attacks on organizations' networks and theft of their intellectual property (IP) continue to increase. There were an estimated 354 million privacy breaches from 2005 to 2010 in the United States alone.
- Attacks can continue in organizations for years before they are uncovered—if they are discovered at all.
- All organizations should classify all their documents with the aim of identifying the ones that need persistent security protection.
- Persistent security tools like information rights management (IRM) should be enforced on price lists, proprietary blueprints, and computer-aided design (CAD) designs. Printing these documents should be highly restricted.
- Most legacy or first-to-market providers of IRM focused on internal sharing, and are heavily dependent on Microsoft Active Directory (AD) and lightweight directory access protocol (LDAP) for authentication. They were not built for cloud use or the distributed enterprise of today, where mobile devices are proliferating.
- Data loss prevention (DLP) started in the form of network gateways (much like firewalls) that searched e-mails, web traffic, and other forms of information for data that was defined as internal. When it detected such data, it blocked it from leaving the perimeter or monitored its use.
- Soon agent-based DLP solutions were also introduced, performing the same action locally on users' computers. The next step brought a consolidation of many agent- and network-based solutions to offer a more comprehensive solution.
- Combining IRM and DLP technologies is the best available approach to securing e-documents and data. Other encryption methods should also be utilized, such as e-mail encryption and full disk encryption (FDE).
- The use of thin-client and thin-device architecture can reduce security threats to confidential information assets.
- Document analytics monitor the access, use, and printing of documents and creates real-time graphical reports of document use activities.
- Document labeling is an easy way to increase user awareness about the sensitivity of information in a document.

(*continued*)

(*continued*)

- Stream messaging is a way to conduct sensitive business negotiations and activities without leaving a business record. Legal counsel must be consulted and clear policies for regular e-mail versus stream messaging must be established and enforced.

Notes

1. IBM, "Smarter Security & Resilience," www.ibm.com/smarterplanet/us/en/business_resilience_management/overview/index.html, retrieved March 30, 2012.
2. Ibid.
3. Byron Acohido, "MasterCard, Visa Warn Security Breach May Compromise Data," *USA Today*, January 23, 2009, www.usatoday.com/money/perfi/credit/2009-01-21-visa-mastercard-credit-security-breach_N.htm, retrieved August 18, 2011.
4. Jim Finkle, "'State Actor' behind Slew of Cyber Attacks," Reuters, August 3, 2011, www.reuters.com/article/2011/08/03/us-cyberattacks-idUSTRE7720HU20110803, retrieved August 18, 2011.
5. Ibid.
6. Ibid.
7. Ibid.
8. Peter Abatan, "Persistently Protecting Your Computer Aided Designs," Enterprise Digital Rights Management, www.enterprisedrm.info/post/1423979379/persistently-protecting-your-computer-aided-designs, retrieved August 18, 2011.
9. Ari Ruppin, March 20, 2011 via e-mail.
10. Ibid.
11. Ibid.
12. Data Loss Prevention Experts, "DLP Product Guide for RSA Conference Expo 2011," January 17, 2011, www.dlpexperts.com/dlpxblog/2011/1/17/dlp-product-guide-for-rsa-conference-expo-2011.html, retrieved August 22, 2011.
13. Ibid.
14. Ibid.
15. Sharon Gaudin, "Security Breaches Cost $90 to $305 per Lost Record." Information Week, http://www.informationweek.com/news/199000222, retrieved May 15, 2012.
16. Ibid.

17. Peter Abatan, "Preparing for Staff Layoffs/Resignations Where Confidential Information Is Concerned," Enterprise Digital Rights Management, www.enterprisedrm.info/post/1230356519/preparing-for-staff-layoffs-re signations, retrieved December 24, 2011.
18. Ibid
19. Ibid.
20. Ibid.
21. Peter Abatan, "Persistently Protecting Your Computer Aided Designs."
22. Peter Abatan, "Is Your Price List under Lock and Key?" Enterprise Digital Rights Management, www.enterprisedrm.info/post/1120104758/is-your-price-list-under-lock-and-key, retrieved August 18, 2011.
23. Ibid.
24. Ibid.
25. Ibid.
26. Andrew Jaquith, "Own Nothing—Control Everything: Five Patterns for Securing Data on Devices You Don't Own," ComputerWeekly .com, September 8, 2010, www.computerweekly.com/Articles/2010/09 /10/242661/Own-nothing-control-everything-five-patterns-for-securing-data-on-devices-you-dont.htm, retrieved August 18, 2011.
27. Ibid.
28. Ibid.
29. Ibid.
30. Ibid.
31. Ibid.
32. Ibid.
33. Ibid.
34. Charlie Pulfer, "Document Labeling in SharePoint," September 13, 2009, http://blog.contentmanagementconnection.com/Home/21196, retrieved August 25, 2011.
35. Ibid.
36. Ibid.
37. Excerpted by permission of the publisher, from *The E-Policy Handbook: Rules and Best Practices to Safely Manage Your Company's E-Mail, Blogs, Social Networking, and Other Electronic Communication Tools,* by Nancy Flynn, p.57. © 2009 Nancy Flynn, AMACOM, division of American Management Association, New York, NY. All rights reserved.
38. Ibid., pp. 68–70.

PART V

Rolling It Out: Project and Program Issues

CHAPTER 13

Building the Business Case to Justify the Program

Implementing a successful information governance (IG) program to safeguard confidential information assets requires all the essentials of any successful project, from building the business case and executive sponsorship to testing and auditing the program.

Determine What Will Fly in Your Organization

The requirements for a business case to justify a project vary by organization, culture, and management style. Some require a strict internal rate of return (IRR), hurdle rate, or return on investment (ROI) to be calculated before moving forward. Others require justification of hard costs, then look at these alongside the intangible, soft benefits of the automation to complete the justification. Yet other organizations understand the inherent efficiencies of automation and their impact on labor costs, especially with the added advantages of security and risk reduction, and base a management decision on intuition or gut feel. Finally, there are organizations that base the decision on a purely budgetary or tax basis, that is, they have determined the capital budget and which projects to compete using those allocated funds.

But with a project of this type, protection against the worst-case scenario may be sufficient to justify an IG program. Critical questions to raise during the decision-making process include: What would happen if our internal documents and e-mail messages were leaked to the press during merger talks? What if our competitors obtained copies of our patented designs—in China? What if during litigation an opposing party was able to gain access to our strategy documents? What if employees gain access to coworkers' human resources files? These types of serious data emergencies can only be prevented with successful IG.

> The approach to project justification varies by organization, but in the case of securing sensitive e-documents, painting a worst-case scenario of a document breach may be all it takes.

And just as the September 11th attacks and Hurricane Katrina changed the realities of disaster recovery and business continuity plans, the WikiLeaks scandal changed the realities of e-document security. One needs to go no further than to cite this clear example in recent history to show the impact of such breaches.

The first step in launching a program to secure confidential information assets is to understand what key factors qualify a project as viable in a particular organization. Once that is known, steps to build the business case that satisfy or exceed those requirements can be taken.

Strategic Business Drivers for Project Justification

A fully implemented program for securing confidential information assets includes the implementation of information rights management (IRM) technology, data loss prevention (DLP), or other related technologies. These technologies monitor and inspect e-mail and attached e-document traffic in the network, as well as access information management applications. *IRM will allow the organization to secure e-documents throughout their use, providing complete Document Lifecycle Security (DLS).*

The added capabilities of document labeling and usage analytics provide real-time surveillance and analysis that can flag anomalies as they occur. The capabilities of these combined technologies allow the organization to closely monitor e-document traffic and remotely control e-documents—benefits that the organization did not have previously. *The benefits of these capabilities are immeasurable, since an organization may never be aware of intruders or malicious insiders who quietly stockpile valuable information assets*; therefore, it is impossible to know what business catastrophes have been prevented. *But on the surface, most executives can understand what a tremendous sea change this offers in terms of e-document security.*

Especially after WikiLeaks.

A complete program for securing information assets also includes confidential stream messaging or other types of secure messaging for key executives. Under strict IG guidelines, a secure messaging tool allows the free flow of ideas in confidence, without an unnecessary record being created.

An overall e-document and information asset security program also necessarily includes the implementation of an electronic document and records management system (EDRMS) or an electronic records management (ERM) system, with supporting IG policies and controls. This enables the organization to capture and declare information and documents as official business records. The records are maintained with accurate and secure metadata and audit trails to provide context along with the content. The EDRMS/ERM software locks the records, preventing modifications, changes, or accidental file deletion, thereby protecting them and ensuring authenticity, a great benefit in legal matters. Records are maintained in the software until the retention period has been met, which further assists in meeting regulatory and legal requirements. Once the retention requirements have passed, the disposition process is initiated, according to the records' retention policy, which means that some may be scheduled to be destroyed. This qualifies as *defensible disposition,* which reduces the organization's risk of keeping records that could be detrimental in future legal or regulatory proceedings. Any records placed on legal or audit hold are suspended from the disposition process until the hold has been removed, which helps ensure compliance with IG policies in the e-discovery and auditing process.[1]

Forming and enforcing the IG policies developed during this project will help transform the corporate culture into one of greater security awareness and compliance. More concretely, though, following these IG guidelines and policies will help secure the organization technologically in all its pursuits, regardless of application or media type. Any business documents or records that utilize social media, mobile computing, e-mail, IM, or web applications, whether running internally or externally, will be governed appropriately by rational, prudent business methods. *This will bring the organization a wealth of benefits in business agility, compliance, litigation readiness, and competitiveness, while protecting information assets from erosion, misuse, or theft.*

With the full implementation of an IG program, *a standard classification system* is used to standardize naming conventions for electronically stored information (ESI). This classification must be in place before any automated system can be implemented. Physical records are generally filed following standard alphabetic, numeric, or alphanumeric filing rules, but e-records are rarely filed consistently (in the Windows directory format); most are filed on an ad-hoc basis.

Most organizations have a number of automated business processes in areas such as accounting, human resources (HR), and customer relationship management (CRM). In instances where software applications have replaced manual processes, the data are maintained within the applications. *These systems typically do not include records management features.* The data in these systems is dynamic, so changes to the system can change the representation of the records. For example: The name of a general ledger account on the chart of accounts is changed. Any reports or statements printed after the change, including reports from before the change, may reflect the change rather than the original. The records contained within the application remain in the system until IT purges the data from the database.[2]

Often an organization creates e-records but does not manage them properly. Physical records are being replaced by scanned versions, without allowing for the e-records' lifecycle management according to a standard retention and disposition schedule. Organizations often scan records using digital printers and desktop scanners for ease of access. The physical records are usually filed and retained in addition to the electronic copy, creating duplicate copies of the same record. This causes confusion over the authenticity of the records and adds to labor and production costs during litigation or regulatory proceedings.

In addition, if retention periods are not consistently applied to the same types of records across the organization, compliance with IG policies cannot be tracked. It is nearly impossible to identify electronic records holdings or ESI compliance with legal statutes, as applicable.

When electronic records are not tracked using a central or systematic process, organizations cannot prove compliance with the records retention policy. In the event of a discovery request in the case of litigation, audit, or investigation, the organization has no mechanisms to indicate what records existed or if they have been destroyed in compliance with the records retention schedule. Organizations that do not track their records or the e-record destruction process are at risk of non-compliance.

In the event of litigation, investigation, or audit, this non-compliance could result in adverse actions if requested records cannot be located, regardless of whether they were destroyed following the records retention schedule or simply lost. When organizations do not have a systematic process for tracking records and their authorized destruction, compliance with current regulations and IG policies cannot be proven. A robust IG program, including the implementation of an automated EDRMS/ERM application, provides this evidence with reports and audit logs.

The regular use of *digital signatures* to safeguard e-documents helps reduce business process cycle times by avoiding the disruptions that occur waiting for signature approvals. This enables business to be carried on in a much more geographically dispersed manner, both within and between organizations. But more important to the security aspect is that the *attached e-documents can confidently be certified as authentic, and the signer's identity is assured.*

Secure printing should also be included in an overall program to safeguard information assets. Secure printing helps ensure that confidential information assets are not compromised when output to a printer. There are various methods to securing the print functions, the most basic being entering a PIN code when sending the documents to print, and then re-entering it at the physical machine in order for the documents to be output.

Benefits of Electronic Records Management

Implementing ERM represents a significant investment. An investment in ERM is an investment in business process automation and yields document control, document integrity, and security benefits. The volume of records in organizations has often exceeded the employees' ability to manage them. ERM systems do for the information age what the assembly line did for the industrial age. The cost/benefit justification for ERM is sometimes difficult to determine, but there are real labor and cost savings. ERM also provides a number of intangible benefits, while the requirements are clearly justified. There are many ways in which an organization can gain significant business benefits, tangible and intangible, with ERM.[3]

Tangible Financial Benefits

- **Space savings.** The financial benefits for ERM are often difficult to quantify. While saving space is a significant financial benefit, the space used for physical records storage is usually unusable as office space. Organizations often store records in basements or warehouses, where they are vulnerable to water, mildew, dust, and other environmental threats, as well as rodents and insects. During the records survey process, studies often find many records are copies of records maintained by other departments or are duplicated electronically. To fully assess the space savings of implementing ERM, a records inventory would be required to identify all of the records, whether they are originals or duplicates, if they can or are being stored electronically, and if they have met their retention requirements. Without a tracking system for these records, it is not impossible to accurately estimate the space savings.
- **Additional cost savings.** Additional cost savings can be realized through reduction in printing, postage, faxing, filing, and archiving costs. With ERM, the records in off-site storage would be scheduled for destruction in a timely manner.
- **Disposal of furniture and consumables.** A small benefit may be expected in cost avoidance of additional filing cabinets and the disposal of obsolete filing cabinets. There will be decreased expenditure on file folders and other filing supplies, and so on; however, this savings is minor.

■ **Hardware savings.** Implementing an ERM system will result in reduced costs for network and shared drives, including the cost for maintenance. When employees store their documents and records on the
repository, the requirement for the network and shared drives will be
reduced.

Intangible, Non-Financial Benefits

■ **Management and control of business documents and records.**
By using an ERM repository for documents and records, costs are
saved through reduced maintenance, handling, and physical storage
costs, and by gaining full control over the lifecycle of documents and
records. Records need to be securely managed, while being made
easily accessible to those who have a valid business need and right
of access.

■ **Reduced risk.** Organizations can reduce the risk of adverse actions
and financial penalties resulting from litigation, government investigation, or audit, by implementing ERM. Through company-wide ERM
implementation, the organization can identify ESI and records. ERM
provides organizations with tools to systematically identify, manage,
protect, and dispose of records and information in the normal course
of business, and also engage in audits to provide proof of compliance
with legal and regulatory requirements including records management
policy and records retention schedule. ERM provides legal departments
with search tools to locate ESI required for litigation, sequester or protect ESI, and prepare ESI for discovery according to the document
retention order.

■ **Productivity benefits.** ERM provides productivity benefits by enabling
employees to work more efficiently and accomplish more with the same
staffing levels. This is achieved by reducing the time spent copying
paper records (for ease of access), looking for lost or misfiled records,
and recreating records. It also increases productivity by making the
records needed by employees instantly available. Also, customer service
(both external and internal) is usually improved.

■ **Legislative and regulatory compliance.** Organizations are increasingly being required to conform to new regulations that effectively man-
date the use of enterprise-wide ERM. Specific legislation and guidelines
are designed to protect the public and govern records management in
organizations, setting the standards for the highest level of security and
transparency.

From a simple browser interface, employees will have access to the
declaration of records, disposal and retention schedules, authentication
and audit features, security, search and retrieval functionality, and the
storage of contextual metadata.

By providing an up-to-date, relevant, accurate, and more complete set of records, ERM will provide increased document auditability, which can be used to justify an organization's past actions and decisions.

- **Higher evidential weight.** With ERM, records presented as evidence in support of litigation will be complete, accurate, and credible. By comparison, collections of paper records and unstructured electronic records seem incomplete, unreliable, and not closely tracked or audited. In any future litigation, there will be processes for identifying the electronically stored information and protecting required records by placing them under a legal hold. The integrity of electronic records may also be used to facilitate complete discovery of evidence.
- **Record security.** ERM provides a highly secure, flexible framework, including options to protect against unauthorized access, accidental deletion, overwriting and version-control issues, and physical storage device failure. ERM provides protection through the full lifecycle management of records from creation to disposal.
- **A structured and trusted information base.** A properly configured ERM system can provide information that is reliably up to date and complete. Effective ERM ensures that all users who need access to information, regardless of where it is held and maintained, can access it in a timely and simple manner. This results in avoiding duplication of records. ERM will allow rapid storage and retrieval of information to support a more effective decision-making cycle.
- **Better decision making.** Many benefits of ERM combine to facilitate the making of decisions more quickly, *and the decisions will be based on better information.* Better decision making can be extremely valuable, although the value cannot be quantified.
- **Improved search capability.** Records would be available across departments and functional areas. With the records being stored in their native formats or as PDFs, they can be searched via full-text search capabilities. Additional, more granular, refined searches are available. Keep in mind that images (scanned or otherwise) not converted by optical character recognition (OCR) software cannot be searched for keywords.

Storing the records in a searchable format can provide employees with research opportunities that rely on textual searches. Often, specific industries, such as health care and legal, require industry-specific dictionaries to be loaded so industry terms and jargon are recognized correctly.

For employees, searches can be tailored to a specific set of data and saved. Saved searches are used by employees who search for the same information often. A saved search could recall specific search requirements so the user only needs to enter minimal criteria rather than start from scratch. The time savings can be substantial.

Presenting the Business Case

Timing is everything. Once a team understands what their organization requires to prioritize and fund a project, then they must work toward fulfilling those requirements. The business case will be different for each organization, as the business environment, corporate culture, funding process, and competitive position varies between organizations.

The project can begin with a broad justification based on a key business driver, something that compels the organization to move forward. Then, as the actual implementation costs become known—including computer hardware, software, training, management time, and maintenance fees—a specific business case can be drawn to implement.

Chapter Summary: Key Points

- The first step to launching a program to secure confidential information assets is to understand what key factors qualify a project as viable in a particular organization.
- A fully implemented program for securing confidential information assets would include the implementation of information rights management (IRM) and possibly data loss prevention (DLP) technologies to secure e-documents from creating to final disposition. Additional technologies such as digital signatures, document labeling, and access control combined with sound IG policies and enforcement will help assure complete document lifecycle security (DLS).
- The use of digital signatures in an overall information governance (IG) program for e-document security certifies documents as authentic and unaltered, and the signer's identity is verified.
- Tangible financial benefits derived from the implementation of an electronic records management (ERM) system include: hardware savings, disposal of furniture and consumables, and space savings. Intangible benefits include: reduced risk, improved search capability, better decision making, a structured and trusted information base, record security, stronger legal evidence, legislative and regulatory compliance, and productivity benefits.
- Timing is everything. Funding an IG project to secure confidential information assets requires developing a solid business case and presenting it at the right time.

Notes

1. Charmaine Brooks, via e-mail to the author, August 21, 2011.
2. Ibid.
3. Ibid.

CHAPTER 14

Securing Executive Sponsorship

G aining sponsorship at the senior management level is always crucial to projects and programs. It is not possible to require managers to take time out of their other duties to participate in a project if there is no executive edict. Ideally, in this case, the informational governance (IG) program for securing information assets is driven by the CEO. With CEO sponsorship come many of the key elements needed to complete a successful project, including allocated management time, budget money, and management focus.

It is important to bear in mind that this IG effort is truly a *change management* effort, in that it aims to change the structure, guidelines, and rules within which employees operate. *The change must occur at the very core of the organization's culture.* It must be embedded permanently, and to do so, the message must be constantly and consistently reinforced. To achieve this kind of change requires commitment from the very highest levels of the organization.

> Executive sponsorship is critical to project success. There is no substitute.

If the CEO is not the sponsor, then another high-level executive must lead the effort and be accountable for meeting milestones as the program progresses. *"Executive Sponsorship is one of those project success factors that are required for any project to succeed. An absent Executive Sponsor greatly increases the likelihood of project failure."* (italics added)[1] It will fade, fizzle out, or be relegated to the back burner. Without strong high-level leadership, when things go awry, finger pointing and political games may take over, impeding progress and cooperation.[2]

The executive sponsor must be actively involved, tracking project objectives and milestones on a regular, scheduled basis. He or she must be aware of any obstacles or disputes that arise, take an active role in resolving them, and push the project forward. If this is absent the IG initiative will not survive competition with other projects when budgeting priorities are pressured.

Executive Sponsor Role

The role of an executive sponsor is high-level, which requires periodic and regular attention to the status of the project, particularly with budget issues, staff resources, and milestone progress. The role of a project manager (PM) is more detailed and day-to-day, tracking specific tasks that must be executed to make progress toward milestones. Both roles are essential, and the savvy PM brings in the executive sponsor to push things along when more authority is needed, but reserves such project capital for those issues that absolutely cannot be resolved without executive intervention. It is best for the PM to keep the executive sponsor fully informed, but to ask for assistance only when absolutely needed.

At the same time the PM must manage the relationship with the executive sponsor, perhaps with some gentle reminders, coaxing, or prodding, to ensure that the role and tasks of executive sponsorship are being fulfilled. "More importantly, the successful Project Manager knows that if those duties are not being fulfilled, it's time to call a timeout and have a serious conversation with the Executive Sponsor about the viability of the project."[3]

The executive sponsor serves a few key purposes on a project:

1. **Budget.** Ensures an adequate financial commitment is made to see the project through, and lobbies for additional expenditures when change orders are made or cost overruns occur.
2. **Planning and control.** Sets direction and tracks accomplishment of specific, measureable business objectives.
3. **Decision-making.** Makes or approves crucial decisions and resolves issues that are escalated for resolution.
4. **Manages expectations.** Since success is quite often a stakeholder perception.
5. **Anticipates.** Every project that is competing for resources can run into unforeseen blockages and objections. Executive sponsors run interference and provide political might for the project manager to lead the project to completion, through a series of milestones.
6. **Approves.** Signs off when all milestones and objectives have been met.

An eager and effective executive sponsor makes all the difference, if properly managed by the PM. It is a tricky relationship, since the PM is always below the executive sponsor in the organization's hierarchy, yet the PM must coax the superior into tackling certain high-level tasks. Sometimes a third-party consultant who is an expert in the project at hand can provide the initiative and support for requests made of the sponsor and provide a solid business rationale.

Project Manager: Key Tasks

Here are the fundamental steps a successful PM will need to take to ensure an executive sponsor rises to the role and advances the project towards a successful conclusion:

1. **Expectation management.** The PM should meet with the executive sponsor and review expectations not only for the resources required but the impact the project's completion will have on the organization's operations. In addition, *it is critical that the ground rules are laid out up front as to what the project manager expects of the executive sponsor—and vice versa.* Clear lines of communication need to be established. One way to address this need is to schedule weekly status meetings between the PM and executive sponsor to review progress and resource needs. "Like managing the expectations of any stakeholder, the successful Project Manager will want to identify the Executive Sponsor's interests and expectations in the project up front, and ensure those align with the goals of the project."[4] *The aforementioned six executive sponsor role points are a good place to start the conversation.*

   The discussions should also include working out the game plan for updating the executive sponsor on project status, tackling thorny issues, and communicating requests for more time and resources.

2. **Approvals: Obtain acceptance on objectives and metrics.** "The Executive Sponsor should approve the objectives and measurement metrics for project completion, normally outlined in the Project Charter."[5] The program objectives should directly align to the executive sponsor's own objectives; for instance, reducing the resources needed to respond to compliance requests in order to cut variable expense levels in their functional area by a targeted percentage. The acceptance criteria should be definitively measurable, meaning it should have measureable objectives (e.g., reduce the cost of file production requests for litigation by 20 percent) and be time-constrained (e.g., by fiscal year end) so it is

very clear when the project has achieved those objectives and can be declared complete. By ensuring the objectives are tied to the executive sponsor's objectives, "the successful Project Manager will be assured to get the Sponsor's attention when the project objectives are in jeopardy of being attained."[6]

3. **Engage.** During initial discussions when expectations are hammered out until they are clear, the guidelines for communication between the PM and executive sponsor should be laid out. The executive sponsor should be appropriately engaged, but not *overly* so. Certain types of tasks must be owned by the PM, and high-level guidance and support is owned by the executive sponsor. This means the latter must also communicate the project's progress to C-level peers. In other words, a steady stream of supportive and firm memos should be issued by the sponsor to keep executive-level peers and the CEO (if appropriate) apprised of the project's needs and progress. The successful PM will attempt to manage the sponsor's input by including in their status updates whether or not assistance is being requested. It should be spelled out clearly.

It is a balancing act. The successful PM keeps the executive sponsor in the loop but does not waste precious political capital requesting assistance for issues that can be solved without it. And when the executive sponsor *is* asked to address a thorny issue, the PM should prepare several alternative approaches and stand ready to make a recommendation.

4. **Final approval.** This should be a logical and simple step, provided approvals of a sequence of milestone accomplishments have been made by the executive sponsor. But it is *critically important*. Once the PM can check off completion of the pre-established acceptance criteria, "the Executive Sponsor should be able to sign off on project completion without hesitation."[7]

So why is it extremely important to gain final sign-off? Sign-off means more than completing the project (or major phase) and releasing resources. "Signoff says there is no more work to be completed, the project has met its objectives and delivered on its expected value, and that all stakeholders identified needs from the project have been met. It means that the successful Project Manager has met his or her obligations to the organization."[8]

In the case of an ongoing effort, such as an IG program to secure information assets, there will be a series of sign-offs as major milestones are accomplished and new business processes and technologies are put into production. Resources will be shifted accordingly as the program progresses and matures.

It's the Little Things

There some additional smaller tasks and activities that the project manager can ask the executive sponsor to take up to improve the project's odds of success. Here are some little things an executive sponsor can do to push the project to success:

- **Coach.** Show active support and involvement—perhaps by dropping in on project status meetings and inserting some nuggets of advice and encouragement.
- **Cheerlead.** Make sure that project wins, however small, are celebrated and recognized.
- **Commend.** Take the time to single out personal contributions and reward team members in some way—be it with a half-day off or free lunch—to show that efforts are noticed and appreciated.
- **Communicate.** Keep executive levels apprised of progress and laud the project's progress in other meetings, newsletters, and internal memos.

There are many other small ways an executive sponsor can positively impact a project, and they can be encouraged by a proactive PM. "It never hurts to ask, and a successful PM is always looking for ways to leverage every resource on the project team roster, [including] the executive team sponsor."[9]

Active, engaged, and fully invested executive sponsors are "paramount to project success," according to Roger Kastner. In order to be successful, the PM must constantly communicate, court, and interact with the executive sponsor to ensure they fulfill their role in the project for task awareness and "willingness to participate when necessary."[10]

Evolving Role of the Executive Sponsor

The role of the executive sponsor necessarily evolves and changes over the life of the initial effort, during the implementation phases, and on through the continued program to secure confidential information assets. To get the project off the ground, he or she must make the business case and get adequate budgetary funding. But an effort such as this takes more than money—it takes *time*. Not just time to develop new policies and implement new technologies, but the time of the designated PM, program leaders, and needed program participants.

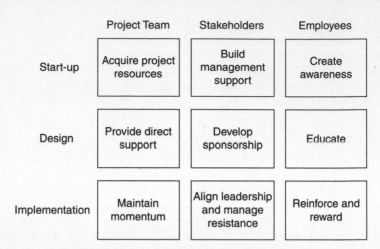

FIGURE 14.1   Matrix: Key Responsibilities of the Executive Sponsor

In order to get this time set aside, the program must be made a top priority of the organization. It must be recognized, formalized, and aligned with organizational objectives. All this upfront work is the responsibility of the executive sponsor.

Once the program team is formed, team members must clearly understand why the new program is important and how it will help the organization meet its business objectives. This message must be regularly reinforced by the executive sponsor; he or she must not only paint the vision of the future state of the organization but articulate the steps in the path to get there.

When the formal program effort commences, the executive sponsor must remain visible and accessible. They cannot disappear into their everyday duties and expect the program team to carry the effort through. They must be there to help the team confront and overcome business obstacles as they arise, and they must hail the successes along the way. This requires active involvement and a willingness to spend the time to keep the program on track and focused.

The executive sponsor must be the lighthouse that shows the way even through cloudy skies and rough waters. They are the captain that must steer the ship, even if the first mate (PM) is seasick and the deckhands (project team) are drenched and tired.

After the program is implemented, the executive sponsor is responsible for maintaining its effectiveness and relevance. This is done through periodic checks, audits, and testing, and scheduled meetings with the ongoing program manager.

Chapter Summary: Key Points

- Engaged and vested executive sponsors are necessary for project success. It is not possible to require managers to take time out of their other duties to participate in a project if there is no executive edict or allocated budget.
- The executive sponsor must be: 1) directly tied to the success of the project; 2) fully engaged and aware in the project; and 3) actively eliminating barriers and resolving issues.
- The role of the executive sponsor evolves over the life of the program effort. Initially, the focus is on garnering the necessary resources, but as the program commences, the emphasis is more on supporting the program team and clearing obstacles. Once implemented, the responsibilities shift to focusing on maintaining the effectiveness of the program through testing and audits.

Notes

1. Roger Kastner, "Why Projects Succeed—Executive Sponsorship," February 15, 2011, http://blog.slalom.com/2011/02/15/why-projects-succeed-%E2%80%93-executive-sponsorship/, retrieved August 22, 2011. © Robert Kastner and Slalom Consulting. Used by permission. All other rights reserved.
2. Ibid.
3. Ibid.
4. Ibid.
5. Ibid.
6. Ibid.
7. Ibid.
8. Ibid.
9. Ibid.
10. Ibid.

Safeguarding Confidential Information Assets: Where Do You Start?

Projects focused on securing confidential e-documents begin for a reason, that is, usually there is some compelling *business driver* in a crucial area that arises that makes it imperative for the organization to tackle and solve the problem. The primary business driver for a document lifecycle security (DLS) project could be one of several things. Here are a few examples:

- A newly discovered security breach that could have compromised the enterprise's competitive position.
- A new regulation that must be complied with, such as a 2010 state requirement in Massachusetts, which *requires* that any personal information sent through e-mail or stored on desktop computers and removable devices *must be encrypted*.[1]
- The desire to protect company blueprints, designs, or product lifecycle management (PLM) data, as the business begins a new venture overseas.

So, *typically, there is a key business driver that causes the project to gain interest, executive sponsorship, allocated budget, management time, and resources.*

> A key business driver is required to fuel a project or program forward.

Business Driver Approach

The purpose of the project should be stated in terms of formal objectives. The more measureable metrics that can be attached to those objectives, the better. For instance, the business objective may be stated as, "Our department seeks to secure 100 percent of Document Types A, B, and C for their full lifecycle within 120 days." The project has a fixed timeframe and a narrow scope. Testing and auditing the information governance (IG) policies and technologies managing those document types can verify the level or percentage of documents that have, in fact, been protected once the new IG policies and document lifecycle security (DLS) technologies have been implemented.

The question is still, "Where do you begin?" That is, "Which documents need to be protected?" The answer is that first you determine the roles and responsibilities of a representative cross section of personnel in the target area. Then find out what key document types they work with and inventory critical target-area documents by type.

All documents will be categorized as one of four basic types:

1. Public facing: Open to all the public.
2. Internal: Open and available to the entire organization.
3. Restricted: Limited access, based on roles and responsibilities.
4. Top secret: Highly confidential documents that should not show up in any folder or search within the organization. Only a few privileged individuals have access to these documents under tight access control and security restrictions.[2]

The top secret and restricted documents are the subsets to focus on initially, especially the former. In subsequent project phases some of the documents that are open internally may need to be considered for inclusion as well.

Common sense dictates here: Although IT people do not know much about the documents that businesspeople in their organization use, those who handle the documents daily *know inherently* which ones are highly confidential and need to be protected. Talk with them.

Classification

Usually, these critical e-documents will have some sort of existing classification or filing system, folder structure, or taxonomy to organize and categorize the documents. *The fastest, easiest, and most efficient way to implement a document security program is to leverage the existing taxonomy or classifications.* That way there is less change, less training, and less maintenance of the system and program.

> Leveraging an existing taxonomy is the nimblest way forward.

Ultimately, organizations should have an enterprise-wide taxonomy in place that standardizes the classification of documents and records across the entire organization. To conduct a complete enterprise-wide inventory of every document and record type is much broader in scope, and there would need to be a top-level executive sponsor, a very strong business driver, and significant funding to justify a project of that scope. It takes a great deal of data collection, interviewing, consultation, and analysis to determine and document the entire universe of data the organization works with, and then decide just how to group them by document type in a new, enterprise-wide taxonomy—and also determine what to do with exceptions.

An enterprise approach is not necessary for a successful first implementation in a high-value target area. In fact, the goal should be to form the correct IG policies, implement technologies, and demonstrate significantly improved security in that particular area, and to formally sign off on the project. Then the implementation can be expanded to areas that are next on the priority list.

Document Survey Methodology

Gathering information about the target area's most critical documents and records to determine which have the most value and must be protected follows a best practice methodology that consists of:

1. Preliminary investigation.
2. Analysis of business activities.
3. Identification of document and records management requirements.
4. Assessment of existing processes and procedures.
5. Identification of requirements for managing documents.
6. Redesign or development of new processes and procedures.

The optimal method for the preliminary investigation uses a combination of techniques and is referred to as a document survey or inventory.[3] The survey is usually completed using a combination of questionnaires and interviews, but if DLP technology, data governance software, document analytics, or other technology tools to monitor document usage are available, they should be utilized to speed the inventory and mapping process. Also, the technology tools provide clear, unambiguous reports that are not subjective. Interviews are time-consuming and have a subjective quality, although they do uncover facts and nuances. Interviews can provide keen insights into the organization, its corporate culture, history of compliance, information asset security issues, and other characteristics and information specific to the organization.

The interviews are optimally conducted in small departmental groups to foster an interactive environment, and the preferred approach begins by asking questions of a general nature—looking for open-ended responses that have not been influenced.

During the interviews, employees are encouraged to be open regarding the challenges facing them in performing their tasks and ideas for improving their e-document security and document management processes.

The selection of a representative group of participants in the investigative process is a key factor in the ultimate success of the information gathering. Also, employees need to know what to expect during the interviews and how much time to allow so that interviews are maximally productive.

In addition to the interviews, analyze existing documentation or previously validated analysis, including policies, procedures, retention schedules, and regulatory and legal research.

Interviewing Staff in the Target Area

Each staff member that you interview should be able to tell you "what [critical documents and] records they use, why they need the [documents and] records, and how they use them. This will help you to determine how long the records need to be kept and what their final disposition should be." *They also know which documents are sensitive and why they should be kept confidential.*[4]

Narrowing the focus of the interviews down to those representatives in the target area that can provide the most salient information is key, as there will not be time to interview everyone. A cross-level approach spanning multiple levels of the organizational hierarchy will provide the most complete picture of how confidential or sensitive documents are used. That means it may be best to start with lower-level clerical or administrative staff and make your way up through support staff, supervisors, midlevel managers, and senior managers. "The people who work with the [documents and] records can best describe to you their use. They will likely know where the [documents and] records came from, if copies exist, who needs the [documents and] records, any computer systems that are used, how long the records are needed and other important information that you need to know."[5] You can then create a complete document inventory of the target area and begin to prioritize the documents and to set up a records retention schedule, should documents rise to the level of becoming business records, (as defined by the organization). *But the core focus should be on identifying those most sensitive documents and tracking their use throughout their lifecycle.*

Selecting Interviewees

It is important to dig down and get to the level where the documents are actually created and worked with and to interview staff below the supervisory level. For example, managers may not use documents the same way that frontline workers do. In addition, the managers may not even know exactly how their staff actually uses the documents and records. To gain a good understanding of the full use of critical e-documents you must document their use at multiple levels of the organization.

Setting Up Interviews

Once interviewees have been identified, then it's time to schedule meetings with them. There are online scheduling tools to facilitate this, such as doodle.com, and some e-mail and calendar programs include scheduling features as well. Since staff members often have hectic work schedules, it is important to give them as much advance notice as possible so that they may be able to attend.

The interviews should be scheduled and tracked through the project manager (PM) and the appropriate business unit managers. The time and place of the interview should be confirmed with all staff. In certain cases, it may make sense to include a line manager and a key support staffer at the meeting so that you can get their perspectives on how the documents and records are used.

It is essential that all interviewees understand the objectives and benefits of the document lifecycle security (DLS) project or information asset protection program. Set out those objectives and benefits up front, in initial meetings and at the beginning of each interview. A summary document or memo may help solidify this.

There is no specified length for the interviews as they may vary from person to person. However, a good rule of thumb is no longer than one hour. When scheduling, remember to allow enough time between interviews in case one unexpectedly runs over. This will also provide ample time for you to document the interview before the next one begins.[6]

Tips for Planning Interviews

Take the following considerations into account when planning interviews:

- **Proximity.** Ideally, the interview should be conducted at the person's workspace. If not, it should be as close to the workspace as possible.
- **Advance Notice.** Consider providing the interviewee with questions in advance so they may contemplate answers, collect their thoughts, and gather preparatory information.
- **Verification.** It may be helpful to make any research and/or inventory documentation available in advance of the interview so that it can be verified.
- **Sensitivity.** Be mindful that often people feel their job is threatened when their area is being studied. Put them at ease and clearly state the goals for the project and the objectives of the interview in support of it.[7]

Preparing Interview Questions

The PM should develop a list of questions about the use and storage of confidential e-documents to complete an inventory of them. Third-party consultants will have prepared these in advance and will be able to fine-tune them. At times, open-ended questions are a good approach, such as "How would you solve this issue?" It gives interviewees a chance to voice their concerns and to contribute to the ultimate solution for the project. If using a detailed questionnaire, be sure to walk the interviewee through it. Regardless of the method used, the end result is most important—obtaining the most useful and accurate information possible.[8]

Necessary Information

Interview questions should cover the following:

- Department, program, or service area being targeted.
- Its primary function and activities.
- Confidential or sensitive e-document types.
- Regulatory, legal, and governance requirements the target area must comply with.
- Core business processes, and their sequence.
- Document retention and final disposition requirements.
- Information management applications utilized.

Drafting Questions

Questions should have a focus on uncovering those most sensitive e-documents, how they are created, where they come from, where they go, and how they are stored. Questions should be adjusted for appropriateness of organizational level (i.e., do not ask clerical staff questions that are management level, and vice-versa). Tailor the questions, narrow their scope, and zero in on the most useful information for the project or program.

It is important to know a brief history of the target area, as it can provide a context for the document use and security appraisal. But the core focus should be on *e-documents,* how they are used, how they are secured, and their retention and disposition schedules.[9]

Prioritizing: Document and Records Value Assessment

Once critical e-documents and records have been identified, their uses documented within the target area, their value needs to be determined, at least to the degree that they can be generally prioritized. Documents will have primary and possibly secondary values. Logically, the most valuable documents need to be secured first with the most protections.

The business records' values will also determine the final disposition of the records when they have reached the end of their retention period.

> Documents can have value in different ways such as financial, legal, technical, or administrative.

Start by tracking the use of the documents themselves through the business process; identify each step either through a narrative or a business process flow diagram, or both. Note the job description of each person who acts on the documents in the process and exactly what they *do* with the documents. Consider key types of (document, information asset) values. Documents and records can have "*administrative, financial, scientific/technical, legal, evidential or informational value.*"(italics added)[10]

Use your organization's strategic plan and goals to determine which types of values carry more weight, and then sort the group of documents types, prioritizing them as best you can. This is akin to letting cream rise to the top of fresh milk—you then skim the cream (i.e., the most valuable documents) and go back to the users, perhaps in a roundtable meeting, and hash out which documents to secure first, considering various methods and technologies to secure these most valuable of information assets.[11]

Second Phase of Implementation

Once the first project phase is completed and the initial target area's critical e-documents are secured, there are a few options for moving forward to continue to lock down and secure the organization's confidential information assets.

Often, these second-stage areas may be with core information management systems like enterprise resource planning (ERP) systems, financial and accounting systems, PLM systems, customer relationship management (CRM) systems, and the like. E-document security software such as information rights management (IRM) needs to plug in to these systems to protect the data and documents stored in the applications.

These core information management applications are certainly high-value next-step targets. And they will show substantial improvements in DLS protection that are important for the enterprise. But these may not be the most prudent ones to target after the initial phase.

Although integrating document and data security into core enterprise applications is commonly the second phase, *organizations would be well-advised to look at their vital records program,* ensure that these most critical records are protected, and that IG policies are updated. This is particularly important in today's fast-changing business technology environment, where security threats abound, both inside and outside the organization.

The enterprise cannot operate without its vital records, and therefore they are the most important ones to keep secure in order for the enterprise to continue to be viable. This raises them to the top of the list of candidate areas to target.

Unfortunately, many organizations will fall into the trap of not dealing with their most serious issues, instead plucking off the showy applications that have easy appeal, the ones which vendors will push for and that resonate with executives. They may, in fact, get by without any negative ramifications or disruptions in operations; but still, the most judicious path is to target the organization's vital records quite early on in the phased roll-out of document lifecycle security (DLS) capabilities.

Chapter Summary: Key Points

- Projects focused on securing confidential e-documents are usually launched because a business driver has made it an imperative in a target area.
- First, determine the roles and responsibilities of a representative cross section of personnel in the target area. Then, find out what

key document types they work with and create an inventory by document type.

- Schedule interviews to uncover document use and prioritization; taking into account interviewees' limited time these should not exceed one hour.

- Workers in the trenches often use documents in ways their superiors do not.

- The fastest, easiest, and most efficient way to implement the document security program and technologies is to leverage the existing taxonomy.

- It is important to demonstrate success in a key target area that is limited in scope. Often second-stage areas may be combined with core enterprise information management systems, although this may not be the most prudent approach.

- Organizations considering a next step of implementation should look at their vital records program to see where gaps or vulnerabilities exist and then apply updated information governance (IG) policies and security technologies.

Notes

1. The State of Massachusetts, "201 CMR 17.00: Standards for the Protection of Personal Information of Residents of the Commonwealth," www.mass.gov/ocabr/docs/idtheft/201cmr1700reg.pdf, retrieved August 26, 2011.
2. Paula Lederman, via e-mail to the author on August 25, 2011.
3. Charmaine Brooks, via e-mail to the author, August 24, 2011.
4. Government of Alberta, "Records and Information Management," July 2004, pp. 71–76, www.rimp.gov.ab.ca/publications/pdf/SchedulingGuide.pdf, retrieved December 25, 2011.
5. Ibid.
6. Ibid.
7. Ibid.
8. Ibid.
9. Ibid.
10. Ibid.
11. Government of Alberta, "Records and Information Management," July 2004, pp. 113–199, www.rimp.gov.ab.ca/publications/pdf/SchedulingGuide.pdf, retrieved December 26, 2011.

CHAPTER 16

Procurement: The Buying Process

G etting a good start is important. Always begin a project or program based on a defined business need. This is the only way the project will have the steam to carry it to completion. Next, determine the potential business impact of solving the need. This is where cost justification and a return on investment (ROI) come into play. Many times it is best to use ranges, as it is difficult to make exact ROI projections. The project team may have several scenarios, based on differing assumptions.

Evaluation and Selection Process: RFI, RFP, or RFQ?

Start with a clean slate and inventory all critical document types in the target area. Keep the focus narrow. There may be some redesign of document-based business processes that are required, irrespective of technologies or vendor offerings. Ask the question, "What is the absolute best way to do this process?" Then apply technology to speed it up and increase security and control.

> Never begin a project or program without a clearly defined business need.

Then, take this inventory of critical documents—including volumes, projected increases, and basic business process steps—and define the requirements any vendor must meet to successfully implement it. These requirements will become the basis for evaluating potential solutions.

There are several ways to approach the procurement process. The one that is the best fit for your organization will depend on its timeframe, budget, corporate culture, and the nature of the project itself. Although issuing a request for proposal (RFP) is the most common procurement approach, there is not necessarily a preferred approach. The one that suits your organization and its situation may not be the RFP route and, in fact, may end up combining several methods.

In this chapter, several basic approaches to procuring software, hardware, and professional services are reviewed and key caveats and tips are provided.

Request for Information

A good way to start the buying process is with a *request for information* (*RFI*). An RFI is a simple, short request sent to potential bidding vendors to gather basic information about their firms and solution offerings. An RFI can also help you gather ballpark pricing information that will help you establish your budget or consider alternative solutions if the pricing is much higher than expected. An RFI lets these companies know that an organization is entering the sales cycle and allows them to plan for the resources they will need to address the opportunity.

One thing that most buying organizations don't realize is that these potential bidders have a choice: They do not have to respond to information requests. And if a supplying organization makes the determination early on that the deal is wired for another vendor, or that it has little chance in winning the business, it may make the decision not to compete. So it is important to maintain an unbiased approach to keep the vendors' interest and arrive at the best solution at the best price.

> An RFI should be limited to 20 questions or less. It is used create a snapshot of potential vendors and to provide more information for an RFP.

It is critical not to waste vendor resources in the evaluation phase as vendors can *and will* refuse to compete. This can lead to an embarrassing situation (e.g., not enough bidders) for the project team and can lead to a project failure or non-decision.

A basic RFI should contain only 10–20 questions and should let the vendor know when to expect an RFP document that provides the details needed to supply a suitable bid. It also helps to winnow out the vendors to determine which are viable and which are not.

Basic RFI questions could be:

1. How long has your firm been in business?
2. What were the last two year's revenues and profit/loss overall? In the e-document security (or information rights management [IRM] or data loss prevention [DLP]) division?
3. Describe your product/solution offerings and provide detailed data sheets.

4. Provide at least two profiles of major customers of yours related to our project. They do not have to be named but rather can be referred to in general terms.
5. Does your firm focus on particular vertical markets?
6. How many employees do you have? How many did you have three years ago?
7. Is there any pending litigation with existing customers?
8. How is your support structured and staffed?
9. What are your support escalation mechanisms for solving customer problems?
10. Can your firm provide or make arrangements for escrow of software source code in the event of financial default?
11. What is your pricing structure and cost per user? Is pricing for concurrent users or dedicated seats? Do you offer enterprise licensing?
12. What is the cost of support? When do support costs commence?

Additional questions specific to the project should also be included, but the RFI should not exceed 20 questions and should not ask for much detail. Make sure that enough information about your upcoming project is provided to give the vendors the opportunity to respond with salient answers, and to pique their interest. Also, provide enough information about the number of archive documents, daily incoming documents, and the number of users so that bidders can provide ballpark pricing. The bidder should understand that you are trying to develop a project budget and need their estimates to do this.

Request for Proposal

An *RFP* is used to make a major business purchase (e.g., software, hardware, professional services) when it is clear that many vendors can provide a solution. Typically, project requirements and specifications are clearly defined in an RFP, meaning the buyer is looking for the best fit, as determined by a vendor's total bid. Frequently, an RFP is the best approach when price is not the leading factor in the organization's decision. Also, an RFP is helpful since cross-functional skill sets from the issuing organization must be considered, and a range of departments (e.g., IT, records management, human resources, legal, risk management, and others) are consulted. If a third-party consultant is used, they will solicit input from these groups and develop the detailed questions and rating system for the RFP.

> An RFP is issued when requirements are clearly defined and there is a field of qualified vendors to select from.

The RFP process can be costly and time consuming and may not always produce the expected results, even after extensive vendor evaluations, demonstrations, reference checks, and revisions to both the RFP and resultant proposals. Having the original RFP and original vendor responses allows buyers and bidders to review the process based on the documentation and determine what may have gone wrong.

The RFP process also serves the purpose of educating the purchasing organization's project team on a technology they are not familiar with, and that can be a moving target, since the technologies are changing rapidly and implementation issues are unique. For the vendors, the RFP provides a detailed set of specifications for customizing the bid.

The RFP provides a common blueprint for both sides to understand the project needs, and it aims to provide a fair and objective way to evaluate the bids. The RFP is the beginning of what will be a long-term relationship with the winning vendor. It provides an open forum so bidding firms may ask questions about requirements and specifications in the RFP. At times, the vendors may question some of the requirements.

Providing a *bidders' conference* to allow for questions is a good way to keep the process open and transparent while allowing an RFP to be fine-tuned and clarified based on vendors' feedback.

The buying organization may also question vendor responses and request a revised response and quote. For instance, if one vendor has bid very little training compared to the other vendors, it would need to address that issue and the buying organization would then take the revised response into consideration.

The final RFP and final winning proposal will often change in the course of evaluation. An RFP can be a significant undertaking that require resources from different departments. E-documents span across all departments since several key departments, such as IT, legal, records management, risk management, and even human resources, may play a role.

Creating an RFP for a document lifecycle security (DLS)/information governance (IG) project will require time and resources from multiple departments.

The key steps in writing an RFP are:

1. **Identify need.** This may be spurred by an information breach, a lawsuit, or new regulations, but some initial analysis will be required to get the funding and operational priority for the project. The initial high-level analysis should focus on risk/return and delineate what might occur, in the potential worst case if nothing is done. This step may be undertaken by a small team from IT, records management, and the legal department.
2. **Allocate budget.** This is crucial to get the project moving. Underfunded projects die and waste management time and resources.

3. **Select and formalize the project team.** This should include individuals from key departments as well as those who will be responsible for implementing and supporting the new technologies. The basic team should include individuals from the aforementioned departments, as well as corporate communications, education, purchasing, finance, and operations, and any other teams that manage efficiency or business process optimization.
4. **Undertake a detailed analysis of requirements.** This will include historical, current, and projected document and transaction volumes, document value analysis, business process analysis, and technological requirements. Also any e-document security breaches and their (potential) impact.
5. **Survey the marketplace.** Look for a broad range of vendors that may satisfy the buying organization's requirements.
6. **Solicit basic information from vendors.** Usually in the form of an RFI or query letter sent ahead of an RFP. This will give the buying organization information as to technological capabilities, ballpark pricing, and additional ideas for the RFP.

Don't drag the process out and drain vendor resources. A long, drawn-out process with an overly complex RFP *is not recommended*. Ask the relevant questions and get to the short list as fast as you can, usually within 90 days. See the demonstrations and presentations, do your reference checks, and narrow the list to two to three viable competitors. Then the competition heats up.

If the decision has already been made and the executive sponsor or project manager (PM) are trying to justify it through a RFP process, the vendors will soon sniff this out, and the project team will be sitting there with no valid competitors to compare.

Request for Quote

A *request for quote* (*RFQ*) is used to solicit bids when detailed requirements are known or a project is relatively straightforward. Often this applies to adding disk drive capacity, buying additional PCs, or expanding networks. It can also apply to buying an enterprise license for information rights management (IRM) software once a pilot has been conducted, or there is another source of confidence about a particular vendor (e.g., that is the vendor of choice for other enterprise-wide solutions).

Negotiated Procurement

A *negotiated procurement* is a way to acquire a new system when the buying organization wants to make a rapid decision and requirements are known.

Often a trusted consulting firm will be engaged to solicit bids, negotiate with vendors, and make a recommendation for procurement. This approach can be a better fit than RFP when cost is a leading issue.

Evaluating Software Providers: Key Criteria

Often, project teams focus on a detailed list of features when evaluating and selecting software and hardware. They create a complex matrix of priorities and weights to score the vendors and *voilà:* A winner emerges.

There are two main problems with this approach:

(1) The manipulation of weights and scoring values can skew an evaluation toward a bias that some members of the team may hold.

(2) It fails to aptly consider the big picture and the long term, which may be the most important considerations.

There are (at least) 10 key issues that must be considered when evaluating software and hardware vendors:

1. *Technological fit:* Does the vendor have the right type of solution considering the business needs and technological infrastructure environment? Can they integrate with the current and planned IT infrastructure (including operating systems, databases, e-mail systems, hardware platform support, line of business systems, and legacy systems)?
2. *Company viability:* What are the vendor's financial strengths, operating history, and culture? It is safe to rely on them for the long term?
3. *Track record:* What is the vendor's history of implementation success and ongoing service? Has the software and hardware been reliable in the past?
4. *Support:* Does the vendor offer adequate staffing, response time, and service-level agreements (SLAs)?
5. *Access to senior management:* Are clients and prospects able to communicate with senior management, as needed? Is senior management involved enough in the purchase and support processes?
6. *Partnerships:* Does the vendor have partnerships with third parties that present a particular value or hindrance?
7. *Technology architecture and scalability:* What is the architecture and scalability of the vendor's service? How well does it meet the needs of the buyer's organization?
8. *Total cost of ownership (TCO):* What will the purchase cost? Be sure to understand up-front costs, as well as software and support fees.

9. *Ease:* How easy is the system to implement? How easy is it to use? Remember that complicated processes often result in failure of adoption at the knowledge-worker level.
10. *Training:* Does the vendor offer training recommendations and capabilities that meet the buying organization's needs?

Technological Fit

This comes down to the basic technological suitability of the vendor. Most vendors in a particular market segment have the tendency to say they can essentially be all things to all companies but this is fundamentally untrue. There are always *basic* scenarios where they fit best.

If your need for features requires a lot of customization to the software, it may not be the right solution. Generally, the more out-of-the-box capabilities offered that meet your requirements, the better. But often vendors will profess to be able to *integrate* when they really mean *interface.* Interfacing involves writing some custom software code that makes your organization a one-of-a-kind installation and therefore more difficult to support.

If your business scenario is one that stretches their capabilities, or their basic architecture conflicts with the direction your organization is moving, it may not be a fit. Suppose your organization is an all-IBM shop planning to move to all Microsoft platforms within two years. Some of the vendors on your short list might have tight integration with Microsoft, and perhaps even some helpful conversion tools. The decision must lean toward those vendors.

Other details will need to be negotiated, such as recourse in the event of default and gross performance guarantees. The result both parties are looking to avoid is for the buyer to be so disappointed in the system after implementation, they want to give it back after it has been installed and entrenched into daily operations. Try to work things out.

Often, an outside consultant can bring the pressure to bear since they hold the keys to the vendor's future success, and the vendor does not want their failure widely reported. Again, litigation with the software vendor should be considered the last line of defense.

Company Viability

Once the field of prospective vendors has been narrowed down to a possible three or four, the project team should look at each prospective vendor's current financial statements. If the vendor is privately held, sometimes this information is difficult to obtain from them directly.

They may be hiding something or they may, in fact, have nothing to hide. Additional information about financial strength can be found from services like Hoover's and Dun & Bradstreet. Also, some assumptions can be made if the vendor will reveal their current and historic staffing levels, as workforce growth can be an indicator of financial strength and stability. The rate at which they are adding installed customers can also be considered when financials are not available. Another option is to ask for the financial statements and offer to sign a nondisclosure agreement.

The business viability evaluation should necessarily consider the number of years the vendor has been in business. There is not much difference in a vendor that has been operating for 10 years and one that has been operating for 20—in fact, the older organization may be more wedded to older technologies. But if one firm has been operating for five years or less, they should be scrutinized more closely. The project team may want to ask for a software escrow agreement that can be invoked in the event the vendor becomes financially unstable or goes out of business.

Some vendors may tout their rapid growth as a sign of their success and viability. But it depends on *how* they supported that growth. Companies that have been funded with venture capital or have gone public through an initial public offering (IPO) will be pressured to grow topline revenues by investors seeking a greater return. Often, this is not healthy for the company. The amalgamation of technologies and corporate cultures can quickly cause real problems in integration and performance, both from a technology and human standpoint. Too many competing technical architectures and fiefdoms can sometimes spell risk for customers.

Organic, slower growth is usually the sign of a healthy, stable company. Overall, look at viability as a big-picture evaluation that considers more than just current financial statements or number of installed customers.

Track Record

This may seem obvious but it is not as easy to evaluate as it may seem. Vendors will provide the project team with a host of press releases and contact information from happy customers. What is needed to complete an evaluation on this measure is to find out what has happened in the trenches. Yes, call the organizations and contacts provided—but go further. Ask those references for names that are not on the list, both inside their organization and at other recent clients. Most vendors have had some projects that have gone wrong. What is important is how they handled those challenges and how satisfied the customer ended up being.

Support

This element is absolutely crucial. Since most vendors typically make 18 to 20 percent of the initial software/hardware purchase price *each year* in support, this is their bread and butter. It is also critical for the success of your project. Check into response times, escalation procedures, and contractual obligations the vendor makes to supporting installations.

Although most software and hardware diagnostics are performed on-line today, proximity helps. The closer the planned installation is to the headquarters of the vendor, the better the support will be. They can quickly dispatch a top expert, or you can have lunch with the CEO. There is simply more access to more resources. Even a nearby branch office will help.

This does not mean you exclude vendors from out of your state or region. A lot can be accomplished with remote diagnostics. But certainly, the first line of support should not be located in India or Malaysia if your organization is based in the United States.

SLAs will delineate hours that support is available, guaranteed response time (and that return phone call is different from actually solving your problem), escalation procedures (which deal with how and when the service problem is sent up the chain of command), and other support details. The project team may also want to specify the level of credentials and experience for those responding when there is a serious problem. And, if a problem lingers, resulting in system downtime, the client and vendor can negotiate gross performance guarantees and specific financial penalties to be paid to the client organization. A daily rate of $1,000 is a good place to begin negotiations since the vendor will never agree to be responsible for any damages caused by their lack of support or software performance. That takes litigation, which all parties want to avoid if at all possible.

Access to Senior Management

This is particularly important in large projects, or in the pilot stage of potentially large projects. It is always a good idea to negotiate the final terms and conditions of a contract with an executive who is at least two to three levels above the field-level salesperson. The higher the level, the better. Of course, the CEO is the ideal choice. High-level executives feel valuable when they walk out of a meeting with a signed contract. This establishes a base for a strong relationship between the client and the executive, which can help an organization achieve a priority status in the future.

Try to schedule the meeting for 10:30–11:00 AM so there might be the possibility of spending more time with the executive at lunch. When assurances are gained from an executive, and business cards and handshakes are exchanged, the project gains extra leverage and this improves its chances for success. If things start to go awry, it is time to pick up the phone and make any issues known to that key vendor executive.

Partnerships

Strong vendors have strong strategic alliances with third-party vendors. These alliances allow them to capitalize on an exchange of technology or services while minimizing costs. Alliances create leverage. Often these third-party relationships can spell the difference in project success. Suppose that your vendor of choice is a small integrator, yet they have an alliance with IBM. The project team may want to negotiate for IBM to be the prime vendor (like a general contractor) on the project to ensure its success. The smaller integrator will then work as a subcontractor and the project risk is reduced. Of course, it will cost more for IBM to assume this risk.

Technology Architecture and Scalability

The project team will need to look at more than just pretty demonstrations of user interfaces. Demonstrations always look nice. What is needed is to look under the hood to see how the software was designed, and evolved. Often, systems are interfaced to add functionality. There is a big difference in interfacing disparate systems, integrating different systems, and a single system that was designed holistically from the ground up. In each case, vendors will claim their system is seamlessly integrated. But if their original product was designed to be optimized for, say, the IBM OS/400 operating system running a proprietary database, and then years later they made it work with IBM AIX, and now they have reworked it for all Microsoft Windows platforms without rewriting the system from the ground up, there will be system overhead created from inefficient software design. This means that as your project increases in number of users, the system performance will lag. So it is just as important *how* a vendor arrives at a particular solution as getting there itself.

Total Cost of Ownership

Most inexperienced IT buyers can be easily fooled by savvy software sales-people. It is not just the sticker price that your team must consider but the total cost of ownership (TCO) over the life of the installed system, usually considered over a range of three to five years. TCO includes not only initial implementation price but also change orders (and the change order approval process), which occur when changes to the project are made outside of the original proposal. This can be a real *gotcha*.

Timing and pricing of software support fees are also critical. Questions to ask include: Is there a 90-day or one-year warranty period with no support fees? What percentage are the fees of the list price? (An annual rate of 18 to 20 percent is average.) What are the planned increases and maximum annual increases? What are the costs of hardware maintenance, increases, and trade-in/upgrade costs? All these questions must be asked to gain a true picture of the TCO.

Ease

Some systems are commercial off the shelf (COTS) and are easily implemented. There will be a number of parameters to set up but these are like simple switches you can turn on or off. Other systems are very complex and require much custom information technology (IT) development work and additional training. These work well when your organization has very complex requirements and the IT staff to support them, but the implementation is difficult, time consuming, and costly. And ongoing support is also costly, since you will have installed a one-off system. These are trade-offs that your organization will want to consider.

Remember also that systems that are easier to use succeed more readily because knowledge workers adopt them more readily. This can be the difference between a project's success or failure.

Training

If a vendor does not include training, or if training is grossly under bid (less than 10 percent of the system implementation cost), *it is telling*. Often, they are cutting back to compete on price. The project will suffer. Sometimes, they just don't understand how crucial training is to implementation success. The client organization should consider the training staff's credentials, processes, and availability when making software and hardware purchase decisions. *The perfect system won't work without user acceptance, and user acceptance depends on training.*

Negotiating Contracts: Ensuring the Decision

Poorly crafted contracts are harbingers of project failure.

Unfortunately, when problems arise mid-implementation, it is often too late. The key principle to keep in mind is that litigation or arbitration is *never* the preferred way to clarify a contract: It should be so clearly written that both sides understand its terms and they never have to go back to the contract to enforce it.

There is an odd incongruity: It seems that the larger the organization, the worse it is at negotiating contracts. Maybe that is due to the layers of bureaucracy, but more likely it comes down to contract negotiators' failing to respect expenditures outside their area. If contracts are considered with the scrutiny of a small business owner who is very cautious with money, many potential problems can be avoided.

First, when negotiating a major contract, understand the company's motivations. Remember, the salesperson has a boss, and that boss has a boss, and so on, so there is built-in pressure to sign deals as large as possible, as fast as possible, and without giving up a lot of unusual terms that will be difficult to get approved or achieve.

Similar to car dealers, technology vendors feel more pressure at the end of each fiscal quarter, and that pressure is at a fevered pitch in the final month of the vendor's fiscal year. Their performance will determine annual bonuses, promotions, and quota performance. Many times, someone's job is on the line. No deal equals a loss of employment and whole collection of personal and financial problems. Sign the deal this month and the salespeople are heroes, don't sign the deal, they lose their jobs. This is reality. As a buyer of technology, the best shot at a good deal is available at these times. *So make sure to find out how the vendor's fiscal year runs and when it ends.*

Second, gauge the strategic importance of the project to the vendor. If it is the deployment of a relatively new product or technology set, the vendor is more highly motivated to agree to terms that are advantageous to the client organization. This is because racking up sales and references is the surest way to make the new technology sell faster. If the current project makes the client organization the first or second customer, there is much greater leverage than if it is customer number 52. That's a fact, and it can be used as leverage to get performance guarantees, price concessions, and additional add-on products and services.

> Never sign a vendor's standard contract without modifying the terms and conditions to include some specific assurances.

Third, and related to the previous point, is the potential for future revenue for the vendor. This could mean the project at hand or from the greater marketplace. If the current project is a $300,000 pilot project to prove a concept, and the carrot at the end is a $3 million enterprise deal, the vendor is going to be more flexible in initial negotiations in order to establish a beachhead. In like manner, if the project is the first in a key industry segment the vendor wants to penetrate, and he or she can see the additional revenue a signed contract will bring, the vendor will again be more flexible in negotiations.

Typically customers/end users sign a standard contract. *Never do this.*

Standard contracts are heavily weighted in the vendor's favor. Decipher every phrase and dig into the contract language at a detailed level.

This doesn't mean starting from scratch—a very difficult thing to do—but considering negotiation of performance warranties, SLAs and prescribed penalties in the case of nonperformance.

It is recommended that the vendor's response to the RFP be folded into the contract, so that its official responses are contractually binding. If a vendor claims to have a feature or functionality, it should be able to contractually stand by its contention. This prevents vendors from responding with anything to get the deal and holds them legally accountable if they do.

Once the project team gets to the contract negotiation stage, it should have a very detailed project plan with a timeline and specific milestones along that timeline. Include this in the contract. As a practical matter, it is best to tie payments to milestone achievements. So when the project is halfway done, they have been paid half the money. This sounds like common sense, but we have found many examples of naive negotiations by end-user organizations. Here are a few:

- A large southern U.S. nuclear power facility wanted to replace its existing document imaging and workflow system with a more advanced one. It started by conducting a small pilot in a relatively obscure area—stockholder services—at around $200,000. That seems like a good move. But the requirements were so light it didn't make for a good trial run (for the purchasing organization). Then, for whatever reason, the vendor convinced the purchaser to pay the entire next phase of the project—a $1 million license fee—up front. The problem was that when the implementation got into the engineering areas of the company with more complex requirements, it came out that the software had a fundamental architectural weakness: It could not handle sub-indexes beneath the primary indexes. The software couldn't be completely redesigned and the vendor had received all the money, so the deadlock ended in litigation. This could have been avoided by a more relevant pilot area selection and progress payments tied to milestone successes.
- Years ago, AT&T's tax department called on IMERGE Consulting to review a document management system decision it was making. It had a proposal on the table from a Big 5 consulting firm (which was also their audit firm in the pre-Sarbanes-Oxley days) but something didn't seem right. The business need was there. They were duplicating efforts when presenting their business case to states and municipalities to minimize AT&T's tax burden. They could save millions in taxes and penalties by forming expeditious and detailed responses. In evaluating the proposal, we found that no monthly maintenance fees were included, no Oracle license fees were included (and they would be required), and the proposed solution was overpriced and not a good fit. We brought in a couple of viable competitors, negotiated the cost down by more

than $1 million, and forced the Big 5 consultants to render a complete proposal. AT&T's staff voted for the recommended alternative solution, which had two CEOs from different parts of the world flying in to agree to terms. Despite this, the staff was overruled by a distant manager with ties to a West Coast Big 5 firm, justifying the contract by saying "we have such a good business relationship with them anyway." Of course, people got promoted, quit, or otherwise moved on, and the project was fraught with problems in implementation.

- The City of New Orleans had negotiated an outsourcing contract for $25 million with a major provider. The Civil Service Commission felt that something was amiss since the contract would displace the entire IT staff, yet no IT staffers were slated to be laid off. When inspecting the contract, it took less than five minutes to determine some major flaws, the biggest of which was that the contract could be modified with the stroke of a pen by one person to increase it to over $50 million. Also, the outsourcing company could not be held liable for any damages in the event of a problem; service levels were not defined; and no training was included. In fact, the contracting company did not have to achieve any milestones at all and it would be entitled to payments of more than $400,000 per month—retroactively for six months! A public hearing ensued, which proved somewhat embarrassing to city officials, but the contract was amended to include training to appease the Civil Service Commission, and the project moved forward, ultimately toward disaster. Within less than four years, the City's CIO and the crooked contractors pleaded guilty to corruption and bribery charges and were sent to federal prison.

- A state agency decided to bring in a specific best-of-breed software vendor to cure its IT ills. It confected a process whereby the business processes of the organization would be redesigned to fit the software functionality—the exact opposite of normal best practice approaches. In evaluating consultants, it was determined that the project evaluation was biased and incomplete, and the entire bid process had to be halted while a best practices review took place. A year later, nothing had moved forward toward implementation.

More Contract Caveats

What will vendors *not* agree to under any circumstances? They will not agree to guarantee to save the enterprise time or money on a certain task. They will not agree to a performance guarantee that involves interaction or interfaces with another vendor's product. *But if pressed hard, they will agree to warrant that their software performs as advertised.*

What if the vendor goes out of business? The client organization normally would get the vendor to agree to put the software source code into escrow, in the event they go bankrupt. But that is not good enough. A case in point: IBM owned 25 percent of Image Business Systems (IBS), an early document-imaging entrant. No one thought it could fail. Its customers had the escrow provision in their contracts, but it could be invoked only in the event of a formal bankruptcy. The financially ailing IBS downsized to just two employees, then it held up its customers by forcing them to pay $200,000 each to get the source code—it later went out of business anyway. To avoid this situation, you can negotiate escrow provisions that are invoked when certain liquidity or other financial ratios indicate a company is on the rocks.

In summary, do the required homework, justify the project based on business need, and use both carrots and sticks to formulate a contract that enforces achievement of milestones and software performance. Then move forward with the enterprise's new partner into an era of productivity and results.

How to Pick a Consulting Firm: Evaluation Criteria

If the client organization chooses to engage a consulting firm to assist in making IG and DLS project decisions (or any IT-related decision), there are some key criteria to consider:

- **Are they vendor-independent?** You must find a consulting firm without economic ties to a particular vendor or vendors, as these ties—and financial pressures—necessarily color their evaluation. Some firms will say, "We have ties to all the major vendors, so we know them and we'll select the best one for you." This doesn't wash, since each vendor agreement has certain quota levels, commission levels, bonus levels, and payment terms. So naturally, the consulting company (really an integrator or reseller) and salesperson will tend to maximize their profits by selecting the system that is best for them, not your organization.

  There must be no economic interest tied to the recommendations.
- **Will they live with their recommendations?** Some consulting firms are independent, but they won't see a project to fruition. They will help you generate an RFP, but they won't evaluate the vendors, assist in negotiation, and oversee the project implementation successfully. This way, they can never be blamed for making poor decisions.

  Firms like this don't have the real-world expertise that is derived from actual implementations. There are problems that do not manifest themselves until the project proceeds. Napoleon said, "No battle plan ever survives an encounter with the enemy." This means that things change once you are engaged in a project implementation. For instance, software documentation is not always correct, and there are other nuances that are found only during implementation. So, you must ask if they are able to go beyond the theoretical to the real and willing to be held accountable for their recommendations.

- **Do they have the breadth of knowledge required?** Many firms in the IT consulting marketplace focus on skill sets and technologies that have become out-of-date. So their recommendations will reflect this focus, and they won't have the current experience in IT to make sound recommendations. They are likely to go with whichever firm they have established a relationship with, rather than the optimum choice for the implementing organization.

  When beginning a project, it is advisable to delve further and determine if the consulting firm has expertise in newer technologies like IRM, social media (SM), DLS, cloud computing, electronic records management (ERM), e-mail archiving, and collaborative software.

  Also, many firms do not have broad multidisciplinary expertise in areas like DLS, records management, business process management, knowledge management, and change management.

  The key to the decision is: Does the consulting firm have the independence and expertise in the breadth of methodologies and technologies to determine a truly optimal solution?

- **What related work have they done?** Look at specific application areas, industry vertical markets, and project-specific business process and technological requirements. The more closely related the firm's experience, the more relevant, and the more likely the firm will perform well.

- **How many top-notch, experienced people does the firm have?** Often firms will parade out a few top people to impress you and close the deal, then you won't see them again as underlings are thrown at your project. So ask, "Who will be assigned to this project? Can you contractually guarantee these people and suitable replacements in the event of illness or other factors?"

- **What do their clients say about them?** Good, strong firms will have no trouble providing references to call to verify their credentials—as many as needed to make the project team comfortable. To really do the required homework, dig deeper and contact others in the end-user organization that worked on the project (who were *not* named by the consulting firm) to determine a consensus.

- **What do their peers say about them, (i.e., what is their reputation in the industry?)** Determine this by looking at how many presentations the firm gives at major conferences, how many articles they have written as experts on related topics, and by asking disinterested third parties about the firm's reputation.

- **How stable are they?** This comes down to how long they have been established, and how long top people stay at the firm.

Consider all the previous factors and make an overall judgment as to whether a third-party consulting firm is needed, and then find the one that best fits your project.

When making a software/system decision, determine whether a vendor can meet your requirements and whether or not the bidding firm would be a good partner over the long term. After all, it's a marriage of sorts.

Chapter Summary: Key Points

- A request for information (RFI) is a simple, short request sent to potential bidding vendors to gather basic information about their firms and solution offerings.
- A request for proposal (RFP) is used to purchase software and hardware when it is clear that many vendors can provide a solution, project requirements and specifications can be determined, and price is not the leading factor in the organization's decision.
- It is recommended that the vendor's response to the RFP be folded into the contract, so that its official responses are contractually binding.
- A request for quote (RFQ) is used to solicit bids when detailed requirements are known or the project is very simple.
- A negotiated procurement is a way to acquire a new system when the buying organization wants to make a rapid decision and requirements are known. Often a trusted consulting firm will be engaged to solicit bids, negotiate with vendors, and make a recommendation for procurement at a discounted price.
- Ten key issues that must be considered when evaluating vendors are: 1) technological fit, 2) company viability, 3) track record, 4) support levels, 5) access to senior management, 6) partnerships, 7) technology architecture and scalability, 8) total cost of ownership (TCO), 9) ease, and 10) training.
- Poorly crafted contracts are the harbingers of failed projects. There is an odd incongruity: It seems that the larger the organization, the worse it is at negotiating contracts.

(continued)

(*continued*)

- Never sign a vendor's standard contract. Always add additional assurances.
- Financial and career pressure builds for vendors to a greater intensity at the end of each fiscal quarter, and is at a fevered pitch in the final month of the vendor's fiscal year end. This is the best time to negotiate contracts.
- Vendors will not agree to guarantee to save the enterprise time or money on a certain task. They will not agree to a performance guarantee that involves interaction or interfaces with another vendor's product. But if pressed hard, they will agree to warrant that their software performs as advertised.

CHAPTER 17

Maintaining a Secure Environment for Information Assets

Keeping an enterprise's confidential information assets secure requires vigilant and consistent monitoring and auditing to ensure that security measures are effective and information governance (IG) policies are followed and enforced. If proper controls are in place this should become a regular part of the enterprise's operations.

Monitoring and Accountability

This requires a continuous tightening down and expansion of protections and the implementation of newer, strategic technologies. Information technology (IT) developments and innovations that can foster the effort must be steadily monitored and evaluated, and those technology subsets that can assist in providing security need to be incorporated into the mix.

The policies themselves must be reviewed and updated periodically to accommodate changes in the business environment, laws, regulations, and technology. Program gaps and failures must be addressed and the effort should continue to improve and adapt to new types of security threats.

That means accountability—some individual must remain responsible for an IG policy's administration and results[1]—perhaps the executive sponsor for the project becomes the chief security officer (CSO); or the project manager for the initial target area becomes the chief IG officer or IG Czar; or the chief executive officer (CEO) continues ownership of the project and drives its active improvement. The organization may also decide to form an IG board, steering committee, or team with specific responsibilities for monitoring, maintaining, and advancing the program.

However it takes shape, a program to secure confidential information assets must be ongoing, dynamic, and aggressive in its execution in order to remain effective.

Maintaining a program for securing confidential information assets requires that someone is accountable for continual monitoring and refinement of policies and tools.

Continuous Process Improvement

This requires implementing principles of continuous process improvement (CPI). CPI is a "never-ending effort to discover and eliminate the main causes of problems. It accomplishes this by using small-steps improvements rather than implementing one huge improvement. In Japan, the word *kaizen* reflects this gradual and constant process as it is enacted throughout the organization, regardless of department, position, or level.[2] To remain effective, the program must continue using CPI methods and techniques.

Maintaining and improving the program will require monitoring tools, periodic audits, and regular meetings for discussion and approval of changes to improve the program. It will require a cross-section of representatives from IT, legal, records management, compliance, risk management, and functional business units participating actively and citing possible threats and sources of information leakage.

Why Continuous Improvement Is Needed

While the specific drivers of change are always evolving, the reasons that organizations need to continuously improve their program for securing information assets are relatively constant and include:

- **Changing technology.** New technology capabilities need to be monitored and considered with an eye to improving, streamlining, or reducing the cost of securing information assets. The program to secure critical e-documents needs to anticipate new types of threats and also evaluate adding or replacing technologies to continue to improve it.
- **Changing laws and regulations.** Compliance with new or updated laws and regulations must be maintained.
- **Internal information governance requirements.** As an organization updates and improves its overall IG, the program elements that concern critical information assets must be kept aligned and synchronized.
- **Changing business plans.** As the enterprise develops new business strategies and enters new markets, it must reconsider and update its

program for securing information assets. If, for instance, a firm moves from being a domestic entity to a regional or global one, new threats will exist and new security strategies must be formed.

- **Evolving industry best practices.** Best practices change and new best practices arise with the introduction of each successive wave of technology, and with changes in the business environment. The program should consider and leverage new best practices.
- **Fixing program shortcomings.** Addressing flaws in the program that are discovered through testing, monitoring, and auditing; or addressing an actual breach of confidential information; or a legal sanction imposed due to noncompliance are all reasons why a program must be revisited periodically and kept updated.[3]

Maintaining the program requires that a senior-level officer of the enterprise continues to push for enforcement, improvement, and expansion to secure confidential information assets. This requires leadership and a consistent and loud message to employees. The security of information assets must be on the minds of all members of the enterprise; it must be something they are aware of and think about daily. They must be on the lookout for ways to improve it, and they should be rewarded for those contributions.

Gaining this level of mindshare in employees' heads will require follow-up messages in the form of personal speeches and presentations, newsletters, corporate announcements, e-mail messages, and even posters placed at strategic points (e.g., near the shared printing station). Everyone must be reminded that keeping e-documents and information assets secure is everyone's job, and that to lose or leak confidential information harms the organization over the long term and erodes its value.

Chapter Summary: Key Points

- Keeping an enterprise's confidential information assets secure requires vigilant and consistent monitoring and auditing to ensure that information governance policies are followed and enforced.
- Information technologies that can assist in advancing the program must be steadily monitored, evaluated, and implemented.
- To maintain and improve the program will require monitoring tools, regular audits, and regular meetings for discussion and approval of changes to the program to continually improve it.

(continued)

(*continued*)

- Organizations need to continuously improve their program for securing information assets due to 1) changing technology, 2) changing laws and regulations, 3) internal information governance requirements, 4) changing business plans, 5) evolving industry best practices, and 6) fixing program shortcomings.
- Maintaining the program to secure information assets requires that a senior-level officer of the enterprise continues to push for enforcement, improvement, and expansion of the program to secure confidential information assets.

Notes

1. Mark Woeppel, "Is Your Continuous Improvement Organization a Profit Center?" June 15, 2009, www.processexcellencenetwork.com/process -management/articles/is-your-continuous-improvement-organization-a- prof/, retrieved September 12, 2011.
2. Donald Clark, Big Dog and Little Dog's Performance Juxtaposition, "Continuous Process Improvement," March 11, 2010, www.nwlink.com/ ~donclark/perform/process.html, retrieved September 12, 2011.
3. Kahn, Blair, *Information Nation: Seven Keys to Information Management Compliance*, AIIM International, 2004, pp. 242–243.

Conclusion

Information assets are the largest component of an enterprise's value. Their importance cannot be overstated, and properly securing them can spell the difference between success and failure. Typically, extensive measures are taken to protect an organization's physical assets, while its valuable information assets are left at risk.

In March, 2012, Richard Clarke, the former cybersecurity and cyber-terrorism advisor for the White House who presciently warned of the 9-11 attacks more than two months in advance, stated that Chinese hackers sponsored by their government have been spying and stealing the intellectual property U.S. companies, which, over time, may seriously cripple America's business competitiveness.[1] In an interview with the Smithsonian, Clarke stated, "I'm about to say something that people think is an exaggeration, but I think the evidence is pretty strong. *Every major company in the United States has already been penetrated by China.* My greatest fear is that, rather than having a cyber-Pearl Harbor event, we will instead have this death of a thousand cuts. Where we lose our competitiveness by having all of our research and development stolen by the Chinese. And we never really see the single event that makes us do something about it. That it's always just below our pain threshold. That company after company in the United States spends millions, hundreds of millions, in some cases billions of dollars on R&D and that information goes free to China.... After a while you can't compete" (italics added).

Business and governmental leaders are the stewards of their organization's information assets and they must be held accountable for their security and integrity. Organizations are faced with more malicious threats and potential information leakage vulnerabilities than ever before. These threats are going to continue to escalate and increase in sophistication. When these attacks are successful—whether detected or not—they erode the victim organization's information assets, competitive position, public image, and stakeholder value. There are real costs when information assets are compromised. Successful attacks can even put a company out of business.

These threats must be dealt with in a systematic and determined way. All the information platforms an enterprise uses must be considered, from basic e-mail to high-value information management applications. Access to these platforms and their critical data may be through mobile devices, cloud computing services, social media applications, or other means; and information governance (IG) policies must be formed and enforced to manage and control information access and use.

IG policies must be implemented using the latest technology tools. These tools may include information rights management (IRM), which secures e-documents directly through their lifespan; data loss prevention (DLP) technology, which can stop the exit of sensitive information from the organization's firewall and assist in discovering and mapping out data flows; electronic records management (ERM), which manages and controls the most critical business records; digital signatures, which authenticate users and speed approval processes; e-mail and instant messaging (IM) encryption, which keep daily information from prying eyes; stream messaging for confidential electronic communications with no record; and secure printing methods or other emerging technologies that enable total document lifecycle security (DLS).

A program to secure confidential information assets requires a strong executive sponsor, a solid business case, and ongoing enforcement and improvement using continuous process improvement (CPI) methods and techniques. It is not a one-shot deal.

Organizations must strive to protect their information assets, and it is a long-term effort that requires constant attention and focus. They may never be able to completely halt all information leakage, but with IG methods, technology tools, and vigilant enforcement, they will have the capability to lock down and secure their most critical information assets.

And their ability to do so may ultimately, over time, determine the viability of their business over the long run.

Note

1. Emil Protalinski, ZDNet.com, http://www.zdnet.com/blog/security/richard-clarke-china-has-hacked-every-major-us-company/11125?tag=nl.e589, March 27, 2012, retrieved March 30, 2012.

Digital Signature Standard

The Digital Signature Standard (DSS) (Federal Information Processing Standard [FIPS] 186-3), specifies algorithms for applications requiring a digital signature, rather than a written signature:

> *Signature generation uses a private key to generate a digital signature; signature verification uses a public key that corresponds to, but is not the same as, the private key. Each signatory possesses a private and public key pair. Public keys may be known by the public; private keys are kept secret. Anyone can verify the signature by employing the signatory's public key. Only the user that possesses the private key can perform signature generation.*
>
> *A hash function is used in the signature generation process to obtain a condensed version of the data to be signed; the condensed version of the data is often called a* message digest. *The message digest is input to the digital signature algorithm to generate the digital signature. The hash functions to be used are specified in the Secure Hash Standard (SHS), FIPS 180-3. FIPS approved digital signature algorithms shall be used with an appropriate hash function that is specified in the SHS.*
>
> *The digital signature is provided to the intended verifier along with the signed data. The verifying entity verifies the signature by using the claimed signatory's public key and the same hash function that was used to generate the signature. Similar procedures may be used to generate and verify signatures for both stored and transmitted data.*[1]

Note

1. NIST, Federal Information Processing Standards Publication, June 2009, http://csrc.nist.gov/publications/fips/fips186-3/fips_186-3.pdf, retrieved August 15, 2011.

Regulations Related to Records Management

Records management practices and standards are delineated in many federal regulations. Also, there are a number of state statutes that have passed and in some cases they actually supersede federal regulations, so understanding compliance in the state or states an organizations operates in is key.

On the federal level, public companies must be vigilant in verifying, protecting, and reporting financial information to comply with requirements under Sarbanes-Oxley and the Gramm-Leach-Bliley Act (GLBA). Healthcare concerns must meet the requirements of HIPAA, and investment firms must comply with a myriad of regulations by the Securities and Exchange Commission (SEC) and National Association of Securities Dealers (NASD).

Following is a brief description of current rules, laws regulators, and their records retention and corporate policy requirements. *(NOTE: This is an overview, and firms should consult their own legal counsel for interpretation and applicability.)*

Department of Defense Rule 5015.2-STD

DoD Rule 5015.2-STD requires systematic records management, both physical and electronic, including the declaration, creation, classification, management, maintenance, preservation, reproduction, and deletion of records.

National Archives and Records Administration (NARA)

The National Archives and Records Administration:

- Oversees physical and electronic recordkeeping policies and procedures of government agencies, requiring adequate and proper documentation on the conduction of U.S. government business;

- Defines formal e-records as machine-readable materials created or received by an agency of the U.S. federal government under federal law or in the course of the transaction of public business;
- Requires that organized records series be established for electronic records on a particular subject or function to facilitate the management of these e-records.

Gramm-Leach-Bliley Act

The Financial Institution Privacy Protection Act of 2001, Financial Institution Privacy Protection Act of 2003 (Gramm-Leach-Bliley Act) was amended in 2003 to improve and increase protection of nonpublic personal information. Through this Act, financial records be properly secured, safeguarded, and eventually completely destroyed so that the information cannot be further accessed.

Healthcare Insurance Portability and Accountability Act of 1996 (HIPAA)

The Healthcare Insurance Portability and Accountability Act (HIPAA) requires that security standards be adopted for: 1) controlling who may access health information; 2) providing audit trails for electronic record systems; 3) isolating health data, making it inaccessible to unauthorized access; 4) ensuring the confidentiality and safeguarding of health information when it is electronically transmitted to ensure it is physically, electronically, and administratively secure; and 5) meeting the needs and capabilities of small and rural healthcare providers.

Patriot Act (Uniting and Strengthening America by Providing Appropriate Tools Required to Intercept and Obstruct Terrorism Act of 2001)

The Patriot Act: 1) requires that the identity of a person opening an account with any financial institution is verified by the financial institution, and they must implement reasonable procedures to maintain identity information; and 2) provides law enforcement organizations broad investigatory rights, including warrantless searches.

Sarbanes-Oxley Act (SOX)

SOX requires that: 1) public corporations implement extensive policies, procedures, and tools to prevent fraudulent activities; 2) financial control and risk mitigation processes be documented and verified by independent auditors; and 3) executives of publicly traded companies certify the validity of the company's financial statements.

SEC Rule 17A-4

SEC Rule 17A-4 requires that: 1) records that must be maintained and preserved be available to be produced or reproduced using either micrographic media (such as microfilm or microfiche) or electronic storage media (any digital storage medium or system); and 2) original copies of all communications, such as interoffice memoranda, be preserved for no less than *three* years, the first two in an easily accessible location.

CFR Title 47, Part 42—Telecommunications

CFR Title 47, Part 42 requires that telecommunications carriers keep original records or reproductions of original records, including memoranda, documents, papers, and correspondence that the carrier prepared or that were prepared on behalf of the carrier.

CFR Title 21, Part 11—Pharmaceuticals

CFR Title 21, Part 11 requires: 1) controls are in place to protect content stored on both open and closed systems to ensure the authenticity and integrity of electronic records; and 2) generating accurate and complete electronic copies of records so that the Food and Drug Administration (FDA) may inspect them.

Listing of Technology and Service Providers

Information Rights Management

Adobe
345 Park Avenue
San Jose, CA 95110
(888) 649-2990
www.adobe.com/products/livecycle/rightsmanagement/

Avoco Secure, Ltd.
7th Floor, 16 St. Martin's-le-Grand
London EC1A 4EE
(415) 839-9433
www.avocosecure.com

Bitscape
39270 Paseo Padre Parkway #244
16 St. Martin's-le-Grand
Fremont, CA 94538
(510) 493-2448
www.bitscape.com

Boole Server
Fluxer UK Ltd
32 Beltran Road, London SW6 3AJ
(0)20 7193 6345
www.booleserver.com

Brainloop
One Broadway, 14th floor
Cambridge, MA 02142

(800) 517-3171
www.brainloop.com

Check Point Software Technologies, Ltd.
800 Bridge Parkway
Redwood City, CA 94065
(800) 429-4391
www.checkpoint.com

Content Raven
121 Bartlett Street, Suite B
Marlborough, MA 01752
(508) 786-0500
www.contentraven.com

Covertix
Ha'atsmaut St.
BeitYaakobi
P.O. Box 9041
Even Yehuda, Israel 40500
97297657726
www.covertix.com

eDocument Sciences, LLC
147 Fairlawn Drive
Amherst, NY 14226
716-836-2509
www.edocumentsciences.com

EMC
176 South Street
Hopkinton, MA 01748
(866) 438-3622
www.emc.com/products/detail/software/irm-services.htm

Fasoo
Nuritkum Square, 1605 Sangman-dong,
Mapo-gu, Seoul, Korea (121-795)
82-2-300-9102
www.fasoo.com

File Open
101 Cooper Street, Suite 202
Santa Cruz, CA 95060
(831) 706-2170
www.fileopen.com

Giga Trust
607 Herndon Parkway, Suite 302
Herndon, VA 20170 USA
(703) 467-3740
www.gigatrust.com

InDorse Technologies
424 West 33rd Street
New York, NY 10001-2662
(800) 610-9210
www.indorse-tech.com

LockLizard
Longlands Park,
Ayr, KA7 4RJ, Scotland
(800) 707-4492
www.locklizard.com/

Microsoft
One Microsoft Way
Redmond, WA 98052
www.microsoft.com

Next Labs
2 Waters Park Drive, #250
San Mateo, CA 94403
(650) 577-9101
www.nextlabs.com

Oracle
500 Oracle Parkway
Redwood Shores, CA 94065
(800) 392-2999
www.oracle.com/technology/products/content-management
   /irm/index.html

Seclore Technology
B 1084, Oberoi Garden Estate,
Chandivli, Andheri (E), Mumbai 400072, India
91-22-4015-5251
www.seclore.com

Secure Islands
Givat Ram Campus
The Hebrew University of Jerusalem
Jerusalem 91391, Israel

972-2-6522941
www.secureislands.com

Vitrium Systems
502-1168 Hamilton Street
Vancouver, BC, Canada V6B 2S2
(866) 403-1500
www.vitrium.com

WatchDox
2685 Marine Way #1212
Mountain View, CA 94043
(800) 209-1688
www.watchdox.com

Zafesoft
560 South Winchester Blvd, Suite 500
San Jose, CA 95128
(408) 572-5590
www.zafesoft.com

Data Loss Prevention

CA (formerly Computer Associates) DLP
One CA Plaza
Islandia, NY 11749
(800) 225-5224
www.ca.com

Code Green Networks
385 E. Moffett Park Drive, Suite 105
Sunnyvale, CA 94089
(888) 473-3668
www.codegreennetworks.com

Fidelis Security Systems
1601 Trapelo Road, Suite 270
Waltham, MA 02451
(800) 652-4020
www.fidelissecurity.com

McAfee (formerly Reconnex)
2821 Mission College Blvd.
Santa Clara, CA 95054
(888) 847-8766
www.mcafee.com/us/

Palisade Systems
400 Locust Street, Suite 700
Des Moines, IA 50309
(888) 824-0720
www.palisadesystems.com

Trustwave (formerly Vericept)
70 West Madison Street Suite 1050
Chicago, IL 60602
(888) 878-7817
www.trustwave.com

RSA
174 Middlesex Turnpike
Bedford, MA 01730
(877) RSA-4900
www.rsa.com

Symantec DLP (formerly Vontu)
350 Ellis Street
Mountain View, CA 94043
(424) 750-7580
www.symantec.com

Trend Micro DLP
10101 N. De Anza Blvd.
Cupertino, CA 95014
(800) 228-5651
us.trendmicro.com/us/products/enterprise/data-loss-prevention/
    index.html

Verdasys
404 Wyman St. Suite 320
Waltham, MA 02451
(781) 788-8180
www.verdasys.com

Confidential Stream Messaging

VaporStream
10 S. Wacker Drive Suite 1835
Chicago, IL 60606
(877) 572-0628
www.vaporstream.com

Digital & Electronic Signature Systems

Access Smart
27762 Antonio Pkwy, L1-461,
Ladera Ranch, CA 92694
(949) 218-8754
www.smartaccess.com

Adobe
345 Park Avenue
San Jose, CA 95110
(888) 649-2990
www.adobe.com/security/digsig.html

A Green Sign
8226 Douglas Ave, Suite 625
Dallas, TX 75225
(877) 445-4307
www.agreensign.com/digital-signature.html

Alpha Trust
8226 Douglas Ave, Suite 625
Dallas, TX 75225
(866) 613-7446
www.alphatrust.com

Articsoft
6575 South Jackson Court
Centennial, CO 80121
(866) 243-3350
www.articsoft.com

Formotus
3633 136th Pl SE, Suite 202
Bellevue, WA 98006
(206) 973-5060
www.formotus.com

Arx
855 Folsom Street, Suite 939
San Francisco, CA, 94107
(866) 327-9754
www.arx.com

Brother Soft
275 Shoreline Drive, Suite 500
Redwood Shores, CA 94065-1413
www.brothersoft.com

Communication Intelligence Corp
275 Shoreline Drive
Redwood Shores, CA 94065
(650) 802-7888
www.cic.com

Elock
1800 K St, Suite 622
Washington, DC 20006
(202) 470-0965
www.elock.com

Epadlink
650 Cochran Street, Unit 5
Simi Valley, CA 93065
(800) 520-3464
www.epadlink.com

Formotus
3633 136th Pl SE, Suite 202
Bellevue, WA 98006
(206) 973-5060
www.formotus.com/SignatureCapture.html

RJS Software
2970 Judicial Road, Suite 100
Burnsville, MN 55337
(888) 757-7638
www.rjssoftware.com

Secure Soft
4 VasileConta
Piatra Neamt 610115 ROMANIA
www.signfiles.com

Silanis
200 Decarie Boulevard
Montreal, Quebec H4P 2P5 Canada
888-SILANIS
www.silanis.com

Topaz Systems
650 Cochran St., Suite 6
Simi Valley, CA 93065
(805) 520-8282
www.topazsystems.com

XYZMO
Haiderstraβe 23
4052 Ansfelden, Austria
+43 (0) 7229 88060-0
www.xyzmo.com

Electronic Records Management

Autonomy (HP is in acquisition talks at this writing)
US Headquarters
One Market Plaza
Spear Tower, Suite 1900
San Francisco, CA 94105
(415) 243-9955
www.autonomy.com

EMC
176 South Street
Hopkinton, MA 01748
(866) 438-3622
www.emc.com

File Trail
111 North Market Street, Suite 715
San Jose, CA 95113-1108
(408) 289-1300
http://filetrail.com/FT_Home/Index.asp?gclid=

GimmalSoft
Three Galleria Tower
13155 Noel Road, 9th Floor
Dallas, TX 75240
(214) 800-2300
http://www.gimmalsoft.com/Pages/default.aspx

Hyland
28500 Clemens Road
Westlake, OH 44145
(888) HYLAND-8
www.hyland.com

Infolinx
10800 Connecticut Avenue
Kensington, MD 20895
(800) 251-8399
http://infolinx.com/

IBM
1 New Orchard Road
Armonk, New York 10504-1722
(800) 426-4968
www.ibm.com/us/en/

Integro
88 Inverness Circle East, Suite N106
Englewood, CO 80112
(888) 575-9300
www.integro.com

Iron Mountain
745 Atlantic Ave
Boston, MA 02111
(800) 899-4766
www.ironmountain.com

Laserfiche
3545 Long Beach Blvd.
Long Beach, CA 90807
(800) 985-8533
www.laserfiche.com/en-US

OmniRIM
39 Plymouth Street
Fairfield, NJ 07004
(800) 899-3975
www.archivesystems.com/products/omnirim-records-
    management.aspx

Open Text
275 Frank Tompa Drive
Waterloo, Ontario
(800) 499-6544
www.opentext.com/2/global.htm

Oracle
500 Oracle Parkway
Redwood Shores, CA 94065
(800) 392-2999
www.oracle.com

RecMan for Google Apps
555 California Street, Suite 4925
San Francisco, CA 94104 USA

(415) 659-1521
http://recman.net/

Email Archiving

Autonomy (HP is in acquisition talks at this writing)
US Headquarters
One Market Plaza
Spear Tower, Suite 1900
San Francisco, CA 94105
(415) 243-9955
www.autonomy.com

AXS-One/Unify
301 Route 17 North
Rutherford, NJ 07070-2581
(201) 935-3400
http://axsone.com/

C2C
134 Flanders Road
Westborough, MA 01581
(508) 870-2205
www.c2c.com

CommVault
2 Crescent Place
Oceanport, New Jersey
(888) 746-3849
www.commvault.com

CA
One CA Plaza
Islandia, NY 11749
(800) 225-5224
www.ca.com

Critical Technologies
3601 S Broadway, Suite 1400
Edmond, OK 73013
(405) 650-1234
www.criticaltech.com

Dell MessageOne
1 Dell Way
Round Rock, TX 78682
(888) 782-3355
www.dellmodularservices.com

EMC
176 South Street
Hopkinton, MA 01748
(866) 438-3622
www.emc.com

Forsythe
7770 Frontage Road
Skokie, Illinois 60077
(800) 843-4488
www.forsythe.com/na/

Proofpoint
892 Ross Drive
Sunnyvale, CA 94089
(408) 517-4710
www.proofpoint.com

GFI
15300 Weston Parkway, Suite 104
Cary, NC 27513
(888) 243-4329
www.gfi.com

GlobalRelay
286 Madison Avenue, 7th Floor
New York, NY 10016-6368
(866) 484-6630
www.globalrelay.com

GWAVA
100 Alexis Nihon Suite 500
Montreal, Quebec, Canada
(866) 464-9282
www.gwava.com

HP
Hewlett-Packard Company
3000 Hanover Street
Palo Alto, CA 94304-1185
(650) 857-1501

IBM
1 New Orchard Road
Armonk, New York 10504-1722
(800) 426-4968
www.ibm.com/us/en/

MessageSolution
1851 McCarthy Blvd., Suite 105
Milpitas, CA 95035
(408) 383-0100
www.messagesolution.com

Messaging Architects
180 Peel Street, Suite 333
Montreal, QC Canada H3C 2G7
(866) 497-0101
www.messagingarchitects.com

Metalogix
1601 Trapelo Road
Waltham, MA 02451
(877) 450-8667
metalogix.com

Open Text
275 Frank Tompa Drive
Waterloo, Ontario
(800) 499-6544
www.opentext.com/2/global.htm

Oracle
500 Oracle Parkway
Redwood Shores, CA 94065
(800) 392-2999
www.oracle.com

Overtone Software
44 Montgomery St., Suite 2040
San Francisco, CA 94104
(866) 517-4100
www.overtone.com

Postini/Google
1600 Amphitheatre Parkway
Mountain View, CA 94043
(650) 253-0000
www.google.com/postini/

Quest Software
5 Polaris Way
Aliso Viejo, CA 92656
(800) 306-9329
www.quest.com

Sherpa Software
456 Washington Ave, Suite 2
Bridgeville, PA 15017
(800) 255-5155
www.sherpasoftware.com

Symantec
350 Ellis Street
Mountain View, CA 94043
(424) 750-7580
www.symantec.com

Waterford Technologies
19700 Fairchild, Suite 300
Irvine, CA 92612
(949) 428-9300
www.waterfordtechnologies.com

ZL Technologies
2000 Concourse Drive
San Jose, CA 95131
(408) 240-8989
www.zlti.com

ZyLab
7918 Jones Branch Drive, Suite 530
McLean, VA 22102
(866) 995-2262
www.zylab.com

Glossary

Authenticity Verified content and author information as original for the purposes of electronic records management (ERM); in a legal context, proof that the e-document is what it purports to be when electronically stored information (ESI) is submitted during the e-discovery process.

Backup A complete spare copy of data for purposes of disaster recovery. Backups are non-indexed mass storage and cannot substitute for indexed, archived information that can be quickly searched and retrieved.

Capture Capture components are often also called input components. There are several levels and technologies, from simple information scanning and capture to complex information preparation using automatic classification.

Certificate of Authenticity Attests to the authenticity of a reproduced record.

Classification Systematic identification and arrangement of business activities and/or records into categories according to logically structured conventions, methods, and procedural rules represented in a classification system. A coding of content items as members of a group for the purposes of cataloging them or associating them with a taxonomy.

Cloud Computing Cloud computing refers to the provision of computational resources on demand via a network. Cloud computing can be compared to the supply of electricity and gas, or the provision of telephone, television, and postal services. All of these services are presented to the users in a simple way that is easy to understand without the users' needing to know how the services are provided. This simplified view is called an abstraction. Similarly, cloud computing offers computer application developers and users an abstract view of services, which simplifies and ignores much of the details and inner workings. A provider's offering of abstracted Internet services is often called *the cloud*.

Data Loss Prevention (DLP) Data loss prevention (DLP, also known as data *leak* prevention) is a computer security term referring to systems that identify, monitor, and protect data in use (e.g., endpoint actions), data in motion (e.g., network actions), and data at rest (e.g., data storage) through deep content inspection, contextual security analysis of transaction (attributes of originator, data object, medium, timing, recipient/destination and so on) and with a centralized management framework. Systems are designed to detect and prevent unauthorized use and transmission of confidential information.

Declaration   Assignment of metadata elements to associate the attributes of one or more record folder(s) to a record, or for categories to be managed at the record level, providing the capability to associate a record category to a specific record.

Destruction   The process of eliminating or deleting records, beyond any possible reconstruction.

Destructive Retention Policy   Permanently destroying documents after retaining them for a specified period of time.

Discovery   May refer to the process of gathering and exchanging evidence in civil trials; or, to discover information flows inside an organization using data loss prevention (DLP) tools.

Disposition   The range of processes associated with implementing records retention, destruction, or transfer decisions, which are documented in disposition authorities or other instruments.

Document   Recorded information or object which can be treated as a unit.

Electronic Records Management (ERM)   Electronic records management is the management of electronic and non-electronic records by software, including maintaining disposition schedules for keeping records for specified retention periods, archiving, or destruction. (For enterprise rights management, *see* Information Rights Management [IRM].)

Electronic Record   Information recorded in a form that requires a computer or other machine to process and view it and that satisfies the legal or business definition of a record.

Electronic Records Repository   A direct access device on which the electronic records and associated metadata are stored.

Electronically Stored Information (ESI)   A term coined by the legal community to connote any information at all that is stored by electronic means; this can include not just e-mail and e-documents but also audio and video recordings, and any other type of information stored on electronic media. ESI is a term that was created in 2006 when the U.S. Federal Rules of Civil Procedure (FRCP) were revised to include the governance of ESI in litigation.

E-mail Encryption   E-mail encryption refers to encryption or scrambling (and often authentication) of e-mail messages, which can be done in order to protect the content from being read by unintended recipients.

Event-Based Disposition   A disposition instruction in which a record is eligible for the specified disposition (transfer or destroy) upon when or immediately after the specified event occurs. No retention period is applied and there is no fixed waiting period as with timed or combination timed-event dispositions. Example: *Destroy when no longer needed for current operations.*

File Transfer Protocol (FTP)   File transfer protocol (FTP) is a standard network protocol used to copy a file from one host to another over a transmission control protocol (TCP)–based network, such as the Internet. FTP is built on a client-server architecture and utilizes separate control and data connections between the client and server. FTP users may authenticate themselves using a clear-text sign-in protocol but can connect anonymously if the server is configured to allow it.

Full Disk Encryption (FDE)   Full disk encryption (FDE) uses disk encryption software or hardware to encrypt (scramble) every bit of data that goes on a disk or volume. Disk encryption prevents unauthorized access to data storage. FDE (also called *whole disk encryption*) is often used to signify that everything on a disk is encrypted, including the programs that can encrypt bootable operating system partitions. However, they must still leave the master boot record (MBR), and thus part of the disk, unencrypted. Some hardware-based FDE systems, however, can truly encrypt the entire boot disk, including the MBR.

The Healthcare Insurance Portability and Accountability Act (HIPAA) Enacted by the U.S. Congress in 1996. According to the Centers for Medicare and Medicaid Services (CMS) website, Title II of HIPAA, known as the administrative simplification (AS) provision, requires the establishment of national standards for electronic health care transactions and national identifiers for providers, health insurance plans, and employers.

Information Rights Management (IRM)   Information rights management (IRM) is often referred to as enterprise rights management. IRM applies to a technology set that protects sensitive information, usually documents or e-mail messages, from unauthorized access. IRM is technology that allows for information (mostly in the form of documents) to be remote controlled. This means that information and its control can be separately created, viewed, edited, and distributed. IRM is sometimes also referred to as enterprise digital rights management (E-DRM). This can cause confusion because digital rights management (DRM) technologies are typically associated with business-to-consumer systems designed to protect rich media such as music and video.

Metadata   Data about data, or detailed information describing context, content, and structure of records and their management through time. Examples may be the author, department, document type, date created, length, and so forth.

Migration   The act of moving records from one system to another while maintaining their authenticity, integrity, reliability, and usability.

Optical Character Recognition (OCR)   A visual recognition process that involves photo-scanning text character-by-character.

Phishing   Phishing is a way of attempting to acquire sensitive information such as user names, passwords, and credit card details by masquerading as a trustworthy entity in an electronic communication. Communications purporting to be from popular social websites, auction sites, online payment processors, or IT administrators are commonly used to lure the unsuspecting public. Phishing is typically carried out by e-mail or instant messaging, and it often directs users to enter details at a fake website that looks and feels almost identical to the legitimate one. Phishing is an example of social engineering techniques used to fool users, and it exploits the poor usability of current web security technologies.

Policy   A high-level overall plan, containing a set of principles that embrace the general goals of the organization and are used as a basis for decisions.

Preservation   The processes and operations involved in ensuring the technical and intellectual survival of authentic records through time. Record information created, received, and maintained as evidence and information by an organization or person, in pursuance of legal obligations or in the transaction of business.

Record Category   A description of a particular set of records within a file plan. Each category has retention and disposition data associated with it, applied to all record folders and records within the category.

Records Management   The field of management responsible for the efficient and systematic control of the creation, receipt, maintenance, use, and disposition of records, including processes for capturing and maintaining evidence of and information about business activities and transactions in the form of records. A set of instructions allocated to a class or file to determine the length of time for which records should be retained by the organization for business purposes, and the eventual fate of the records on completion of this period of time.

Social Engineering Social engineering is the act of manipulating people to perform actions or divulge confidential information (as opposed to gaining assets by breaking in or using technical hacking techniques). While similar to a confidence trick or simple fraud, the term typically applies to trickery or deception for the purpose of information gathering, fraud, or computer system access; in most cases the attacker never comes face-to-face with the victim. Social engineering has also been employed by bill collectors, skip tracers, and bounty hunters.

Secure Sockets Layer (SSL)/Transport Layer Security (TLS) Secure sockets layer (SSL) and transport layer security (TLS) are cryptographic protocols that provide communications security over the Internet. SSL and TLS encrypt the segments of network connections above the transport layer, using symmetric cryptography for privacy and a keyed message authentication code for message reliability.

Structured Data/Records A collection of records or data that is stored in a computer; records maintained in a database or application, such as Lawson or Facets.

Taxonomy A hierarchical structure of information components, any part of which can be used to classify a content item in relation to other items in the structure.

Time-/Date-Based Disposition A disposition instruction specifying when a record shall be cut off and when a fixed retention period is applied. The retention period does not begin until after the records have been cut off. Example: Destroy after two years.

Time-, Date-, and Event-Based A disposition instruction specifying that a record shall be disposed of after a fixed period of disposition time after a predictable or specified event. Once the specified event has occurred, then the retention period is applied. Example: Destroy three years after close of case. In this example, the record does not start its retention period until after the case is closed—at that time its folder is cut off and the retention period (three years) is applied.

Total Cost of Ownership (TCO) All costs associated with owning a system over the life of the installation and implementation—usually considered over a range of three to five years. TCO includes implementation price and change orders (and the change order approval process), which occur when changes to the project are made outside of the original proposal. Timing and pricing of the software support fees are also critical TCO components, and may include warranty periods, annual fees, planned and maximum increases, trade-in and upgrade costs, hardware maintenance costs, and other charges that may not be immediately apparent to buyers.

Transfer   Moving records from one location to another, or change of custody, ownership, and/or responsibility for records.

Unstructured Data/Records   Data/recoreds that are not expressed in numerical rows and columns but rather, are objects such as image files, e-mail files, Microsoft Office files, and so forth. Structured data/records are maintained in databases.

Zero-Day Attack   A zero-day (or zero-hour or day-zero) attack or threat gives the victim organization zero time to respond. It is a computer threat that tries to exploit computer application vulnerabilities that are unknown to others or the software developer, also called zero-day vulnerabilities. Zero-day exploits (actual software that uses a security hole to carry out an attack) are used or shared by attackers before the developer of the target software knows about the vulnerability.

About the Author

R**obert F. Smallwood** is a founding Partner of IMERGE Consulting and heads up its E-Records Institute, a specialty consulting practice, as Executive Director. Mr. Smallwood is a 30-year veteran of the information technology industry and has been recognized as one of the industry's "25 Most Influential People" and "Top 3 Independent Consultants" by *KM World* magazine. He consults with Fortune 500 companies and governments to assist them in making technology decisions and implementations. Some of his past research and consulting clients include Johnson & Johnson, Apple, Miller-Coors, AT&T, the Supreme Court of Canada, Xerox, and IBM. He has published more than 100 articles and given more than 50 conference presentations on document, records, and content management. He is the author of *How to Manage Social Media Business Records* (CreateSpace, 2011), *Taming the Email Tiger* (BB Publishing LLC, 2008), and several other books.

Index